Born in London in 1936, Tarquin Olivier spent his early childhood in Hollywood with his mother Jill Esmond, where he acted in seven films. After military service in the Coldstream Guards, he graduated from Oxford University, and then spent two years in Southeast Asia, living among farmers and fishermen. This resulted in a book, *The Eye of the Day* (1964). His career in business has been mostly with Thomas De La Rue, the leading banknote printers. He has now set up his own company for the development of feature films.

He has a son and two daughters by his first wife, and now lives with his second wife, Zelfa, in London.

My Father
Laurence Olivier

Tarquin Olivier

HEADLINE

First published in 1992
by HEADLINE BOOK PUBLISHING PLC

First published in paperback in 1993
by HEADLINE BOOK PUBLISHING PLC

10 9 8 7 6 5 4 3 2 1

ISBN 0 7472 3988 6

Printed and bound in Great Britain by
HarperCollins Manufacturing, Glasgow

HEADLINE BOOK PUBLISHING PLC
Headline House
79 Great Titchfield Street
London W1P 7FN

CONTENTS

Part Four

For Zelfa

I am no good at love
My heart should be wise and free
But I kill the unfortunate golden goose,
Whoever it may be,
With over-articulate tenderness
And too much intensity.

I am no good at love,
I betray it with little sins.
For I feel the misery of the end
In the moment that it begins,
And the bitterness of the last 'good-bye'
Is the bitterness that wins.

Noël Coward

ACKNOWLEDGEMENTS

The letters are reproduced by the kind permission of Joan Olivier for my father's, my step-sister Suzanne Farringdon for her mother Vivien Leigh's, and Graham Payn for my godfather Noël Coward's. I am also indebted to Bernard Levin for allowing me to reproduce part of what he wrote in *The Times* following my father's death.

For the pictures every effort has been made to obtain the relevant reproduction rights and to ensure that the details are correct, and my thanks go to those from whose collections the photographs were taken. My thanks also for the colour transparency for the cover portrait by Bernard Hailstone, kindly lent by E.T. Archives of London, and for the photograph of the Salvador Dali portrait kindly lent by Wildenstein, 147 New Bond Street, London, W1.

I am grateful to the British Film Institute for the use of their film archives and stills library, and also to Barry Norman of the Theatre Museum for making so much material available to me. Most of the early photographs are taken from 16mm black and white home movies filmed by my parents more than sixty years ago. This was made possible by John Bulmer letting me use his cutting room in George and Dragon Hall to select each best frame for enlargement to 8in by 10in stills.

In writing as personal a book as this it has been a pleasure to rely on the encouragement and good judgement of my publisher Alan Brooke; my literary agent Gillon Aitken; Peter Hiley – who became Company Secretary to Laurence Olivier Productions in 1947 and ever since has been affectionately described as 'general factotum' – a family friend and counsel who read the manuscript as a check on its truthfulness; and on my old friend David Lloyd-Jacob whose comments were invaluable.

I should like to thank my son and daughters: Tristan for the loan of his wide-angle camera, Isis and her husband Paul for helpful comments of their generation, and Clavelle for the Notley hazelnut and lovers' knot artwork; last and most of all my wife Zelfa who was with me throughout, in Kensington and in Turkish homes from home: Sedef, Bebek and Kandilli.

FOREWORD

Countless articles and many biographies have been written about Laurence Olivier and Vivien Leigh, together with references to my mother Jill Esmond. The direction of these writings has largely become fixed, as each effort has fed from its predecessors. My father's autobiography has naturally been taken as gospel for source material.

I once helped a biographer, Anne Edwards, when she wrote about my step-mother Vivien Leigh. She handled my limited contribution with discretion, but friends and relations read the whole upsetting story, the horrible bits, the intimate revelations, and assumed wrongly that I was their source. Since then I have declined to give assistance to biographers.

My direct recollections start from around the time I was three. To these can be added the indirect ones of earlier years, passed on to me as I grew up. They were more than enough to underscore for me how far from the truth the various records were. There was much more happiness and love than has ever been written of – especially in my father's autobiography, where he wrote: 'I was desperate to get married . . . she admitted to me that she was in love elsewhere and could never love me as completely as I would wish.' Apart from the reference to my mother there is an implication which does him injustice too: that he married for ambition to the exclusion of his youthful romanticism.

As the *Evening Standard* wrote following her memorial service in 1990, a year after his:

'Lasting trauma was caused to Miss Esmond by Lord Olivier's 1982 autobiography, *Confessions of an Actor*. Although he was harshest in his revelations concerning the psychiatric illness of his second wife, Vivien Leigh, when the book appeared Miss Leigh had been dead for fifteen years, so it was the somewhat less barbed comments on his first wife, whom he left very publicly to pursue his infatuation for Miss Leigh, which caused the most pain.

'Tarquin Olivier, 53 today, the actor's son by Miss Esmond, said: "My father's autobiography appeared to have been written in a blind and bitter rage. Both my mother and I were extremely pained by some of the things he wrote, but she cared for him until the day he died, and was much too loyal ever to respond publicly."'

This was fairly reported, but it does not demolish the wall of untruth which has become ever more solid with each succeeding biography, and even featured in her obituaries.

This is a book mainly about Jill, Larry, Vivien and what it was like to grow up among them. It is personal, and not based on interviews in the manner of biographers, nor on the massive researches which have not prevented some more recent efforts from being so wrong.

Apart from my recollections I have dozens of wonderful letters he wrote to me, revealing more urgent insights than anything anyone, including himself, wrote many years later. I am deeply grateful to his widow Joan, as executor of his will, for allowing me to reproduce them.

After my mother's death, I came across in her attic neat stacks of letters she had written to her mother which reveal the fullest picture yet of the early years of her marriage to Larry, and the direction she gave his career. Even earlier researches point to influences which strengthened his own approach to acting and directing, a school of realism which had been practised by Jill's parents, the leading dramatic couple of their era.

During the war I was evacuated to America with my mother whom my father had left for Vivien Leigh. His determination to join the armed forces led to his most frustrating time, redeemed by his love for Vivien, and by being invited to make 'Henry V', widely regarded as his finest achievement. So in Part Two I have described their war years in England and ours in California as a context for his letters, and to highlight his film which blazed forth like a beacon over the land.

The intimacy which then grew between us for fifteen years is reflected in his letters to me. They give the flavour of the man, the father, the actor, as he was at the time, with a vividness which outshines any mere recollection. Of those who survive him I am the one who knew him best at that stage. After I began a life of my own in

1959 and after he married Joan Plowright it was she who became his closest confidante.

There is then an interval of seventeen years which I do not describe because the closeness between us had been replaced by our separate careers and obligations to our new families. At the end of his life we did become close once more and this is reflected in the final chapter.

My aim in writing this book is to set the record straight, but the material at my disposal has yielded far more. I have had to use much which is familiar simply to give a shape to life, but only where crucial. There is much which is entirely new. The sense of discovery, recollection, and rediscovery has given me the greatest pleasure.

Part One

1

England

'He was a funny looking man,' my mother said. She described to me the poor dentistry intended to disguise the gap between his front teeth. 'His smile made him look surprised. He seemed unsure of his ground. But as soon as I saw him I knew: he was the man I was going to marry.'

In March 1928 when they were both twenty-one, she saw him in the dim backstage of a London theatre. He was awkward and bony. His eyebrows met in the middle and extended across his temples leaving the narrowest forehead. Beyond her physical description was a man dedicated to being an actor, to being other than himself, given to mimicry, impersonation, losing himself in roles which had no existence save in him. He was extraordinary.

She was a handsome young actress, a success from a wealthy theatre family, all of which he craved in a wife. He was wild, romantic, and with an impetuousness he never lost he fell in love at once, at first sight, hugged this new emotion round himself and brought it to bear upon her. She wanted more time but knew that she was captivated.

His passion for performing had started while a chorister aged nine, at All Saints, Margaret Street, near Oxford Circus. As I later discovered when a chorister and soloist at school the emotions engendered were more glorious than any thus far, at the dawn chorus of a lifetime. You *were* your voice, singing to the glory of God; and because the outpourings were linked to prayer in a hallowed place there was a feeling of safety which allowed expression without fear of ridicule.

At school his mimicry was more original, but had been less understood than his singing. For most people it was too much, but Jill loved it. She had been brought up in a theatrical atmosphere. Although she herself was no mimic she told her stories with enthusiasm, a good choice of words but few gestures. She was down-to-earth, nonetheless lively and imaginative. She had been to the Royal Academy of Dramatic Art, and at the age of fifteen played in a West End production of 'Peter Pan'. Her voice was well modulated, her attitude professional and her looks enabled her to obtain the best parts early on, including the lead in 'Eliza Comes to Stay', written by her father. Her first big success, after three years, was as Sorel Bliss in Noël Coward's 'Hay Fever'. He gave her a first edition of his play and signed it: 'For Jill, from the Great God Coward!'

Larry, on the other hand, was born into what he described as genteel poverty, although with illustrious antecedents. The Oliviers were originally French Huguenots, one of whom was Louis XV's Court Painter, whose miniatures are still with the family. Many of them had left France after the Revocation of the Edict of Nantes in 1685. Most descendants became clergy, but there had been soldiers and other professional people; a generation older than Larry a painter, and the first Labour peer, a founder with the Webbs of the Fabian movement – no thespians apart from the acting often endemic in the clergy.

Larry's father, known to the family as 'Farve', had taught at a school where he fell in love with the headmaster's sister, Agnes. They had started married life setting up a school of their own to run, after an engagement of several years saving up the capital required, and she was dismayed at his sudden decision to follow his father's footsteps into the Church. He became a melodramatic preacher in Blakian style: a St George, much to the inconvenience of his family and the surprise of Agnes, who had never wanted to be married to a clergyman.

Larry was born on 22 May 1907 at 26 Wathen Road, Dorking. His father had moved his family down in living standards to assume his first religious post as Curate. The semi-detached house now has a blue plaque commemorating his birth which I unveiled eighty-three years later, after his death the previous summer. It is a friendly dwelling with a manicured garden behind it; the room where he was born is tiny.

He was their third child, after his sister Sybille, and brother Dickie. He felt left out and unwanted by his father. In furtherance of Farve's proselytising quest they moved to the slums of Notting Hill, then to Pimlico, and then again to Letchworth in Hertfordshire. There, when

Larry was only twelve and still at choir school, with utter unexpectedness, his mother died.

He found it difficult to speak of her even in old age and during his most relaxed and forthcoming moments, and then only of the void her death left within him. He could never recollect the inner beauty he said she had. Her parents were well-born country people, the Crookendons. She had widely spaced brown eyes, high cheek bones, and a soft mystery. While he delighted in imitating everyone else, he never 'did' her. He couldn't. She was the only one in the world he could never externalise through imitation.

His gift of athletic hell fire was from Farve; his poetic sensitivity was from her. His powers to observe, mix and reproduce, to 'create' a true version of a human being whose country he had never been to, whether a Mexican priest or an Arab prophet were I believe hers, if such gifts came from anyone; as if, like Cathy saying 'I am Heathcliff', it were true to say of him that he was his mother, whom he had lost.

He would harp upon his father, had nightmares about him and made him sound like a man of ice: the piercing steel blue eyes and marvellous physique, the great cricketer who found fault with everyone else. He referred to him as a sententious old misery who played for effect rather than from conviction, as if religion were a lie that Farve enjoyed shaming others into believing. He impersonated Farve in life, and also, once, in the theatre. He had been afraid of him.

He was sent to St Edward's, Oxford. The boys teased him for his unco-ordinated gangly body and his puniness. He longed to score a goal at football or make some runs at cricket. But he did win praise for his acting, even for playing the role of Kate in 'The Taming of the Shrew'. This astonished him: they had been genuinely impressed, even his persecutors, by his playing a girl.

He wanted to be bourgeois and follow his elder brother Dickie by becoming a rubber-planter in India. His father told him not to be silly, he was going to be an actor, and prompted him to win a scholarship and a bursary of £1 a week at Elsie Fogarty's Central School of Speech Training and Dramatic Art. Peggy Ashcroft was a student there too.

He rented lodgings in an attic near Paddington station and just about starved, agonising over whether taking a bus was cheaper than wearing out his shoes. With persistence, and after many rebuffs and tiny beginnings he managed, through Farve's introduction, to be accepted by the Birmingham Repertory Company: the second time his father had been crucial to his career.

One of the plays brought to London by Barry Jackson's company was 'Bird in Hand' by John Drinkwater. Peggy Ashcroft had been his leading lady in Birmingham. Jill Esmond was engaged instead of her as a star for the London public. That was how he met her.

In the play they had to be very much in love. In life Larry's puritanism and total inexperience made him awkward. To ease things, if only for the sake of acting on stage, Jill invited him for a weekend at her mother's country house, just beyond Maidenhead in Berkshire.

Apple Porch stood on a hill. Heavy wooden gates led under an archway of wisteria, between the main house and the servants' wing. There were kitchen gardens, greenhouses and a gardener's cottage by the woods, a croquet lawn, grass tennis court and pergolas of roses. Flower beds sloped down to a sun-dial and a wrought-iron gate to Temple Golf Course. The view over the fairway was of the distant glint of the Thames, and the steeple of Marlow church.

Larry had never seen such a place in his life.

Jill was stylish. Her background was literary and theatrical, her father, the late H.V. Esmond, an actor–manager who had written thirty plays. 'Harry' was survived by Eva Moore who, at sixty, still had star quality, and was admired as an actress by Queen Mary.

Jill told me that Eva took to Larry far more readily than to previous young men. She saw beyond his gaucheness, the machine-stitched suit and the cheap shoes. This young man was original: magnetic but lost. He did not know what was expected of him, like a man drunk with life even when sober: earnest and irrepressible, incorrigible. He giggled and impersonated and tried too hard to be helpful. He couldn't help being an actor all the time.

Eva had started her own career as a dancing teacher when she was fifteen. A year later she played small parts kept secret from her Victorian family: acting was for rogues and vagabonds, close to prostitution. Her father found out when she was seventeen and slammed the door in her face. She left home for various touring companies, on her own, surviving in tiny parts. She had known hunger as Larry had.

It is true that he saw what he wanted: an entourage which included Ivor Novello and many other leading theatre people. Eva, as a producer herself, had wide business contacts. But he was also dying for Jill for her own sake. His autobiographical account of her as not being dazzling but 'would do excellent well as a wife' flies in the face of his young idealism. How often he said to me in my late teens:

'I want to save you from the cretinous romanticism of the Oliviers'. By then he had long come to deplore his puritan youth as a sickening waste of opportunity.

Apple Porch had begun as an eighteenth-century cottage. Larry had a little guest bedroom upstairs, with a porcelain bowl on a washstand, and a copper pitcher of hot water set outside his door every morning and evening. Eva and Harry had had the main house built on around 1900: an oak staircase, heavy with the chimes of a grandfather clock, the drawing-room with Jacobean panelling and an arched ceiling of dull gold. Eva sat at her desk in the morning room which Jill called the Chamber of Horrors because of the illuminations of actors posed in great roles, embellished with tinsel. Larry, on the other hand, liked them so much that Eva promised to bequeath them to him.

Harry had died when Jill was fifteen. His creativity had waned long before and he had taken to whisky. Eva did not want Jill to see him in an uncontrollable state; she had her own career to lead; many others depended on her for theirs; her son Jacky was thirteen and doing well at Radley . . . so she sent Jill away as a boarder at the early age of five to the co-educational school Bedales, in Hampshire. Although liberally enlightened it had no central heating. Jill's first letter home would have horrified Eva, the more so for the little mistakes.

Dear Mum

I hope you are quit well.
It is very cold day.
I have a chilblane on my foot.
I am sorry that Jacky is working so had.
This morning Miss Cross took me inot the
kitchen and told me to take off my stokins
and she got boiling hot worter and told me
to put my feet in and she held them in and
then she put them inot cold worter
and my feet were like lobsters pour me
and then she put stuf on them and I was
very glad when she had finisht.

Throughout the rest of Eva's life it seems that her immense concern for Jill was an obsessive attempt to make up for an unhappy childhood.

Her marriage to Harry, a leading actor, playwright and manager, had been fulfilled and happy, charged with energy from their work, the successes and failures, and the adrenalin which flowed from their audiences. He was a dreamer and she a disciplinarian, a suffragette committee woman. Their son Jacky thought that she had driven Harry to drink. She interrupted his reverie. Each intrusion became sharper. He lost self-control, something snapped, and he wrote an agonised letter from their London house:

21 Whiteheads Grove, Cadogan Terrace, W.1. [Around 1920]

Beloved Beloved Beloved,

After a quarter of a century still Beloved – either you or I or both of us are abnormal. These things don't happen in our profession. (I believe there may be two f's in 'proffession' but now I've written it I'm sure there aren't.)

If I hadn't thrown cold water on that subject last night in the drawing room things would have been different. All was well till I did that. It only shows you how easy it is to destroy and how difficult to rebuild. Can you come back to me next Sunday? Not to the concert, to ME.

I am just answering another appeal from Viola Tree with a stern refusal in spite of the fact that she has billed me all over the Tube . . .

VOL 1. 11. 111. Dads

P.S. about profession. I'm sure there *are*.

There is a photograph of the two of them in the garden at the end of his life, strolling up a path between Michaelmas daisies. His face has the lines of exhaustion that Richard Burton's had, straight features, soft flesh drawn down, terribly sad. Eva had the remains of beauty, but clenched, yet her voice even decades later had a wonderful lightness. I remember her infectious laughter. Jill used to say that if they had played mother and daughter on the wireless they would have had to reverse roles, Eva as skittish daughter, Jill with a lower voice playing the more mature mother. Eva's enthusiasm and love of life, her absurdity . . . 'O Jill, do look . . . The tits are in their nests.'

Even though Harry had lived for some years as hazily as a ghost, his death in Paris of pneumonia elicited an avalanche of letters. He was missed by the entire profession and millions of theatregoers. King George and Queen Mary, who had seen a number of his plays and his Shakespearian performances, offered condolences. As Miss Sybil Thorndike wrote to Eva: 'Doesn't it seem strange that out of a big personal grief comes sometimes a wonderful recognition of warmth that's in the hearts of outsiders?'

This aching void Eva allowed to be filled with her love for Larry. While her entourage had called Gerald du Maurier 'The young Greek god', and Harry 'The genius', she shared Jill's perception of Larry as having the potential for both, especially in his quest for versatility. She came to adore him, sometimes called him 'Harry' instead of 'Larry'. He called her 'Mum'. Despite his horrified denials of fifty years later there is no doubt of his love for her then, as their letters will show.

Reading plays out loud was a constant exercise, far more than a mere parlour game. It resembled rehearsals and was followed by lots of notes and the post-mortems associated with a green room. Of Harry's plays, Larry's favourite was 'The Law Divine'. It is the story of a couple who were happy until the outbreak of the Great War. The husband is called up and his wife becomes obsessed with 'doing her bit'. He returns to a drawing room which has been converted into an office, and a bedroom with a telephone on her side of the bed. His dilemma is whether to retire into the background or revolt against the interrupted home life. This was close to what happened to the Esmonds. The climax of the play is the wife's recollection of the early years, of their love in full flower, running bare-foot along a moonlit beach.

Eva's own son Jacky had tried without success in the theatre and turned his hand to motor racing and other businesses. Her experience as an actress and determination to pass it on centred on Larry. She knew what equipment he needed and the route he had to follow. He was a willing recipient. Much of what she wrote about Harry in her own autobiography *Exits and Entrances*, could have been written about Larry a generation later:

His character studies were real people, not bundles of eccentricities with amazing and repulsive tricks; they were real old people, treated, where it was demanded, with humour, but a humour which was from the heart and spoke to the heart, and not only apparent to the eye of the beholder. His young men were charming, virile and obviously enjoying life. He could play devout lovers, rakes (and what delightful rakes, too, they were!), old men, and mad men, and play them all with more than a touch of genius.

If Larry had inherited his sensitivity and artistic gifts from his mother's genes, her death while he was so young imbued him with the gift of pathos. He himself ascribed his power to move audiences to the effects on him of this loss, which he drew upon when playing in tragedy, whether in the loftiest roles or the most pitiable, to cauterise his trauma.

Harry's early death had not been equally affecting for Jill, but it had left its mark. Their times together had been special. She resembled him and shared his love of literature. She had read Hardy's *Jude the Obscure* aged twelve. She and Larry had much in their backgrounds they were able to share. There were many of their generation orphaned by the Great War, and once this was accepted they had also the universal gaiety of that time. They had house parties and even imposed on them their eternal live readings of plays, often at Larry's insistence. When Jill asked him to do something else for a change he would whisper fiercely: 'Don't you realise . . . I want to be the greatest actor in the world!'

Even so, they did play tennis, cheat at croquet and go for long walks. At night when it was moonless dark, the favourite party game was 'Strike a Light' – a fast-run panting hide-and-seek outside on the golf course. 'He' had ten matches, and whenever called upon had to strike one wherever he was hiding, and dash through the darkness to somewhere else, to crouch in a bunker, lie in the rough grass, stretch along a branch and hold his breath in silent agony.

A grassy knoll divided the rough from the fairway and they would sit on it, and look at the distant lights of Marlow: no cars, just stars, the night sky, the watchful owl. Jill would imitate it, clasping her hands together and blowing: to-woo to-woo.

She had grown up in the countryside. As a girl she had shot rabbits and rooks, and had once had to hide in stinging nettles from the gamekeeper. She was well made and had good legs, but moved awkwardly and bit her nails. Larry was skinny. He used to joke about his feeble arms: 'These little wires which hang from my shoulders' and his hairy chest: six hairs which grew upwards. He could laugh at anything, and made others laugh with him, even at his own shame. For he was deeply ashamed of his undernourished and undeveloped physique, and he set about body-building in addition to his voice training, to improve his 'noble proportions'.

His shame had overtones: moral, spiritual, engendered by a sense of sin imposed at an all-male boarding school for clergymen's sons. The catch phrases were 'self-abuse', and 'inadequacy before God', whose forgiveness had constantly to be sought even for normality. The result was frustrating for Jill, who enjoyed kissing and had a liberal outlook. In 'A Kiss for Two' Harry had written a speech for an Irish soldier, Captain Patrick Delaney, setting out the polarities between nature and bigotry. This was personified by the Esmonds and Oliviers.

It's a legend I'm tellin' ye, an' all true legends begin with 'My Dear and My Judy'. Well, My Dear and My Judy, one fine day Mother Nature, havin' nothin better to do, she made a man. You know what a man is? That's all right then – well, she made a man, and this mighty fine piece of work tickled her to death, it did, and so she went to bed devilish pleased with herself, had a beautiful dream, woke up next morning, went one better than the day before – she made a woman. You can't say you know what a woman is, for she's a mystery to the lot of us. Well, she made a woman, and then she said to the man, 'That sweet lookin' thing's all yours.'

. . . The stuffy old men then started to make laws. Oh, them laws that they made, sure they forgot all about the days of their youth, when their blood was warm, and the sunshine was singin' in their hearts. They just sat there on them cold stones in that old Town Hall, chilled to the marrow, and made them laws to stop love-making.

And while they were at it, there came a tap at the door, and they all gave a jump – which showed you they were doin' something they were ashamed of . . . and there in the sunlight stood a beautiful young woman, lookin' in at them, her eyes all agog with wonder. 'What the devil are you doin'?' says she. 'None of your business,' says they. 'True for you,' says she. An' she took them at their word, and slammed the door, an' she's been slamming the door on them same laws ever since!

For 'stuffy old men' read 'Farve'.

Eva's description of Harry's acting could also describe Larry's, who all his life sought after realism, and it reflects what she passed on to him:

His voice was wonderful; he could put more tenderness, without the least touch of sentimentality, into his words than anyone I've ever heard. To hear Harry say 'My dear', as he did in 'The Law Divine', was to hear all the essence of love-making, with all the love in the world behind it, put into two words.

His gesture was superb; he was not, as so many actors are, apparently afraid of using a big sweeping movement; he was never afraid that a big gesture would look ridiculous . . .

All his movements were good . . . during his telling of the 'Legend', he used that sweeping gesture of his arm. Seated in a chair, leaning forward, carried away by the story he tells, he comes to the words: 'and there in the sunlight stood a beautiful young woman', – out went his arm, his eyes following it, the fingers outspread to take in the whole of the picture, until, when he looked behind him, looked to where his arm and hand had pointed, you might almost have seen her, 'her eyes all agog with wonder'.

The 'Bird in Hand' was a play attacking 'class'. Jill played the Bright Young Thing whose 'common' parents owned a pub. Larry was type-cast as the puritanical young 'squire', in love with love, all anguish and yearning and no deeds, except prissily kissing the *outside* of her bedroom door. It perfectly reflected his then 'cretinous romanticism'.

During rehearsals, with prospects surging for a brilliant First Night and his first West End success, he proposed. She knew he would, was thrilled, and somehow found the words to delay matters without killing his fragile self-esteem. He proposed several times. She loved him too, and knew that one day he would be for her, but she wanted him to mature, to provide a love that was real and more experienced.

She overheard a conversation between director and producer, all about Larry. They agreed that he was a fine young actor, wonderful gifts, exciting . . . But all that hair: 'Makes him look so bad-tempered, almost neanderthal . . .'

Jill repeated this to him in his dressing room, filled his glass with whisky and set to work with a pair of tweezers until he could bear it no more. There were a number of painful sessions, plucking one hair out after another. Later, whenever she looked at photographs of him with his new hairline, she felt as if his looks were partly of her making.

His innocent guilt did bring a kind of determined sweetness to him. An actor friend, Roland Culver, told me how, at about that time, Larry drove him all the way down to Hurley – an hour's drive then, as now, but through hedge-lined roads with only one or two other cars to avoid. He parked beside Hurley Church, where he went to Communion every Sunday, and led the way to the river. He loped along the towpath and sat down on the riverbank, opposite a rock on the far side. He contemplated the rock, turned to Roley, then said, 'Last Sunday – Jill. She dived off that rock.' Then he drove him in silence all the way back to London.

He did not apply Prince Hamlet's advice:

> Be not too tame, neither: but let your own discretion be your tutor. Suit the action to the word, the word to the action, with this special observance: that you o'erstep not the modesty of nature.

Larry's modesty was unnatural. Any forward move from Jill led to his prayers for forgiveness, on his knees. It could not but 'make the judicious grieve', and she was judicious. She was driven mad by his coy immaturity, and decided to give him time to grow up. She escaped to New York, unfortunately still in the 'Bird in Hand' which she had been in for far too long.

He knew that she was right about his problems not being fair on her. They did confide in each other to a very great degree. She took the opportunity she was offered on Broadway for emotional rather than career reasons. It suited him to do the opposite: he stayed behind in London for another play.

2

New York

The departure of an ocean liner carried a sense of occasion: brass bands, streamers, and the resonant diapason of the ship bellowing for the open sea – during the embraces of loved ones admiring the cabins, tearing away just in time to hurry down the gang-plank, and into the cheering crowds. Passengers were people of purpose, set to realise hopes five days and three thousand nautical miles away: the launch of a business or book, the opening of a play, doing a deal, even starting a whole new life.

In a letter to her mother, Jill described the landing at New York, the skyscrapers, albeit through the mist.

April 6th, 1929.

Just an occasional tower looming, most of the thrill had gone as we had had such a long wait, but when we began to pull in it all came back again and gave me a lovely feeling. We docked at about 3 o'clock.

Jack Hawkins came to meet me.

Of course we had lots of photos on the boat and interviews. By five o'clock I was taken by the scruff of the neck and photographed for over an hour. I hadn't had time to change or anything.

I got back to the hotel to snatch a little food and get to the theatre to rehearse as we open in three days.

It was six months before the Wall Street crash. There were secret stills, boot-leggers, wood alcohol, and speakeasies.

Another suitor had preceded her: a sedate stockbroker with a Homburg hat, Donald Krolik. He had reserved her a room at the

Bristol Hotel, West 98th Street, and filled it with flowers. She only mentions him to Eva once, and then as 'Mr'.

There was a heat-wave. She returned very late from the theatre. It was too hot to sleep, the overhead railway clattered outside her window and she spent most of the night walking up and down in her room. When eventually she lay down the bed seemed to roll after her long voyage at sea. She awoke at five, felt wonderful, rehearsed all morning, had her hair done in the afternoon and went back to the Bristol to rest, after changing her room to one on the 8th floor overlooking Broadway.

Jack Hawkins impressed on her how businesslike the theatres were in New York. She found the Booth Theatre very different.

> I've never known anything so slack. No one minds about having no props, or my having no clothes. They just said it was lucky I had brought my own.
>
> My dressing room looks like a bad theatre in the Midlands. I've got it nearly clean now, all but the floor which is strewn with dirt. If this letter seems odd it's only because I am tired and it's very late and we still rehearse. How I hate this play.

'Bird in Hand's' first night went well, reviews were splendid and audiences overflowing. Jill started networking with her letters of introduction from Eva and London's theatre moguls. She wrote coyly of her chances in 'Talking Film'.

In the West End, Larry had been in four plays in the first six months of 1929.

> I'm awfully glad Larry has another job. He is the luckiest fellow I know. I hope I never get in another play that runs as long as this. I've quite forgotten what it's like to act. I'm sure it's awfully bad for one. Still, I suppose being out here teaches one something though God knows what. It's what I wanted so I mustn't grumble – but it does seem a waste of time, unless I can get a picture . . .

Her letters are fond and companionable. She did not confide her real reasons for escape – to give Larry a chance to shake down – but Eva would have guessed. Donald Krolik's being in New York put the wind up Larry. He agonised over the supposed prowess of a Jewish lover. Jill never even found Donald attractive: he became her friend and stockbroker.

Larry decided on a bold and romantic dash over the pond to claim her. He was offered the lead in a thriller, 'Murder on the Second Floor', which had been a success in the West End and was headed for Broadway, with Phyllis Konstamm as leading lady. He seized the chance.

Upon arrival in New York, even before checking into his hotel, he sped to the Booth Theatre and waited in Jill's dressing room as she took her curtain calls. She was radiant with success and thrilled to see him. Absence had made his kisses real. Suddenly, everywhere they went, they were accepted as a couple in love. This was America. They were unofficially engaged, living in separate hotels in deference to society's good opinion. She was admired in her play, and he had just arrived with a glamorous contract and seemed destined to join her in the ranks of stardom.

When his play opened it flopped badly. It ran for one month. Equity rules forbade him from further work in New York that year. This brought to their attention the problems of two people in their profession getting married. Something has so frequently to give, on one side or the other. He had to leave for England.

He proposed to her yet again and this time, knowing how close he was to despair, she accepted him. They went to Tiffany's and he bought an engagement ring. She gave him a cigarette case in three shades of gold: yellow, orange and greenish. He took her out for a slap-up lunch, ordered champagne, fine wines, and at the end of it found he hadn't enough money. Neither of them had a cheque book; she had only a few dollars. So he had to leave as a deposit the cigarette case she had just given him.

Torn away from New York by the failure of his play, and from Jill who was locked into the continuing success of hers, he set sail for England on the *R.M.S. Lancastria*, the same boat she had sailed out on. They had been lionised, doted upon, they were engaged, she was a big star, and he a betrothed Romeo banished by failure. He wrote to her from on board, a touching, reticent letter, a bit muddled, filled with young love, helped perhaps by the Atlantic.

. . . lovely just standing there, with no one but God and you, in the bright moonlight, about full moon I think it was.

The sea is absolutely calm again now, like black glass. A Russian chap joined me later and we sat on top deck playing gramophone records; and I've just come down.

I was just thinking – I was awfully happy up there on the top deck tonight – you know, quite and wholly at peace and contented, and yet I wasn't contented or happy at being in that state.

I suppose our *happiest* moment has just the faintest shadow lurking somewhere near it, some doubt, or fear – fear perhaps of hurting something, some ideal, God, perhaps the moment itself. And then I suppose our really happy moments are when we don't know they're there, and we look back and say, 'I was happy, then'.

Being conscious of happiness always makes one rather step out of the picture and watch oneself being happy. People tell me that's a great gift and should make my life much more interesting but it just seems to mar it somehow, at least not mar it but alter it, and one would prefer the untrammelled happiness of a sweet dream.

But one must go on, eliminating the fears and doubts and feelings of safety and love, until one can be fully conscious of being happy and still enjoy the happiness.

Yet I used to be *like* that – a little while ago. I must have strayed a little from God I suppose. I have been frightfully slack about religion since I've been in America. You must keep me up to that, Jill, it's my only hope of being of use to God and the world and I think everybody should try to be that. Goodnight darling. I kiss you.

He was twenty-two. By Renaissance standards he should have been at his physical and sexual apogee, but he was wandering in the woods. He was very down, alone on a boat, away from theatre people who would applaud a sketch from him in their own language, in fact he was hiding, hence the relief of talking to a 'Russian chap'.

He landed in England in September 1929, without work. He lived in Ralph Richardson's flat while Ralph was enjoying success on Broadway. He went to stay with his father at Addington in Buckinghamshire. Farve had remarried: a fifty-year-old spinster named Isabel, who was called Ibo – her new initials now that she was Mrs Olivier. Larry took to her. She was kind and devout, quiet and cheerful, and had had a softening effect on the old tyrant.

At breakfast Farve opened an egg with his little spoon and scooped out the white, no bigger than a Communion wafer, and held it towards Larry. 'Would you like the top of my egg?' Larry wondered why the mean so-and-so hadn't offered *him* an entire egg. What could this signify to a very young man, engaged to be married, a self-important actor trying to get over a failure? He accepted graciously, then asked might he have an egg too, it was *so* good.

Farve's double standards had also paraded themselves when Larry had introduced Jill to him at lunch in a restaurant. The young couple chose the cheapest thing on the menu. Although Farve must have known that they were not rich, especially his son, the old hypocrite remembered what day it was.

'Ah, Friday.' He cleared his throat. 'Then fish is *de rigueur*.' There might have been sardines, but he ordered oysters, smoked salmon, lobster . . .

'Well,' he beamed at them both, 'if I get outside that, I won't be doing badly.' At the end of the meal the bill was presented. Larry blanched, and paid up like a lamb.

During his stay Farve took him for a country walk so as to be out of Ibo's earshot. He thought it time to explain the intimacies concerning the periodicity of women. Larry remembered the misinformation. 'And remember, my boy, the good Lord has given to mankind a safe period, so that nature can be truly gratified without yielding up the blessed fruit of conception. And this special time: the *middle* of the month,' he nodded with the air of a conspirator. 'A time of perfect safety.' So Larry felt he owed his entire existence to Farve's biological misunderstanding.

By then he had been in many plays and won good reviews even though the productions themselves were unsuccessful. Farve was as convinced as the most supportive West End critic of his son's ultimate success. This gave rise to a wounding change in paternal favouritism. Previously Farve had reserved praise for his elder son Dickie, now returned from his tour in India, bored with rubber-planting. At dinner, preventing Dickie from helping himself, Farve reached across the table for the decanter and set it before Larry. 'Help yourself to some port, m'boy. Dickie, pass him more Stilton.'

Meanwhile in New York 'Bird in Hand' was still running. For New Yorkers the play was an escape from the Wall Street crash and continuing news of suicides to pastoral parochial Jolly Old England. Jill was successful but frustrated. Larry had said that when they were *married* everything would be fine and God would smile on them. She did not much care for his God. She was not an infidel, having what she called knowledge and love of God, but she did have reservations about virgin birth and the cleansing of women after the 'sin' of childbirth. She must have wondered whether, apart from making the heart grow fonder, Larry's absence from her would make him more mature. Loneliness had made her miserable.

At her entreaty, Eva arrived in New York, knowing there was a problem and wanting to help. Jill seems to have needed Eva's reassurance and possessiveness. She even called herself 'Jill Esmond

'Moore', tacking her mother's maiden name on to her own. Eva was sure that Larry was the right man, a noble character with a conscience of gold that merely needed to be melted.

He wrote to Jill on 5 December from a smaller, less romantic place than the Atlantic: the Green Room Club, at 9.15 p.m., surrounded by half-empty glasses, dirty ashtrays and out-of-work actors. At least he had work.

I'm getting keener and keener on this play – re-entitled 'The Last Enemy', I think it's a lovely play – and I'm going to love the part, everybody in it is terribly nice. Oo I'm a lucky boy.

I feel rather a swine being all happy like this, when you're sick to death of 'Bird in Hand' – but you mustn't feel 'Oh Gosh', you know, like that about it darling. Bless you. After all we've got to get on and earn money for bread and butter and things –

Why does one always quote 'bread and butter', ridiculous as if anyone ever lived on bread and butter.

I'm loving you Jilli darling much better now, and at the moment so O so much, and the mental battles are getting less frequent. I should think so too. I'm a bloody fool ever to have them, but they just happen like a very well laid plan before I know where I am.

I have a feeling now all the time of 'getting my house in order' before Jill comes back, but I never seem to do everything I would like to have done when the day is over. Still I'm getting better – and happier than I was. O my dearest Jilli, my dearest one I hope you're happy. Mum seems to be staying with you over Christmas. I'm so glad. Awful to be alone, specially over Christmas – my love to her.

Jilli, what's the matter, why are you so far away, why can't I write to you properly – I've got one of those feelings – You seem snatched away and I can't say anything I want to say as if you were all closed up. No use using endearments or saying I love you when it's like that.

It's 9.35, nearly quarter to five with you – perhaps you're asleep, resting or something, no matinée today. You must be thinking of something very different – funny.

Doesn't matter anyway I love you – Goodnight dear, God bless you. My love to Mum.

I feel all better now, warmer – and I don't know, I love you more easily, as if you're thinking and p'raps loving me.

As soon as it was written he would have folded it away and become totally different: for a new scene. Had he decided to stay in the club he would have joined his fellows. If they were arguing he would argue louder, drinking, he would make them drink more for that was the only possible direction, laughing, he would make them laugh more, because that too for him was a one way street. Had he left, he would have hurled himself into learning his lines, thrust the script under his pillow and woken up next day word-perfect, or so it always seemed when he was pitch-forking himself into a new part.

Jill's letters to him do not survive, only her letters to Eva. Mother and daughter did the rounds of old friends together in New York, and then, after sharing an apartment for a month or so, Eva left for home.

Jill's play went on tour to Chicago. Prohibition was at its height, and after the Crash the amount of alcohol consumed put madness in the air. The manic energy was sharpened by gang wars, cop chases, the organised, mother-loving and outrageous anarchy of Al Capone. Jill was swept up by it all, threw her legs into the air with gay abandon and became all the rage.

> I wore my new pyjama trousers, a silver jumper top, long earrings and hair straight back, eyes heavily made up with green; looked awfully attractive.
>
> Lord what a party: the sort of thing you read about. Everyone was quite blind and had very few clothes on and made a hell of a noise. I was feeling very sad at having seen you off and couldn't get the party spirit. Anyway – whether it was the green eyes or what I don't know, but I was quite the success of the evening. Men fell on top of me from all sides and I only danced a second with each man as I was always being cut in on. Funny, all you have to do is to have a white face, full red lips, long earrings and a sad expression and men think you're marvellous.
>
> Sunday with friends. We talked all day, ending at Pierre's speak-easy where we sat for hours.

On Christmas night 1929 she wrote from the theatre, full of the self-confidence of the 1920s which now sounds absurd, but the freshness is racy. It shows that Noël Coward's characters in 'Private Lives' were just that: characters, not caricatures. They had never known what it was like to be contradicted, or stand in a crowded train, or occupy the same room as the 'working classes', or even speak to a businessman . . .

It's all here –

Today I caught the 11 o'clock train to Hinsdale to spend the day with some friends. I sat next to a typical businessman – well dressed, glasses, small moustache and weak expression, quite harmless.

I asked him if I was on the right train.

I was. And then we chatted. It was an hour's journey and we chatted all the time. He was very anxious to know who I was, so when I got out I told him my name – just Moore. His was Watt.

I had a great day with the Castles, met lots of charming people, played ping-pong and beat everyone and had lots of eggnog and had a really good party but all too short as I had to catch the 5-40 train back. I can't remember anyone's name I met but they were all charming.

On the train back I was standing. No room anywhere. And who should I see but little Watt. He gave me his seat and again we chatted. Then as we neared Chicago he asked if I would have dinner with him so I did.

Poor little man he was so thrilled he didn't know what to do. He named the most expensive Hotel there, then counted his money and said we wouldn't have time to go there, so we went to a cheaper hotel, near the Theatre.

I found him counting his money again, so I suggested that we just have a cup of coffee and a sandwich and he was so relieved.

Inside the cafe she slipped her hands from her gloves.

During our meal he noticed my ring and asked if I was engaged. His face fell a mile. I felt so sorry for him. Anyway on the way to the theatre he told me I had given him the nicest Xmas he had ever had.

Her next description sounds like one of the early scenes in 'Some Like It Hot'. Texas Quinan was a lady much admired by Al Capone who sometimes came to her gin joint. It was quite safe: not the remotest chance of *it* being raided by the police.

Texas Quinan is in front. She's coming round to see us and I think I'm going to join a party of hers at her Night Club. I'm dead tired but it would be a good end to a very queer Christmas.

Texas called for us in her Rolls. She is an amazing person, covered in paint and what a sense of humour. I've never laughed so much before. I was next to her most of the night and what she didn't say was nobody's business.

I got off with lots of awful working men and talked to the most queer people. She is one of the most interesting people I've ever met. She told me to come as her guest as often as I liked so I hope to go there again soon. It certainly was a great night.

Jill was relieved to get away from the theatre and the North Park Hotel. The green Rolls came almost every night to collect her from the stage door and go to Texas's night club – where everything was 'on the house'.

Jill's youth could well have been the inspiration for Noël's 'Poor Little Rich Girl' – cocktails and laughter, but what comes after, nobody knows. In her case, chaste sleep.

With her and Larry on opposite sides of the Atlantic, still to be married, their roles and moods were approaching a turning point. No doubt he did see the advantage of a theatre family such as hers, but his morality at that age would have stopped him being pushed into marriage for that reason alone. His calling Eva 'Mum' underscores the point. This was not blasphemy towards the sacred recollection of his own mother. It was internalising a new truth he had found, and knew he needed as a part of him, both professionally and personally: Eva and Jill personified the best of the acting profession. He needed them to be a part of him.

Jill was his first love. His emotions at the time surprised him at least as much as anyone else in that state. He felt as if love were not only his discovery but his invention, to be worshipped on a pedestal and never to be dislodged or even handled. Such was the fashion of the time.

Whatever the excesses of the 1960s they at least did not throw nature out of the window, to strangle at the end of a noose. In maturity he came to deplore early romanticism, the genuine, wonderful, cruel and often laughable uncertainties of youth untried and untested. He had forgotten how beguiling they were. He wanted to sound as if he had been in charge of himself, to make it seem in retrospect unlikely that he had been wide-eyed and innocent enough ever to fall into what he chose only to remember as a mess. 'Aye merriyed bedly', he intoned, as an Edwardian bore would have done, making us all laugh with him.

In his dotage, he did not make the inherent implication that 'Sheee, on the other hand, married rather well'. The only time he summed up the matter he was rude about both of them: 'Poor Old Jill, she didn't deserve much, but she deserved better than me.' What I like about that statement is that, no matter how hard you try, you cannot chip it away. Its unfairness is irresistible. It repels all boarders. And it's too good to be forgotten.

Jill's letters show what fun she was. Frustrated perhaps by him, she would try everything so long as she could remain uninvolved, except of course with the theatre and Larry. She knew, as did Eva, that he was potentially a great actor. He was irresistibly endearing to her, except when he deliberately tried to be. I suspect that she was not as carried away by his letters as he would have wished.

She was down-to-earth and commonsensical and must have wondered whether he really did believe that marriage was followed by 'happily ever after'. It will be seen that the strength of her love was enough to linger until their deaths after more than fifty years of separation. More important for posterity is that Jill more than anyone else steered him into the winds which filled the sails of his career, and gave momentum to his talent when it most mattered – at the start.

3

Larry and Jill

Jill left America, returned to London and took over from Kay Hammond to star in the West End. Larry's 'The Last Enemy' closed after ten weeks and his next play was scheduled to last only a week.

His first part in a film, 'Murder for Sale', took him to Berlin: a city built for giants, with enormous buildings and statues, laid out with wonderful roses and avenues of trees. They both went, and stayed not only in separate rooms but in separate hotels. Always the party girl, she suggested that they go to all the night clubs. They even decided to try a drag club. She wondered whether it would beat Chicago. It did. This was Berlin.

The 'girls' were gorgeous, décolletées and swirling on the dance-floor. Larry, not to be outdone, dived after the most stunning redhead and was all bravado, an over-acting Rudolph Valentino, cheek-to-cheek and hilarious. Jill sat at the bar and chatted with a balding barman. He leant towards her. 'Is ze man your hussband?' he asked.

'No. He's my fiancé.'

'Oh vell. It is not my affair. But he dances with ze only other woman in the place.'

One day Larry finished early. Jill agreed to meet him at an Art Museum, and correctly told the driver to take her to the 'Kunsthalle'. He, with the same objective and memorising the German by associa-tion, befuddled the chauffeur by asking for the 'Fuchshalle'.

In early summer, as they were not acting, they went to stay together at Apple Porch. Eva hoped this might help them sort out their love life while she based herself at her house in Chelsea: 21 Whiteheads Grove.

They went for walks and lay in sweet embrace, to be surprised in the woods by a deer, which made them feel guilty. It was an ebullient time too, alone together or with friends. Jill was so full of beans that they decided to call her the precise opposite of what she was: 'Poor Old Jill'. No one in history has ever been less Poor, or Old, than Jill. They shared Eva's bed, disconnected the phone and slept clasped in each other's arms. May Larry be forgiven his prayers for forgiveness.

Gradually they became more familiar, jumping on the bed as if on a trampoline. That was fun. Then Larry had her stand on the floor and catch him as he stood on the bed and fell backwards into her arms; the start perhaps of a career of theatrical leaps? Then it was her turn to fall. He was thinking of something else, forgot to catch her and she flumped to the floor not hurt, and it evoked the sweetest tenderness from him.

His abnormal shyness also derived from bad luck. Just after puberty he had developed a tight foreskin. For weeks he tried to bear it. Eventually the pain became excruciating and he had to go to the matron. In a country unused to circumcision after babydom the other boys gave him hell about his 'face-lift'. Then his scrotum became blocked, causing one half to swell up. This required an operation, done too late to prevent one ball from becoming sterile, although still active. The result was for him to associate the orb and sceptre of his manhood with humiliation and pain, over and above church-induced guilt: the ultimate unfreedom.

She insisted that she would not marry unless they first made love and eventually he agreed. It was not much of a success. He said years later: 'Romeo and Juliet? Both virgins: must have been rotten.' It might have been if Romeo had been to a school for clergymen's sons.

His father was having contrary problems with Ibo. Her age of fifty, or perhaps her Christian conscience, or still being a virgin, caused her to stonewall his advances. So Farve and son had much to keep quiet about.

Eva wanted the wedding ceremony to be in the Savoy Chapel where she and Harry had been married. There is a memorial to Harry there, a semi-circular bas-relief, above the door in the porch overlooking the little graveyard. It is an unusual piece, in bronze, of his profile, a hand holding a cigarette, the smoke curling as clearly as in a photograph.

Larry wanted Farve to marry them. Farve refused: the Savoy Chapel had been put to improper use, for marrying those who had been divorced. The fact that he himself had remarried, even though marriages were made in heaven, made no difference to him. So the service was held at All Saints, Marylebone. In this particular wedding, outraged feelings found expression in Eva's refusal to have *him* officiate at the marriage ceremony.

Larry had started to have his shoes and suits made. Gymnastics had improved his physique and his poise, but he still had a raffish and gypsy quality to him. On the day, 25 July 1930, like many a bride-groom, he looked a complete Charley in hired morning clothes: sleeves too short, and trousers failing to hide his actor's love of costume: white spats. A button-hole marched with a pointed pocket handkerchief – gaudy but not neat. He was the proudest of grooms, his brow nobly plucked by Jill, and his Ronald Colman moustache his hour-consuming pride, and the bride he had first proposed to almost two years before was his for ever.

The most illustrious theatre people in England were at the recep-tion in the garden of 21 Whiteheads Grove; people like C. Aubrey Smith, who captained the first English Cricket Eleven to South Africa, and then became an actor and subsequently, with his wife Tor, a pillar of the English Colony in Hollywood; Sir Charles Wyndham; Dame May Whitty; George Alexander; Ivor Novello; Gladys Cooper, and newer friends who had been to Apple Porch and had their eyes opened to Larry's dazzling handsomeness and laughter, like Noël Coward, Ralph Richardson, Sybil Thorndike and Lewis Casson.

For their honeymoon a friend of Eva's, Lady Fripp, offered them her house in Lulworth Cove. She said that there was a cook-housekeeper and a manservant. The couple could have the run of the place. And her two daughters would look after them. Eva, for once lacking in imagination, thought this 'Rather a good thing'.

Cheered away by the adoring reception, they drove to Dorset in Larry's powerful sports car. Upon arrival they found the daughters at a loose end, with nothing to do, bored, the season over. It was raining and they had nowhere to go. So on the very wedding night, the four of them sat for warmth by a log fire and played piquet.

While there on his honeymoon, Larry wrote to Eva. It starts on a note of treacly insincerity which almost sounds sarcastic, an unattrac-tive performance he was sometimes pleased to indulge.

Weston, West Lulworth, Dorset. Wednesday, 28 July 1930.

Hello Darling Mum

I do hope you're as happy as I am Mum darling. You deserve a good bit more than I do. You've worked so hard to make everything perfect for us, and perfect it has been – and Mum dear I'm so terribly grateful to you and I do so hope you're happy about everything. We're having a lovely lovely time down here. The Fripps are being perfect angels.

We had a funny embarrassing sort of evening when we got here, with the two girls. We all four sort of hummed and hawed and didn't know what to say.

And then, catastrophe!

A tragedy occurred next morning, when my razor slipped and cut off half my moustache and I had to do the other side to match and now it's a horrid little thing like this [drawing] – you'd loathe it. I'm hoping against hope that it will grow again before I come back to London.

O Mum darling, I think only you can imagine what Jill is like down here, clambering over rocks and being a pirate and pointing at imaginary fishes and things in the water – life is a perfect joy – and I think she's fairly happy – O she's grand.

All my love from your very happy son-in-law, Larry.

'O Shenandoah I love your daughter . . . !'

The letter is a jejune give-away of the state he was in, a smoke-screen blown clean away by 'and I think she is fairly happy'. He was hardly a knave, marrying for ambition alone, and 'Oh she's grand' begs all sorts of questions.

They moved into 13 Roland Gardens, SW7. Larry had a signet ring made for Jill, a green octagonal blood-stone carved with a squire's helmet, surrounded by a swordbelt, inscribed 'Sicut Oliva Virens' – 'As flourishing as the Olive tree'. It was a design worn by several generations of Oliviers – except for Sydney, who had been Governor of Jamaica, in the Labour Government of 1924 as Secretary for India, and made a peer.

Jill wore the ring all her life. It represented the most generous gift in relation to Larry's financial state – for she was still largely supporting him. They acquired furniture piece by piece as they made the money to pay for it. The first thing they bought was a bleached oak box, to keep the coal by the fireplace.

Before they were settled in or remotely comfortable they had Noël

Coward home for lunch. After all Jill had starred in his 'Hay Fever', and he was deeply fond of her. 'The Vortex' had been his next huge success. Utterly different, it shocked London with its confrontation between a drug-taking son and his addled mother with a toyboy lover, and set Noël up as an *enfant terrible*. His enormous following derived from his impeccable style and his incomparable talent to amuse. Repeating his name, or a mere inflection of his voice, was enough, and in many cases still is seventy years later, to take over an entire conversation. The decade of the twenties was his.

At Apple Porch Jill had invited Noël down several times. There he was able to study Larry from every angle. He found him outrageously funny, with gifts of timing almost as good as his own. He admired Larry as an actor and for his amazing good looks. Through Jill he took a liking to him. He decided to cast him in 'Private Lives', with himself, Gertie Lawrence and Adrianne Allen. Jill was already committed to a film.

Noël later insisted that it took him only four days, while in Shanghai, to write the play. The physical writing may well have needed no longer, but the mental preparation took weeks. He went over and over the plot, characters, motivations, moods and moves, and often treated Jill and Larry as bed-posts. They would challenge some of his ideas and he would explain or rearrange them, so that everything was set forth in his head before he put pen to paper.

He told me himself of the finest speech he ever wrote, at the end of 'Cavalcade'. He had completed the play except for that, put his pen down and gone to bed. He awoke at 7.30 in the morning and without a second's hesitation wrote out the speech. He went down for breakfast. When he returned he found no need to alter a word, not a comma. His mind had worked on it all night.

Larry and Jill asked Noël for lunch at Rowland Gardens. The three of them sat doggedly on hard chairs round a card table, and Noël asked if they would like to have an old sofa of his. They gladly accepted.

Their cook was of a breed now rare. Mrs Johns was a baritone salt-of-the-earth cockney complete with headscarf and varicose veins. In she burst with a tray: 'Din-ner! Toast's 'as 'ard as buggery.' Pause. 'Well it's all very well to laugh. S'posing someone famous was 'ere.' Noël's face must have made *her* laugh.

In 'Private Lives' Larry did not like the role of Victor Prynne, a foil to Noël and Gertie, and he never liked Adrianne Allen, which seems to be a kind of rebellion against her well-ordered mind: everyone called her 'Planny Annie'. Nevertheless Noël persuaded him to take the part: after so many failures in which he had been excellent it was time he became associated with success – on both sides of the Atlantic – and had money to spend.

Noël and Larry together: ribald and spikey teacher with rebel giggler. The two of them regaled me with an outrageous story of their behaviour. In the Pullman carriage of the London North-Eastern Railway they were having a polite lunch with their two actress companions. The steward set the pudding down before them in elegant glass bowls: chocolate mousse. A brown speck landed on the nice white cloth. Staccato conversation continued until Noël saw it. He put down his spoon.

He lined up his flicking forefinger with the speck and aimed at Larry. He fired. It was a good shot and Larry was hit.

Larry scooped up half a spoon of mousse and catapulted it at Noël, but missed. So Noël took up a full spoon and hit again. It ended with them rolling in the aisle, scooping whole handfuls of mousse from their bowls, then from the actresses' dishes, then from everyone else's at the other tables . . .

Jill's enquiries in the movie business provoked the interest of Alfred Hitchcock. He was keen to cast her in his films in Hollywood, but insisted that she drop the 'Moore' and just call herself 'Jill Esmond'. Eva heard of this, flew into a fury and accused her of 'Dropping the Pilot', a grandiloquent allusion to the Kaiser's dismissal of Bismarck in 1888. Jill wrote in desperation, even though she lived only half a mile away:

> Mummy Darling – I don't know what to say . . . the changing to Esmond has nothing to do with my love for you or my resenting being a Moore. You know I've always been proud of that and most awfully proud of you. I tried to explain last Sunday that a double name is not good professionally. As I am either known as Esmond or Moore never both, if I became a star it's too long to top the bill.
>
> I can't bear to hear you talk of dropping the pilot. You must see it's not true. When I spoke of being a shadow I was blaming myself for not having enough guts or individuality to stand on my own feet: you have never smothered me . . . When you love someone terribly you always seem to hurt them more . . . Will you be in town tomorrow. I'm not filming can I see you?

'Private Lives' went to Broadway in early 1931. Adrianne was expecting baby Daniel Massey, so Noël gave her part to Jill. She and Larry took a swish apartment in 34 East 57th Street. With Noël and

Gertie, they were the most glamorous successes of the season. They were everywhere, everyone's most sought-after guests. Nothing was too lavish.

During the daytime Jill targeted on films, films, films. Although Larry had not liked filming in 'Murder for Sale', she argued that the medium did offer a second line of attack for an actor's career and that the rewards for success were enormously greater than in the theatre, especially in Hollywood.

As a medium filming made him nervous and stagey, with the sheer quantity of technicalities focused on him, an audience he could not even see, couldn't address or hypnotise because it was not there: and the style and people were so different from the theatre. There were basics to be learned even though he had been in drama for six years – a whole new language in what was becoming recognised as more of a director's medium than an actor's. Jill led the way.

From New York she wrote to Eva in early 1931.

Apparently Fox are quite anxious to get me. We saw the Paramount test. It's not quite so good as the Fox one but again it's better for me than Larry. RKO test we can't see because it's gone to Hollywood but they say it's very good . . . met Charlie Chaplin the other night.

And Larry wrote:

Hello darling Mum

I expect Jill has told you all about the film tests and things. I can't tell you Mum how thrilled I am at the way she's getting on. She's looked simply lovely in all the film tests. Ever so much better than she's been photographed before, and RKO have offered her an awfully good contract and are mad about her.

Unfortunately my tests haven't turned out so well, but that won't interfere with her in any way.

She's awfully good in the play and has improved beyond recognition and everything is going swimmingly. It's so lovely being together here, and I think she is fairly happy.

Everyone goes about with long faces about how bad everything is and about their handful of unemployed who sell apples at street corners, they don't know the half of it do they? Our unemployed have no apples to sell, that's about the difference.

From Jill:

> RKO seem to think I'm the 8th wonder. They offer £175 a week
> . . . not bad! I told them I would only do it if I could work for 6
> months in the year . . .
>   Larry is a little depressed.
>   I hate the idea of Hollywood but I've been on the stage 7
> years, done nothing really worthwhile and my last London
> salary was £8. London is awfully overcrowded.

And then the first plea:

> You will have to come over to me as I couldn't bear to be away
> from you for a whole year. I'm not a bit excited about it. I hate
> filming and I should probably be on my own as I don't think
> Larry is very keen to go, he has a far bigger career in the theatre
> than I have.

Then:

Times Square Theatre. March 1931

> Life is still very uncertain.
>   Larry still hasn't made up his mind what to do. We went home
> with Noël last week and talked over the situation until 4 in the
> morning. He discussed it from every angle and was very fair and
> said he thought the best thing would be for Larry to come with me.
>   It's a hell of a situation and really from a career point of view
> it's better for Larry not to do films at all, but if it's to be careers
> before everything we should never have got married as it's
> almost impossible to combine the two at the early stages of the
> game. That was one of my arguments to Larry before we got
> married. It's a hopeless situation anyway and much worse when
> you've both got futures to think of.
>   But we have got married and love each other and are very
> happy and we want to get as much from it as we can, so the only
> thing to do seems to be to compromise in careers. I am sure a
> year apart would be very dangerous to us.
>   It's a swine to solve and Larry changes his mind every day. We
> went up to arrange his contract and as he was in such a flap and
> didn't know what he wanted I did it for him.

I felt rather awful doing it all but Noël had said: 'If Larry can't make up his mind you must.' It's all settled – he is to do two pictures at $1000 a week each, then Noël's play in September, then two pictures at $1400 per week.

This was one of the most important turning points in Larry's career. The previous linch-pin, 'Private Lives', was only partly thanks to Jill. Noël might have cast Larry anyway, though there is no doubt her help was considerable. The decision for Larry to go to Hollywood was wholly thanks to her. First, because of her own success in screen-tests. Had she been no good they would not have gone. She was very good, they wanted her. Second, because she did not want to go alone and be separated from him. Third, because she actually signed Larry's contract. She did not relish filming at that stage but she believed in the medium, having spent so much time with the industry's pioneers.

While her practical grip was so effective, the letters also indicate that the emotional side of their marriage was still not good. Throughout her life, whenever Jill spoke about being 'very happy' it meant the contrary, and that she wanted to keep things to herself. Larry's describing her as 'fairly happy' indicates much the same – redolent of their awkward honeymoon. The reason was that something gynaecological was wrong and interfered with their love-making.

'Private Lives' continued to play to packed houses until it closed on 25 April. They decided to have a holiday in the sunshine of Nassau: Noël, Larry and Jill and a few theatre friends. From Miami they took the sea-plane which flew at only a few thousand feet, and descended heels down like a swan into the tropical harbour.

They had private rooms and shared a garden and swimming pool. Noël rose to the occasion, as to every other, like Rabbit with all his friends and relations from the pages of Winnie the Pooh. He organised everybody and everything precisely as he wanted.

He organised that they should all be nude. They flapped and then succumbed, and it was really quite all right. In fact it was rather nice; it made for an all-over, even tan, and as they were all so young, they were quite attractive. Swimming was heaven. At lunchtime Jill stood beside Noël's chair and held the salad bowl for him. He helped himself, then appraised her from toe to top and said: 'Darling Jilli. Have you any idea how lovely you are, just like that?'

After lunch he decided that Larry was far too hairy. While Jill was lying asleep in the sun, he and an obedient friend seized Larry, held him down, and set to work with a pair of scissors south of his stomach. She awoke, went over to them and watched. Larry looked up at her, apologetic and helpless. Noël gave a final snip, blew away the swarf, straightened up and saw her.

'There,' he said. 'That's much better, don't you think?'

'Yes,' she said. 'Much.'

She was firm and well made and fun. Her least good feature was her neck, the lack of which she had inherited from Eva, but that day she had managed to conceal it, by combing her hair down with lacquer so that it hung just above her breasts – at least so it appeared from Larry's viewpoint lying on the ground. Noël stood over her and looked down. 'Jilli darling, why must you wear your hair three feet long, when your head is set prettily, but directly, on your shoulders?'

She came to realise, as her internal problem became more painful, that Noël's titillating behaviour towards Larry had homosexual overtones. Straightforward as ever she confronted Noël and shooed him off.

Larry and Jill went sailing in a dinghy. The breeze was fresh, the sun hot and the spray cooling. They stripped and whipped through the little waves, heeling over, going about and flinging themselves against the gunwales. But they were not used to the sun. They returned in agony, and great swathes of cotton wool had to be soused in witch hazel to soothe their skin.

Back in New York Jill obtained precisely the contract she wanted for herself from RKO. She preferred them to MGM who already had so many stars she felt she would have no chance: RKO had none and wanted to make her into their own.

Before leaving for Hollywood Larry got a rash on his face. They went to a doctor recommended by Noël: Bertie Eskell, who was English. They both decided to have a check-up. Apart from the rash Larry was fine: tired but healthy. Bertie examined Jill. He found a grumbling appendix and an ovarian cyst.

Larry wrote to Eva that this was probably the cause 'Of all the little troubles she's been having lately. So Bertie planned to take this away and the appendix at the same time – making the most tremendous difference to her enjoyment of life.' He spent a full four days in her hospital. The letter, expressing his devoted love for Jill and the intimacy he felt for Eva, was written on the train to Chicago, where he would have to change trains for Los Angeles.

May 15th 1931.

And so the show finishing on Saturday, she went into the hospital on Sunday night – Gertie (Lawrence) by the way was a perfect angel and took us out into the country all Sunday to give Jill some air and take her mind off it.

After dinner we went home and packed her things and went into the hospital. I tucked her up in bed, and stayed with her until the nurse came and told me to go away. A nice room it was, but Jill said the bed was hard but she likes it now.

I can't write very well, Mum, the train's rattling so.

She was operated on at 12.30 pm and Bertie Eskell said the last thing she said was: 'Promise the incision won't show.' She wasn't a bit nervous . . . I was waiting in Bertie's office feeling terrible and inventing all the different ways that he would tell me something had gone wrong – *you* know – when he came down and said she was fine . . .

Then he said I could go and see her at about 5 o'clock when she'd come round. I came back and was taken up. O Mum it was peculiar – all shaky I was. She was lying huddled over on her left side . . . But she knew me alright, and surprised me by lifting her arm and pulling me down and kissing me, then we were alone for a minute.

Funny how when someone one loves is suffering one always wants to torture oneself and suffer too. I did.

Next day . . . I stroked her head for a bit but she was feeling a bit emotional and upset so I went downstairs and watched Bertie perform an operation – and I was so interested that I stayed for a second one. It was awfully funny, Mum, I'm not really a bit squeamish and I stood for 2 hours, watching Bertie sawing people's insides about, without turning a hair.

But I'd go up and see Jilli for a second, and perhaps she'd be having a gas pain, and I'd be all white and trembling in a second – Oh but Mum she was so good, she's got more guts than any-body I've ever met.

I went in again in the evening and stroked her head and she dozed for a bit and I was so tired that Bertie came in and found me fast asleep with my head on the bed.

Noël went in for a second just to whisper Good-bye and pat her hand.

For these last 4 days I've been almost living at the hospital, walking about the passages or sitting in Bertie's room waiting for her to wake up.

The writing becomes shaky.

> Mum you must think I'm drunk or something but it's this train!
> Besides this is a dry county . . .
> Jilli's forgotten all about it now, almost forgotten what it felt like. I don't think I shall tho' Mum, not for ages.
> It will be awful not seeing her. You must miss her terribly, Mum dear. Good-bye now darling. Your Jilli's loving Larry.

He had managed to cajole RKO to grant him twenty-four hours leave of absence so that he could stay with her for the extra, fourth, day. He was unknown as a film actor, with only a screen-test to his name, so he must have been very persuasive for them to rearrange their schedules just for him.

Many years later she told me herself how he had left.

After the operation she was so sore that even with a catheter she could not pee: no matter what they tried she was blocked and everything became more and more painful. In tears Larry had simply had to tear himself away. As he went towards the door to leave she had such an emotional wrench, her arms stretched in yearning towards him, that the blockage was released and she peed and peed and they held each other in their arms and cried with relief.

During her time under general anaesthetic she underwent the phenomenon of her conscious mind leaving her body and hovering above it, just below the ceiling. She saw, perceived, watched her body, the heads and shoulders of the nurses lifting it from the bed to the trolley, and she followed above them, down the corridor and into the lift, out, into the operating theatre.

This self of hers watched precisely what Bertie was doing and heard what was said. A few days later, she convinced him that there was indeed a part of her being that had been conscious and watched from above their heads, while the rest of her had been deeply unconscious, under their hands.

Bertie's skill made a huge difference, most surprisingly to Larry. The experience of seeing the living insides of people started a life-long fascination for their workings. 'Know thyself, be thyself' for him came to mean physical as well as mental knowledge. More significant at the time was seeing over and over again the designs of nature which were dedicated, among other things, to the enjoyment of men. His enthusiastic exposure to matters which his conscience had denied ever existed replaced his unnatural dread with a healthy deference.

For Jill too there was the direct link between the physical and the emotional. The delicate operation released a tiny but crucial constraint that had prevented enjoyment other than anticipation. So she and Larry were at last to find fulfilment, in California.

4

Hollywood

Larry was on his own, the hours of work in filming the usual ones: leaving home before dawn so as to be fully made-up with the other actors, in time for the director and camera crew. Driving to work before the world was up gave him an excitement at being wide awake with the streets so empty. He preferred this rhythm to that of the theatre, when he acted and dined late and rose from bed well after the sun was high.

Jill was a long time recuperating in New York. Her decisive signing of Larry's contract on his behalf had brought him regular employment in Hollywood and the highest salary he had ever earned. He set about preparing for her arrival. In the evenings and over weekends he sought out every estate agent and scoured high and low for a place to match his optimistic heart, worthy of his love. He could not afford a place in Beverly Hills, he did not want one on stilts over the sea alongside Pacific Coast Highway, and there were years to go before Malibu was to become desirable. He wanted a place that overlooked everything, the whole of Sunset Boulevard, the studios, across to the desert and sea, and over to downtown Los Angeles. He found it exactly. When she joined him there she wrote to Eva:

8945 Appian Way, Look-out Mountain Crest, Hollywood

June 20, 1931.

Well Mrs Esmond here we are. I can't quite believe it but it seems that I am actually in Hollywood. I was beginning to feel as if I should never get here.

The house is right on top of Look-out Mountain, built on the

side, and it looks down a canyon full of flowering shrubs and
enormous flowers called Yuccas that stand about six feet high,
and has the most amazing view of Los Angeles and the whole
valley right to the sea and more mountains ahead. It's quite the
most amazing view I have ever seen and at night when the whole
city is lit up it is unbelievable.

It's a white house and some of it is half-timbered and has a
balcony that runs all the way round, and a small garden with fig,
mimosa and other flowering trees, a little hedge and a lawn and
an old English cottage entrance.

Larry's newly demonstrated initiative thrilled her. She rhapsodised
about the size of the bedrooms, bathrooms en suite, dressing rooms
with millions of drawers, 'the laundry shoot where you put your
clothes and they fall right to our own laundry'.

Page after ecstatic page: the living room fireplace twice the size of
Apple Porch's log fire, the beamed ceiling, the baby grand Steinway,
the radio, and lighting which is 'all soft, but we like using the candles
and just a lamp or two'. She described the modernity of the kitchen.
California was fifty years ahead of England.

They had the 'most perfect servants', a German couple who had a
grand 5-seater Ford, while 'we have a 1929 Ford drop-head 2-seater
that goes very well thank-you'.

It's about 20 minutes drive from the studio. There is of course
Sollocks the puppy – he is a bit of a trial but the servants like him
and he is getting better.

The studio is very grand with Spanish gardens. I have a suite
to myself. They have nothing for me yet and I have been ordered
to lie in the sun and get fat so I spend most of my time at the
house. I go down to the studio to fetch Larry and have lunch and
get £180 a week for nothing so I'm not kicking.

She refers to his first Hollywood film, 'Friends and Lovers', at RKO.

Larry, as I knew, looks marvellous on the screen. I've seen quite
a lot of the rushes. The picture is quite good and Larry is lovely.
Everybody at RKO is wild about him. He has another 2 or 3
weeks before he finishes. He loves it out here and says he never
wants to leave.

Last Sunday we went to Ivor Novello's by the sea . . .

We went to a Hollywood First Night and vowed we would never go to another. Awful crowds, police, search-lights and all the stars being mobbed and talking over the radio, and everyone fighting and screaming. The play began an hour late.

I think this place is going to be great fun and as soon as I am really strong I mean to have a grand time. At the moment I think that's all – will you transfer my banking account to your No 3 account as you suggested.

Her links to Eva were all over the place, in every direction, like the roots of a mangrove.

Her perception of His Majesty's Inspector of Taxes was original: 'I think it would be a good idea also to take my name out of the phone book as I do not wish to pay income tax. It's awfully hot today so I'm going out. Good-bye bless you.'

It was a letter which any mother of a twenty-four-year-old would love. But it wasn't enough for Eva, who almost at once said she wanted to come out and stay with them: hardly a moment for them to breathe freely. Jill's first response was to say that she hoped Eva's play carried her through until the autumn. Meanwhile she wanted her to learn to drive as it was the only way of getting about in L.A.: 'If you want to be out for a long time, that is. If I am working I feel you will be rather stuck and you won't want to stay up at the house all day.'

She wrote about sunbathing and becoming tanned and bathing in the sea at Ivor's – his beach rather like a French beach with coloured umbrellas. She and Larry went to a party at P.G. Wodehouse's and met many interesting people. Larry had a moonlit bathe in the pool. Then six of them drove in Robert Montgomery's car right along the coast.

Friday night we gave a party for Ruth Chatterton [one of Hollywood's leading actresses] which was a great success and we all talked till dawn. It makes me laugh, Larry and I giving dinner parties with 6 courses and different wines all beautifully served by our butler! We get the giggles in the middle.

They have no film for me till August, so I may be lent to another studio to play a tough American Wop Gangster's Moll.

She managed to argue herself out of that, preferring to wait than to start with the wrong part. Larry finished his picture and RKO took up their option on his next picture: 'They are all thrilled with him as I knew they would be. We are getting to know some awfully nice people, all really top-notchers.'

Her next letter, 8 July, again has to put off the Old Lady, only five weeks after her own arrival in Hollywood.

> My operation put me 6 weeks back and made me miss my first film.
>
> I want to know definitely before you come out if I am going to be any good. If you said September instead of August I shall have a pretty good idea how things are going. If I've got to fight to get a position I want to be alone as it's easier.

And it ends by saying with the inconsistency of earnestness: 'Now listen, just because I say October instead of September it doesn't mean I don't want you.'

There are no further letters to Eva from Larry, who must at that stage have been wondering how he would cope with a sixty-year-old mother-in-law landing on them. It is hard to imagine how such an imposition could have been contemplated before Jill had even recovered from her operation. She wrote:

> July 25 1931
>
> I am not going to do the Fox picture as the tests were awful.
>
> I have ordered a marvellous wig from the man who makes Ruth Chatterton's and I think that will improve me a bit. I am to test for a picture at Universal, a marvellous part which I should like to do.
>
> Larry is such a wow that he is not going to do his play in the Autumn but is going to stay on until my option is up in December so as to get 3 more pictures.
>
> Le Baron, Head of Production of RKO says he will be a big star in a year. They ran the picture through for us, slow but Larry divine and he is so thrilled with himself that he decided that it would be wiser to make a name here and get a definite position before going back to the stage. So they are drawing up a new contract at more money for him.
>
> Darling there is no reason why you should change your plans so you must come out just the same arriving any time in October.

The original plan had been for Eva to stay with Jill while Larry went to New York to act in a play, but that arrangement was being replaced.

> By the way, Guthrie McClintic has talked a lot about you for the mother in Noël's play ['Hay Fever' on Broadway] but at the moment it is put off. Every actress in London and USA is after this part so please don't mention it.
>   It's our anniversary today. It's been a grand year and we have a hell of a lot of fun together.

After regular massage she was able to take up tennis again. Their zest was infectious, their private moments delicious, alone with a kitten called Frank, having breakfast in bed with yellow baby ducklings wandering all over them. Even Larry's gymnastics were at last adding further nodules of fibre to his 'little wires'. They became friends with Douglas Fairbanks and his wife Joan Crawford.

August 11

I've been working awfully hard. Ruth Chatterton wants me for her new picture which Guthrie McClintic is directing: a very good story. I play the daughter and have a divine drunk scene with her – it would be a grand first picture but – there's always a but – I did a test last week with a young man who was petrified and gave up in the middle.
    More complications, Janus Whale wants me for the lead in 'Frankenstein' that Universal is doing and for the last 3 days I've been testing hard – with false eyelashes and without, with wig and without. If I don't look alright then I never will as the cameraman did 'All Quiet on the Western Front', 'Robin Hood', and God knows what others and we worked all the afternoon on close-ups of me in all different lights.

Larry went at a moment's notice to 'Yellow Ticket' at Fox, which was to be followed by: 'playing opposite Pola Negri at Pathé. He did a test with her where she nearly killed him with passion and poor Larry was very disillusioned as he had always loved her on the screen, but she has become ham and rather fat.'
    That Sunday they drove sixty miles up the Pacific Coast Highway. They came across a beach cove. No one was to be seen. The bathing

was perfect. On the way home they took what they thought would be a short cut. The road wound further and further into mountains, higher and higher among rocks until they were above the clouds and looked over the top of them. They stopped and saw a deer standing quite close, on a crag silhouetted against the sky.

Their friendship developed with Douglas Fairbanks and Joan. They went to outdoor concerts at the Hollywood Bowl with Clive Brook. Their circle spread among welcoming people, including Greta Garbo, happy to receive them.

Thank God we now have 2 cars as Larry is working at Fox Hills which is miles away and I have been at Universal which is the opposite direction and our calls have been the same time.

Sollocks the dog is growing up. He's going to be great fun.

MGM sent for us the other day to play our parts in a film of 'Private Lives' with Norma Shearer and Leslie Howard but we smiled and said NO. I can't see myself as Sybil on the screen, besides I'm the same type as Norma Shearer.

The script is grand, kept nearly all the lines, merely giving it action. The beginning of the 2nd act all takes place climbing the Alps, with Eliot and Amanda in the most parlous positions, hanging on to the edges of rocks when they say: 'Foreign travel is the thing – have you ever crossed the Sahara? My grandmother had a lovely seat on a camel.'

Between filming they took a couple of days off to go to the island of Catalina, some sixty miles south of Los Angeles Marina. They rented a speed boat which Jill drove at full throttle. Larry is filmed naked, walking, sitting down, deliberately shot so that later he could study his movements. His walk is stilted and needs improvement. He dives magnificently.

They go big-game fishing. Larry straps himself into the fighting seat in the stern. He hooks a marlin. His arms and back take the strain, the thick rod bends far over as he struggles to wind in, knuckles whitened, arms pulling and grabbing. The great fish leaps out of the sea. The last shot is of the marlin, dangling on a tail-rope from a high scaffold. Larry stands dwarfed beside it, gleaming with pride. He stands lightly there. The scene goes on too long so he slaps the fish with the back of his hand and wanders off.

They were gaining confidence. Jill's recuperation left her feeling terrific, Larry loved his work and their shared moments reflected all their hopes. None of his films had yet been released which added poignant expectation, encouraged by the studio renewing his contract.

Their panache was right for Hollywood: the mountain-top house, the lavish entertainment, the shameless networking, a Hollywood remake of Harry and Eva's Apple Porch. Larry's mimicry and overacting, his different caricatures, energy and absurdity captivated everyone.

Tallulah Bankhead had an appetite which he was one of the few to deflect. He formed the secret all-male 'Tallulah Club'. It had a striped tie: purple, scarlet and pink. Membership was much sought after but diminished rapidly: the qualification was that you had *not* been to bed with her. 'Happy as Larry' could have been coined for him.

> All the fights are over and I'm going to play Ruth Chatterton's daughter in 'Once a Lady'. Paramount wanted to put in one of their contract girls and jibbed at the money, but Ruth and Guthrie McClintic the director stood firm and so I play it. It's a grand part, all my scenes are with Ruth and so I shall have to be clever about getting my face seen. I couldn't wish for a better first picture.
>
> I did some tests for Universal the other day with a marvellous cameraman and believe it or not I looked quite beautiful. It is amazing what lighting can do. Ivor Novello is in the picture.
>
> I had a cable from Dwight Wyman in New York saying can I possibly play a big leading part there in September: will pay what I ask! I'm getting on! But of course I can't and Ivor wants me for his play to be done in December, so if they don't take up my option . . .

In the middle of filming 'Yellow Ticket' Larry went the colour of saffron and was taken to hospital with jaundice. Jill had problems with her wig: Paramount insisted that *they* make it and not Ruth Chatterton's wig-maker.

While he was in hospital life continued to accelerate for Jill, with dinners at the Fairbanks's, Guthrie's and Ruth's.

Then the old subject returns: expecting Eva in October and suggesting she stay not for three weeks, don't be ridiculous, two months. And do bring Aunt Decima.

Now Decima was indeed the tenth child of the Moore family, even tinier and more formidable than Eva. She too had been a beauty, but her acting career had been taken over by imperial duties. She married the Swiss-born Sir Gordon Guggesberg, whom she accompanied when he became His Excellency the Governor of the Gold Coast. He was a great man, still honoured by the Ghanaians, who years after their Independence put up a statue of him in Accra.

She was indeed a great lady. But as a guest for two months, with Eva, in Larry's house? Unimaginable. Yet, with Larry still in hospital, Jill wrote to Eva that the two sisters must enjoy the last quarter of their lives to the full, grab all they could while they could. Regrets at *not* having done something were so much worse than any other regrets. They should return to England via China. I can picture the two elderly ladies in black lace, with veils, and hats like hydrangeas, intrepid wherever they went.

Living alone was anathema to Jill throughout her life. Now, confronted with hyperactivity and with Larry in hospital, if only for a few weeks, she became thoughtless: 'I'm determined to miss as little as possible in the future. What the hell anyway. Have a good time and enjoy life. I'm feeling extraordinarily well, and apart from Larry being ill and this bloody wig, life is very pleasant.'

By the time he was completely recovered Eva's ten-day journey from England was planned.

Jill was offered the film opportunity of her lifetime in 'Bill of Divorcement'. It was such an important role that weeks were spent in deciding for certain who should play it. The pointers were that she was the favourite.

Larry's two films for RKO, 'Friends and Lovers' and 'Westward Passage', were released and many of their friends flocked to the zany openings. Both were disastrous failures. They lost a fortune. They were simply not good films, but it was of course Larry who carried the can for not being 'box-office', even though everyone thought he was good. His terrible disappointment, after everyone's hopes had been so high, made Jill realise how deep her love was for him, and of course she felt responsible.

He wanted to go home to the London theatre. That was what he understood, knew inside out, that for him was real. He was convinced that Hollywood had been a waste of time for him. Jealousy of Jill's success was inevitable. The house became a gilded cage of disenchantment. Apart from his sense of failure and being referred to as 'Jill's husband' there was also the impending arrival of Eva.

As the discussion on 'Bill of Divorcement' continued the strain on Larry began to tell. Jill either had to risk her marriage and go after the role, or sacrifice her career. He could take no more and needed to leave. He was out of favour in the business just then.

She capitulated, and decided to accompany him home as soon as she was free from her present contract. That film which could have meant so much, launched Katharine Hepburn to international stardom. Larry was accused by his agent David Selznick of being a shit to Jill. Years later he told me he had long been troubled, guilt-ridden for once justifiably, and had asked David Selznick for his opinion: 'Was Jill really ever that good?' Selznick conceded that perhaps Hepburn was the finer actress; but that Jill was good was never in doubt.

Eva arrived alone, to stay, with Jill at work and Larry exiled at home. To judge by the loathing of her that he eventually conveyed to me, she gave him hell for standing between Jill and her success, and was merciless about his failure in the film industry. Eva then played the lead in 'The Old Dark House' and was highly praised. Larry in the attack mode could be excessively strong professionally and personally. When on the defensive he was easy to sink.

All this placed a great burden on Jill. I have tried to understand why she had to cling to Eva. Whatever happened, Eva was forthright in word and deed. She returned to England via the Panama Canal and after going up the Amazon River. With her gone Larry was able to shake off his disappointment. He did not behave like a loser; Hollywood would never have forgiven that. His behaviour impressed them. That everybody liked him was already established.

5

Cheyne Walk

They returned to 13 Roland Gardens but it was sunless and drab after California. As a house it had never meant much to them. When it came to lifestyle, and as an utter rejection of his parsimonious and genteel upbringing, Larry was determined to be king.

'I've found a huge studio. Enormous. Absolutely mad. Next to Chelsea Old Church and overlooking the river. We have to have it.'

Jill saw exactly what he meant, and was wise enough to indulge it. For curtains she chose sixty yards of white satin. They found seven-foot cider presses with trunks threaded like Gargantuan screws, which they converted into lamps with huge shades. They bought bleached oak furniture, a grand piano, and a modern radiogram with a clanking mechanical record changer. They entertained as Eva had done in her heyday and as they had in Hollywood. Their after-theatre parties celebrated an ever-widening circle of friends.

They now had a shared past: an uncertain start together, then happiness, and some serious professional strains. To say their marriage had been flawed or bored would be completely wrong. During the next three years they acted together in a film and three plays, and separately in a number of others.

They both recognised the importance of films as a means of subsidising their theatre acting. His decision to stay with films for a further year was largely at Jill's prompting and very much to his credit because his US films were shredded by critics in England as well. Professional friends and advisers told him what neither he nor Jill wanted to admit, that on screen he was full of emptiness.

They knew that on stage this quality was fundamental to his versatility. He filled the emptiness with what he had observed and selected, after try-outs, for inclusion in the character of his creation. He reached out for these elements, unlike many actors who prefer to mine something from within themselves. His characters became what he collected and retained for them, as with a human being who is largely an assemblage of what he remembers, what he doesn't throw away.

With each character he had to start empty, gobble up as much as he could from the lush foliage of his ideas and observation, for his genius like a chrysalis to form into the perfect *imago*. This constant cleansing of his being to give it room to ingest the qualities of yet another being, the jettisoning of so much, seemed, over later years, to mean that less and less of himself remained; less of his memories, less of once important truths.

The filling which he could assemble so successfully for the stage looked overdone on screen. When he tried to bring it down to size it disappeared and the camera saw a hollow being. Even so he was determined not to be seen to drop the medium after so brief an effort, because it might then drop him for ever. The press may have prompted this.

His looks came to the rescue. They prompted Gloria Swanson, megastar of the 1920s, to cast him as her husband in the film she was producing: 'Perfect Understanding'. This was an offer he couldn't refuse. She wanted to fool her admirers into accepting her as their continuing idol, with a virile youth playing opposite her.

Her shining virtue was her eyes. They had blazed fire from the screen even in earlier days when the medium was less well defined. Now that it, and unfortunately she, had matured her blemishes showed as well. She had no neck, moved badly and her voice was dull. Larry hated the film because it showed his torso as so thin. It was a flop, as Larry and Jill knew it would be when they saw the rushes.

To put things right they acted together on screen in 'No Funny Business'. Its US title 'Professional Co-Respondents' more accurately reflects the story: an agency provides a stand-in to feign dalliance with the spouse of someone wanting evidence for a divorce. An unconvincing plot, even so the film should have been better.

In Melvyn Bragg's television documentary which Larry and I watched together many years later there is a clip of him and Jill dining tête-à-tête, he gauche and she coaxing him into refinement, indicating with the subtlest expression not to order onions. I said how intelligent and lovely she looked. He riposted, 'The camera liked her,' aware that then she had acted him off the screen.

She had tried and tried at home when going through the lines, in the studio, even on the set when it was not too obvious, to get him to bring the right kind of meaning into his eyes. She failed. The blaze of the lights, the scrutiny of an inanimate lens from only a few feet away, the lumpish equipment, were objects he still could not love. It was going to take a panzer division of a director to break him in to that medium.

Jill's own screen capability continued to win her good parts in interesting films. She had a well modulated voice, a fine well-bred face, but she still moved in a roly-poly way and lacked elegance.

Much to Larry's surprise, these further films and his time in Hollywood eventually proved not to have been wasted. He had been remembered around swimming pools and from the screen by the biggest legend of the day: Greta Garbo. She summoned him back to Hollywood and the newspapers in England headlined his glory: he was to be screen-tested as her leading man. If he were chosen, Jill had every intention of renewing her own screen career.

That screen-test proved to be the end of it. The chemistry with Garbo, despite their earlier if brief acquaintance, was wrong. Yet the studios were reminded that he was very much around, was hugely admired on stage in London, and could hardly be blamed for being rejected by so capricious a lady as the Swede.

Here again he and Jill showed resilience at so public a setback. They decided against returning in a huff to the contumely of London. They flew in the opposite direction, literally into the sunset, for Honolulu. They took up surfing, assisted by a couple of Hawaiians who pushed them and their boards through the waves out to sea, where they lay flat and waited for the men to launch them on the advancing slope of a roller. They were captivated by the rush of the pale salt water beneath them, the gathering height of the breakers and the roaring foam as they were hurled up the beach. After a few days he tried it standing, to be centre stage and shout out 'Look at me'.

After his further rebuff from Hollywood their conversation would have dwelt as usual on his real passion: the English theatre. Jill later recalled that their time in Hawaii was the best they had ever had, coupling the great outdoors with his fully achieved sexuality and her completeness at last as a woman. Their safety had for so long been threatened by his constant yin-yang duality where, as he had written, 'The happiest moment has just the faintest shadow lurking some-where near it . . . unable to be conscious of being happy and still enjoy the happiness.' He had now grown out of that.

Their fulfilment heightened his awareness of how much he had within him that he wanted to give. They both deplored the current fad in London theatre, largely in imitation of John Gielgud, of Shakespearian actors using their voices like tremulo violincellos. Although none had such a beautiful voice as Gielgud, and none could approach his poet's understanding of language, many indulged in falsetto ornament, making more of cadenza'd notes than of meaning. Larry's instincts, nurtured by Jill with her background, insisted on the only truth for him that mattered: realism.

They both delighted in exploring the effects of emphasis. For example, in the familiar: 'Friends, Romans, countrymen, lend me your ears' everyone lands heavily on the 'ears'. How much more dramatic and true to life if Mark Antony screamed above the noise of the crowd to 'lend *ME* your ears' – far more chance of getting their attention by being out of scan. And in the description of Cleopatra: 'Age cannot wither her, nor custom stale . . .' with the weight on 'age'; how much more lustful to emphasise with a deep and lingering voice the word '*her*'.

No one can give a complete, nor even a pat, answer to the question of how Larry brought such naturalism and original intelligence to bear on the speaking of Shakespeare. But here there are a few further indicators to show that he did not arrive, Ariel-like and fully formed, as if by magic.

Although Harry Esmond was dead, and his plays all but dead, I have quoted from his widow on his influence as a harbinger to modern naturalism. To emphasise this further I quote from an outside source of impeccable credentials, the 'incomparable' Sir Max Beerbohm, drama critic of the *Saturday Review* from 1898 to 1910.

After regretting that most then 'modern' playwrights tended more and more towards comedy, Beerbohm indicated that Harry Esmond had written one admirable modern tragedy: '"Grierson's Way", a realistic tragedy, dealing with modern life in a Chelsea flat (where there is little opportunity for spectacle).' Nowadays this sounds like a precurser to 'Look Back in Anger': modernism, dramatic realism, if such labels help. The influences of the Esmond family were among those which Larry well and truly absorbed.

Referring to Harry's naturalism in acting, Beerbohm's words, like those already quoted from Eva, could equally well be applied to Larry: 'Mr H.V. Esmond – show me the human being who ever cocked an eyebrow so significantly, or smiled with so poignant a sweetness, at nothing in particular, or drew sighs so deep, interspersed with backward glances so piercing . . .'

This was the school Jill was born into and which she proselytised in her highly charged get-togethers with Larry. In later life she described the quivering self-adoring untouchable warblers forthrightly enough as 'a lot of cock'. In Larry she must have seen that a strong core of hands-on realism best suited his angular and animal nature – that was what she wanted in a man.

In the Hawaiian evenings they continued to do their play readings: 'Don't you realise that I am going to be the greatest actor in the world?'

History records their zest for surf-boarding, an extremely mobile stage which rose up against Larry and broke his toe. That soon mended. Jill's punishment for exuberance lasted a lifetime: the sun and spray damaged the skin of her face, bringing to the surface a myriad purple veinlets which she ever after had to cloud over with pancake make-up.

With Larry's foot in plaster and Jill's face covered in Nivea cream, they explored the outer islands by speed boat, picnicked, and enjoyed the rest of their stay at the Royal Hawaiian Hotel. Then they received an offer by cable for them both to act in 'The Green Bay Tree' on Broadway.

They had not bargained on their growing to dislike the director Jed Harris. His direction was dictatorial. Things did start well, however. Larry had to play the part of a homosexual and asked for guidance: limp wrists and gestures, pansy voice, or what? Harris's advice was inspired: 'Just move and speak, exactly as you do normally, but walk with your knees bent.'

The reviews were excellent, the play a success, especially for Larry, and he loved acting with Jill again on stage. Harris invited them for a weekend in the country with his girl-friend Margaret Sullavan. He gave her hell. To escape from him she rushed out into the pouring rain dressed only in her pyjamas. She came in only at breakfast when she knew she would be safe, with Larry and Jill there too. After that the whole enterprise went sour. Besides hating Harris, Larry's role of a homosexual, which was so totally out of character, began to depress him.

A cable from Noël Coward in London brought rescue with an offer for Larry to play the lead in 'Biography'. And so they returned, after success on Broadway, to their own home.

'Biography' flopped. They were rescued indirectly by their great friend Ralph Richardson. He had been rehearsing the part of Bothwell in 'Mary Queen of Scots', directed by John Gielgud. He couldn't bear it and pulled out, possibly because of his dislike of over-direction, a Gielgud tendency.

This last-minute opportunity for Larry brought him into a close working relationship with John G. whose status was at its height after his highly acclaimed interpretation of Hamlet. It was the first historic costume piece Larry had played. He wore a beautifully embroidered cloak. He was as proud as a peacock and at the weekend wore it on a walk in the country. Later that evening he disappeared. Jill eventually found him hidden in the seat of an old stone fireplace, sliding back and forth on his behind, in deep concentration. He held his elbows out and rubbed them against the brick walls, got tired and resumed sliding.

'What *are* you doing?' she asked.

'You see, Jilli, I've just realised what's wrong with this cloak. It's got to look worn and lived in,' and carried on rubbing the seat and elbows of the beautiful new garment.

One scene in the play had him, the arrogant and overpowering Bothwell, patronising a man played by James Mason, while tossing a coin. At one performance he dropped it. In the haughty tones of Bothwell he said: 'Pick that up,' to which Mason replied, 'Pick it up yourself.' Such unprofessionalism helped James Mason wave good-bye to the theatre. Bothwell would have had him hanged, drawn, quartered and fed to dogs.

Others in the cast were more professional and became life-long friends, of whom only Mercia Relph survived Larry. Her husband George had acted with Eva in 'Caesar's Wife' in 1919 and had often stayed with Mercia at Apple Porch. Two of the other actors, Glen Byam Shaw and George Devine, collaborated with Larry as directors in a number of projects years later.

The star system was then at its height. People would ask not 'What's on?', but 'What's Laurence Olivier, or Gladys Cooper, in?' Directors would take a play and cast stars appropriate to the leading characters in it. This encouraged versatility. It also meant that actors' lives had no security from one play to the next, unlike the ensemble Larry put together in the 1960s at the National Theatre, where actors could be in several overlapping plays in repertory. The director could select the play for an actor, rather than the other way round, where much depended on who your cronies were; hence the parties at Cheyne Walk, with the most amusing people and the ones who had something to offer professionally. Like Hollywood, the West End theatre was largely a 'relationship business'.

As a mascot to their self-confidence Larry and Jill acquired a ring-tailed lemur, a rare creature from the Madagascan rain forests, where there were no monkeys to kill them. Tony was a foot high, with soft fur, patent-leather hands and muzzle, bright round eyes and a long raccoon-like tail. At Cheyne Walk he had a cage. At Apple Porch he slept in a tiny cupboard he found in the panelling above the dining-room fireplace.

At dinner he liked to sit on people's shoulders, every tit-bit held between his hands for nibbling. After balancing on his hind legs he would jump over the table and land on the shoulder opposite. Sometimes he would drink wine, leap with complete abandon and miss.

In the garden he used to sit and spread his hands out to the sun, gurgling with contentment. He clung to Jill or Larry when frightened by a strange dog or a banging door. Perhaps he awakened Jill's maternal instinct, suppressed by her ambition as an actress. She used to wonder whether, if she had a child, she would love it as much.

Larry's next play 'Theatre Royale' was directed by Noël Coward. It was a comedy take-off of John Barrymore whom Larry impersonated, leaping from great heights. It was written by the Americans Edna Ferber and George S. Kaufman, who endeared himself to Larry; they discussed Jed Harris and their shared dislike of him. 'His own worst enemy,' Larry said. Kaufman replied: 'Not while I'm alive.' And when Jill complained how impractical Larry was in the house, not even able to mend a fuse, Kaufman said: 'I can't even hold a hammah.'

The leading lady was Dame Marie Tempest. She took a deep old shine to Larry which was just as well. One night during the fight scene his sword swept out of his hand and he watched it, as if in slow motion, arcing through the air towards her. It walloped her bosom. She screamed. The curtain came down and there were varied forms of panic. Young actors said it was too awful and poor Larry, *weel* his career was finished now, while older ones said it served the silly old girl right. The most vivid anxiety was presented to Jill when she arrived from her own play, to be confronted by the pansy stage doorkeeper.

'Oh Mrs Olivier the most *dweadful* thing happened . . .'

'Yes, *yes*?' she peered into the tiny window. 'What is it?'

'Your husband's sword . . .'

'Is he all right?'

'His sword flew. It did fly, Mrs Olivier . . .'

'For God's sake, how is he?'

'Flew across the stage and struck Dame Marie on the er, the . . .' and he spread his hand over an area well below his stomach, '. . . er, the bweast.'

No doubt Larry's ministrations and shocked sympathy elicited a heartfelt hug from the old actress.

Larry and Jill now prepared to do Romeo and Juliet, and made daily studies of the verse, the possible meanings, the analyses written. Mercia said they seemed marvellously suited to each other, complementary in many ways. On stage there was a certainty that he would indeed be the great actor he was so steadfastly set on being, and Jill's support was the best he could have had.

Had jogging then been fashionable Larry and Jill would have been devotees. They played tennis, and took long country walks at Apple Porch, on regular weekends starting after the theatre on Saturday, and ending on Monday afternoon, for them and as many friends as they wished. For George and Mercia it was like a second home, especially after George had a car crash which did terrible damage to his jaw, for the second time, the first being from a German bullet in the Great War.

Larry's leaps in 'Theatre Royale' drew standing ovations for the excitement they added to an already dramatic performance. He became a matinée idol. Why matinée only? Every night he had to stay behind in his dressing room autographing dozens of theatre programmes after he had taken off his make-up and had a shower. He would sit, squiggling away, careful to ensure that the two 'i's' of Olivier were separately dotted, while alternating sips of Scotch and puffing a cigarette. Once signed, the programmes would be handed back to the fans waiting excitedly outside the Stage Door. He and the rest of the cast had to make their exits, smiling and trying to look happy, even when the pressure of people became alarming and the outstretched hands seemed to threaten, as adored as royalty and as tugged at as pop stars.

His lack of sporting success at school was now more than compensated for by his developing physical power. This magnified his self-confidence, and in turn the force of his already strong stage presence. He was thought by many to be the handsomest man they had ever seen, in an age when looks and masculinity were greater preoccupations than they are now. He always claimed that acting was largely to do with sex appeal. Adulation helped liberate him from his upbringing.

His interest was in acting to the exclusion of almost all else. He had little time to discuss politics or other news. When he picked up a newspaper it was only to turn to the reviews and notices. During the General Strike he had become an announcer on the London Underground and this he turned into a charade he liked to recall: 'Pass right down the car please, thenkyoop, moind the doors.'

His changes of mood, sometimes in mid-sentence, make him a difficult subject for biographers who never knew him. For those not used to this, or growing up as I did under his tutelage, they could be alarming. 'My dear darling boysie how simply splendid to see you and how wonderful you look, and where the fuck did you get that awful tie. Take it off. Jesus, you come here looking like a hobo I can never understand it. I was delighted by your last letter. Now about our holiday . . .'

If he seemed down in the dumps one minute, that did not mean that this state of mind would continue. Usually it meant that he wanted to play that role, the being-sad role, and try it a bit differently. If someone suggested marital discord as a possible topic, by complaining that his wife did not understand him, Larry would certainly be tempted to pretend to the same problem, and invent grievances to joke about. It was a trait quite contrary to the truth and consideration he applied when he consciously put his mind to things. His manners concerning the unconscious day-to-day events were appalling. In a dreaded Truth game, where the object was to award points for various things, Jill once gave him two out of ten for manners. He was furious all the way home.

1935 was to see him become more of an establishment figure, with membership of the Garrick Club. They rented the Dower House, near Apple Porch, in Burchetts Green. It was substantial, Georgian, with a walled garden at the end of a country lane beyond an Elizabethan house of brick and timber. Ivor Novello's Red Roofs was only a mile away.

Larry and Jill spent a weekend with the Duke of Kent and his lovely wife Princess Marina who was a fan of Noël's. It was unsuccessful perhaps because of Larry's switching between being over-the-top and very shy. After dinner they played match houses. Even here Larry managed to overact. As the boring squares of matchsticks reached thirty storeys or so he blurted out to the Duke, who had a match poised: 'Look out! . . . You're shaking the whole of Kent!'

And the Duke replied, 'Yes, the whole of Kent is shaking.' The evening was rescued by Noël playing one of his new numbers.

Larry's leaps on stage continued, including one over a banister with a landfall eight feet below. He took every risk known. Inevitably he missed timing one night and broke his ankle.

The next play 'Ringmaster' had him cast in a wheelchair, with Eva's old friend Dame May Whitty, whom they referred to as Dame May Titty, and Jill. They were directed by their Canadian friend Raymond Massey whom Larry did not respect as an actor, still less as a director, which made him want more than ever to become a director himself.

This ambition was first prompted by his loathing of the intrusive Harris, then John Gielgud who would be so full of criticism and bright little ideas, that the constant stopping, restarting and interruptions prevented the whole play being worked through, for many days, by which time they had forgotten the finely tuned beginning.

Such stop-go was considered usual, even the traditional approach to directing. Larry wanted to make more of the alternative: letting the actors have the earliest possible run-through, however rough, so that they could see themselves and each other's performances in toto and grow into them the way *they* saw them, guided but not drilled by the director, and certainly without constant interruption.

Before starting rehearsals as director of 'Golden Arrow' by Cunard, he worked out all the main moves, using a model theatre a yard square with figures two inches high for each actor. The detail would evolve in rehearsal once the cast knew what the play was about.

Larry's approach to directing was also derived from Henry Esmond; to quote from Eva's *Exits and Entrances*:

> Harry knew that anything, whether tone of voice or gesture or movement is very rarely ridiculous if it is prompted by real feeling. He knew that the real justification for anything an actor may do on stage is 'because I *feel* it', not 'because I think it will look effective'. As a director – and he was one of the very best directors I have ever seen – he got the very best out of his company because he always, when asked 'What do you want me to do here?' answered 'What do you feel you *want* to do?' He nursed his company, and watched them.

That too could very well be written about Larry.

He cast the play with actors who shared his enthusiasm for this approach. In a way that became typical he made a 'Discovery' in his very first production: Greer Garson, a well-educated, red-haired, Irish beauty. Her sparkling green eyes she would have loved to have been only for him. In any audience there were many ladies who sat and lusted. The play flopped, but according to Mercia Relph, Greer did have her way with him, if briefly.

One day at the Dower House he was carving a small chicken to go round a large number of friends – a skill remembered by anyone once impecunious – when a thought hit him. He spun round, carvers held aloft, and declaimed: 'I am going to have a son, and call him Tarquin.'

Larry and Jill had as ever been working on play readings at home.

This time it was 'Macbeth', in which he was to play the title role two years later at the Old Vic, at the end of the Shakespeare season which included him as Henry V and a full-length Hamlet: the season that raised him to the heights of recognition as a leading Shakespearian actor. The line is: 'With Tarquin's ravishing strides toward his design, Moves like a ghost.'

In the comparative cool of my own middle age I asked him whether he had thought the word 'ravishing' meant 'graceful' or some such. 'No. I knew perfectly well it referred to the determination of a rapist.'

My name never became a problem. Nobody had read Shakespeare's tragic poem the 'Rape of Lucrece', nor the novel 'Cage me a Peacock' where Tarquin was a godly sex object; by the time of 'Love Among the Dahlias', where he was a deviate hunch-back, it mattered no more. Sometimes Americans ask: 'Yeah, but what do your friends call you?'

I have always resisted abbreviation, except from those who are very close. Rather like the French 'Tu': when out of place, it grates. The advantage of the name is that once people understand it, they never forget it. The disadvantage is that I often forget theirs.

Swearing by the nine gods and Great Houses apart, there have been occasions when people have been funny about it. I always fancied the idea of the 'Lays of Ancient Rome'. Years later on my way to Hanoi, the clerk in Bangkok read my air-ticket: 'Olivier The Hon. T'. Perfectly correct. The clerk asked: 'Are you Vietnamese?' Curious, I replied 'Noo. Why?' 'Olivier well-known French first name, Tay Hon Tee big noise in Saigon.'

Again, in Los Angeles the Avis car-hire man, educated and black, read 'The Honourable Tarquin Olivier' on my driving licence. He scratched his head. 'Ain't never seen a name like that. No I have not. What kind of a first name is it anyway – "The"?'

Jill and Larry's plans to do 'Romeo and Juliet' together were scuppered when John Gielgud offered him the role in his own production, to his Mercutio and Peggy Ashcroft's Juliet. Long before, Jill had taken over from Peggy as a star when 'Bird in Hand' opened in London. It was difficult for her to wave good-bye to all the preparation she and Larry had done for their own production, but she knew that there was no room for equivocation, that the great John Gielgud was offering Larry an ideal opportunity to come to grips with Shakespeare and make a name for himself as a classical actor.

One consequence of the months of her work with him was that Larry was fixed in his interpretation of the role. Rehearsal time was brief which enabled him to resist the interpretation Gielgud wished to impose. Larry acted a scorchingly passionate Italian with brown skin, the first of many false noses, and padded calves under the tights to make his legs sculptural. His naturalism contrasted with Gielgud's poetry and was at first damned by the critics. His sensualism pulled in large audiences, and eventually even a few of the leading critics came to a qualified admission that his Romeo was a cause of some fascination.

There is a touching fan-letter to him from wise old Eva, whose espousal of realism is evidenced by her autobiography, and her success by *Who's Who in the Theatre* listing more credits for her than almost any other actress.

5 Cresswell Place, The Boltons, SW10

(Undated)

Larry Darling – Your Romeo gave me the greatest joy. I've seen lots, but never one who *was* youth and really in love, and never has one, till now, made me cry. The Banished Scene has never moved me. I expect your power and youth gave me what it has always missed before.

You look fine. In fact I loved every moment of your performance. I've only one *wee* grumble and when we meet I will tell you what it is.

I thought the way the house listened was splendid, not a movement, that one seldom gets these days. John [Gielgud] must be very happy about it all.

Take care of yourself darling, do go gently. You use up so much of yourself. You must rest. A proud mother-in-law & Loving Mum.

Fascinating that she wanted to give him a 'note'. Even Aunt Decima wrote, from the Ladies' Army and Navy Club – where else? – that his performance was electric.

Gielgud saw Romeo with his own poet's eyes and his mellifluous voice amplified his belief that the heights of Shakespeare's music should indeed soar, almost like an aria. His reputation as the great proponent of his day had been founded on his exposition of these qualities. Indeed, his recordings show that, as a poetic interpreter, he was supreme. Larry, on the other hand, was actor rather than poet, and bent the verse to his own portrayal of the young Veronese lover.

They amazed London again by swapping roles. The economics were indeed a marvel: two plays for the cost of a single production, being identical in cast and all save the two male protagonists' costumes. It meant for John Gielgud that he could be the Romeo he wanted, and for the theatregoing public that they had to see the same play twice.

Of the two roles Jill preferred Larry as Mercutio: the Shakespearian young man – tousled, extrovert, provocative and adorably mad, derring-do for anything, but loyal and teasingly loving. How like Larry!

He described his Romeo as trying to play for sympathy when the character's main drive was an erection. But what a beautiful scaffolding he provided; discreetly clad graceful muscles, lank black hair cropped and pious under a skull cap, deep smouldering dark eyes; a stunning series of contradictions. Again, how like Larry!

In November 1935 Jill conceived, the first of what she hoped would be two or three children. She looked forward to stepping off the stage for a while, to reflect Larry's Christian wish to be a father, and her own to be a Mum.

Like other West End actors, they performed in their separate plays on Christmas Eve. Next morning they drove up to stay with Roger Livesey and his wife Ursula Jeans at Sarrat in Hertfordshire, a tiny brick house in a terrace of six overlooking a wide graveyard leading up to a flint church. It was close to Bunny Austen and Phyllis Konstamm who had been Larry's leading lady in 'Murder on the Second Floor' in New York. Two other fine actors were also there, Dickie Hudd, and Robert Flemyng who is the only one of the house-party left to remember how happy they were. They all went to Evensong.

Larry gave Jill a bracelet with a number of charms. First a ruby. Then a crescent clasping a disc with hieroglyphics on each side; when the disc is spun, the message joins together and reads 'Xmas 1935'. Next, half an inch high, is a Virgin in sapphires and a baby in diamonds. Then, the number 6 because they had been married six years before I was started. Finally an onyx target with a tiny diamond in the bull's eye.

On the return drive to Cheyne Walk they looked forward to seeing their lemur Tony again. They were anxious because the maid had once let him out of his cage, thinking he would recognise the authority in her voice as he did with Jill, and behave with sweet reason. Tony had bounded to the window, up to the roof, and swung from the eaves into the neighbour's bedroom where there was an enormously fat woman getting dressed. He loved it. He terrorised her, and was found by Jill prancing up and down, keeping the poor woman cornered in her underwear. As soon as Jill came to the rescue he clasped his hands to his face to show how sorry he was.

This time the maid assured them that he was still in his cage. They went upstairs, Larry to the bedroom to let him out, Jill to powder her nose. Tony was in Larry's arms when she came into the room. As soon as he saw her he knew: she was pregnant, and he flung himself at her in a screaming jealous rage. He bit her hand and clenched his teeth. She had betrayed him. Larry managed to prize open his jaws, wrench him away, struggling, and put him back into his cage where he sat, glowering, shaking.

The passing of the months calmed the hatred in his eyes. He could come out of his cage, was obedient, sullen, went down to the country with them, to the Dower House, to the grocer's shop, and paid visits to Apple Porch. But the love was gone.

Jill heard rumours that Romeo was seeing Juliet after hours. She went to London. Peggy Ashcroft explained that, while romance was to be expected for such passionate protagonists, Jill could rest assured that her pregnancy was sacred and that there was nothing further to worry about from her. Jill felt embarrassed to have asked, but deeply grateful to Peggy.

She spent days at Apple Porch with Eva, to be joined at the Dower House by Larry when he came back at midnight from the Lyric Theatre. He and Ralph Richardson had directed and were playing in 'Bees on the Boatdeck' by J.B. Priestley. They saw eye to eye and worked well together, with a feather-light touch which allowed their actors to experiment. Harry Esmond would have approved.

Anxieties were accumulating over Europe after Hitler's rise to power with his appalling rhetoric about world domination. Larry was to act in the first of a number of morale-raising films intended to stiffen England's sinews in the face of appeasement and the renewed threat of German militarism.

'Fire Over England' was derived from A.E.W. Mason's novel, and produced by Alexander Korda, a Hungarian Anglophile. Larry was to play a passionate young Englishman who had seen his father burnt at the stake by the Spanish Inquisition, and had just managed to escape back to England.

Opposite him was cast Vivien Leigh.

6

Vivien

In May 1935 Larry and Jill had admired Vivien in 'The Mask of Virtue'. She had herself introduced to them at the Savoy Grill where she knew they often lunched, and since they moved in the same circles Jill asked her down for lunch that summer at the Dower House with her husband Leigh Holman, a barrister with a dry wit who was at ease among actors.

It has been alleged that Larry fell in love with Vivien before Jill conceived and that the pregnancy was somehow unfair. This is nonsense. No doubt he noticed Vivien. Everyone did. And no doubt he flirted with her in front of Jill and Leigh. It is true that Vivien had wanted him in 1934 when she saw 'Theatre Royale' and had determined then that he was to be the love of her life: she told me so. But the occasion for intimacy never arose until she was filming with him.

Korda knew that Vivien was married to Leigh, who was distinguished and wealthy, and had a three-year-old daughter Suzanne, and that Larry was married to Jill who was a month or so from giving birth. He would have guessed at Vivien's designs on Larry. He wanted good product. A fling during shooting was recognised as conducive to passion on screen; it's in the nature of the business. His was the position of any producer wanting the grand emotions to blaze forth.

As Korda built up Denham Studios he desired the increased recognition of discovering his own Star, one with a unique quality. Eventually Vivien was the actress he chose. She was a big success in the West End with 'The Mask of Virtue'. Her beauty was flawless, poised and aristocratic; her swanlike neck, her translucent skin and the delicate perfection of her features gave her an ethereal quality which seemed to deny the existence of earth and blood and fire. Yet her compound of these was erotic.

She had been born in Darjeeling, the summer retreat for the ladies and families of the Raj, while her father Ernest Hartley, a Yorkshireman, hung on in Calcutta's heat as a rich exchange broker. He was a delicious character, a gifted amateur actor and womaniser. He married Gertrude, a pale Anglo-Indian beauty, and, given the hypocrisy of the time, was obliged to resign from the Calcutta Club. She was a woman of spirit and energy. She once threw a party for all the women whom she knew had been to bed with him, and their husbands. I wonder how many of them realised, and whether she had devilishly invited one or two who hadn't. So Vivien, like Jill, was sent to a boarding school at a tender age to distance her from paternal misdemeanours.

At her English convent was Beatrice Dawson who was as busy as a bee and was nick-named 'B'. Later in life as she became larger and lazier this was changed to 'Bumble'. The girls had to wear shifts even when having their baths, to hide their nakedness. Repression had the opposite effect on them that it had on boys. Their imaginations blazed. Vivien would spend hours making up lists of dirty thoughts she could confess, so as to make the longest confession of any of the girls and therefore be thought deep, and also be able to peer through the grill at the white-faced young priest sitting so close and listening to every whisper.

One of her schoolmates told me of her skill in anything to do with gym and body movement. If the class was in difficulty the teacher would say: 'Oh Vivien, you show them.' She was also capable of cruelty like every other child. Once at tea Vivien was saying: 'Don't you love it in the hottest bath and lying right back, when you stretch your hands down beside you and spread the fingers wide under the water? Isn't that lovely?' 'Yes, yes, I know just what you mean!' 'Silly little thing, how could you, with hands as ugly as yours?'

She was sent abroad to Heidelberg and then to France and became a good linguist, but at the personal cost of being a constant guest even though one or both of her parents were sometimes in attendance. She never really had a room of her own, an accumulation of her own things, a place for herself to retreat to. As a guest she was a model of neatness, mistress of the art of pleasing, expert in finding the little present that was just right. She was generous, outgoing and determined, but with little emotional ground to concede. She grew up with no firm foundations to fall back on. With uneven support from her mother and father she was vulnerable, a guest in her own life, touching to all who loved her, with the corollary of becoming the most sparkling guest in theirs.

Leigh Holman, the highly civilised and kindly man she married, used to remind me of Ashley Wilkes in 'Gone with the Wind', but with a stronger character. They lived in a little Mayfair house near Shepherd Market: 6 Stanhope Street. When their daughter Suzanne arrived Vivien found she was by no means happy in motherhood. She hated being tied down, and sought more and more to be in the theatre and films.

It was Larry on stage who inspired her. For her he was the most glorious adornment and theatrical genius of all time. She was determined to lay down her life for him.

Denham Studios were an hour's journey west of London. Larry and Vivien began shooting in August 1936. Sometimes they would drive down together when they were in the same scenes. It was obvious almost from the start of shooting that Vivien was out to get him. She later admitted that the most terrible thing a woman could do was to take a man away from his wife when she was expecting a baby.

Jill, great with child and her poor complexion interlaced with mauve veins, was defenceless and looking her worst. Larry still loved the woman who had become the way she was, through him; in his set of sails loyalty was a very strong stay, as was shared suffering. But the combination of Vivien's radiant beauty and acuteness, with the film's demands for passionate embraces, closeness that made exchange of breaths inevitable, mouth-to-mouth kissing, and her determination to have him, proved too much.

It was as old as the apple, as irresistible; the more so because daily they saw the rushes, sitting in the dark together watching themselves passionately kissing on screen. It must have been as alerting as mirrors on the ceiling and once they had grabbed the forbidden fruit it became a drug. The effect on his acting was to make him a blazing lover, which thrilled everyone. Any hollowness discerned by the camera's lens in earlier films was now filled to overflowing. Vivien did that for him.

After filming for three weeks, he was alerted that Jill's birth pangs had begun. He and Vivien had been doing many takes of an embrace. He hurtled into his dressing room, tore off his costume, leapt into slacks and jersey and without pausing to take a shower, sped home.

He rushed upstairs, into the bedroom and flung his arms round Jill.

This was the most terrible, the most unlucky thing he could have done; he smelled of Vivien. This might have meant nothing. But Jill knew. She held his hand; he must have known what was in her mind. He adored her. He sat up with her the entire night. When the contractions came she gripped hard, with the strength of great pain; at the end of her fourteen hour labour with the ultimate need for some surgery, his hands were raw and swollen.

The baby had punctured the membrane and swallowed fluid. The doctor put it in cold water, then hot water, then cold again and just managed to bring it to life.

With the tight shooting schedule Larry returned to work next day. He brought Vivien home with him to show her his son. In a letter to Leigh she described the baby as large, reasonable to look at, but with an unfortunate resemblance to Edward G. Robinson: the effect of a bruising delivery?

This action of his bears examination. It pleads an element of make-believe: his mistress at his wife's accouchement. Perhaps it was supposed to look like the deed of an innocent man, bringing an innocent friend from work to offer congratulations. Part of him would have wished it were so, but another part knew full well he was guilty of the most cruelly timed adultery, with a woman who was married to a blameless husband and had her own little daughter. Their presence side by side was perhaps a double bluff, or a reflection of his craft as an actor – someone trying to convince that he is another, with the accompanying pain of standing outside his own body, watching and not really being a part of anything as it really was.

In their film's love scenes the call was for innocence, where consummation lay chastely over the horizon – at the other side of marriage. Putting on their wistful expressions, so sweet and brave in a threatening world, was quite an act. They were both adept at it, even though they might have leapt into their roles directly from the hurly-burly of a studio dressing room chaise-longue. No time for the preparatory introspection of method acting!

It was a remarkable case of jettisoning one truth for another at speed, or one lie for another. All she wanted was him, with guilt put to one side. He had been seduced, and loved it, by someone who made him feel better than he had ever felt. But as the actor, all innocence on the surface, looking down at his own wife and baby, he was probably storing up in his memory how what he was doing really made him feel, so that he could later make more excruciating a characterisation which demanded such knowledge.

Larry was an attentive father, proud of pram-pushing, fond of bath-time and bottle-feeding, easily persuaded that the baby loved him. His exuberance, never far off, led him to declamations which evoked shrieks of terror from his son, whom he then comforted, panic-stricken. His over-concern at the baby's apparently unbreathing sleep prompted anxious prods to discover if life prevailed: more shrieks and more comforting, deep sighs and cuddling.

Jill needed a rest from childbirth, from London, from the near presence of the woman who threatened all that they had hoped for as man and wife. She sought the kind of sunshine and sea she and Larry had loved in Nassau, California, and Hawaii. The Mediterranean beckoned.

They checked into the Hotel Quisisana in Capri, wondering whether the magic of the place would work. Within only a few days they were landed upon by Vivien, determined to prize them apart, accompanied by an elderly male chaperone. Larry, seeing the two women concurrently, realised, as did Jill, that he had quite simply been taken over by Vivien. They were all photographed together, with Jill's unmade-up mauve-veined face swollen with sunshine, and perhaps with crying.

Back in London she tried everything she could to hang on to him. She attempted to get to know Vivien. They lunched together and Vivien took the opportunity to discover all she could of Larry's likes and dislikes, how she could improve herself in his eyes. Like Jill, she loved him for his sake as well as for her own. As Jill later said to me: 'Real passion – I've only seen it that once. If you are ever hit by it, God help you. There's nothing you can do.'

She went to Vivien's house with its tiny rooms filled with exquisite feminine taste. Although her own style was less precious she admired the place. Despite herself she could not help liking Vivien. Aware that Vivien was making it happen, she would sit unbelieving: she had gone there to fight for her family.

Vivien asked her about breast-feeding. Jill admitted that she had tried but nothing happened. So the baby was immediately put on a bottle and she felt a failure as a mother. 'Not as much a failure as me. You see, Jilli darling,' and Vivien explained that she had breast-fed Suzanne and hated it. It pulled her breasts down and they had never recovered their shape. It had put her off babies for ever.

Vivien, although fluent in French and German, was not then as well-educated as has been claimed. She wished to be. She recognised that Jill's theatrical and literary background was invaluable when it came to seeking which writers to explore. Jill was reminded of her own earlier years with Larry, and his quest to make up for not having had a higher education. She was astonished to find herself passing on all she could to Vivien, as though they were the closest of friends. Next time they met Vivien would have read what Jill had suggested and be keen to discuss it. She learnt fast.

Much delayed, the Christening was held, with nothing resolved, on 9 December in Chelsea Old Church: Farve officiating. It was his first grandchild so he was determined to be moving. For the baptism itself he was so carried away that he forgot the font had a cupola, and he repeatedly hit his head on it. Larry and Jill could still giggle.

For her the baby felt heavier and heavier. A photograph taken afterwards outside the church shows her puffy-faced and defeated, over-burdened with a large three-and-a-half-month-old baby. In the background is Farve, lean and unknowing. Larry stands obsequiously, leaning towards his wife and baby, improperly dressed, trilby in hand, tweed cape out of place, as if he had hurried there from somewhere else. Looking across Jill and the baby and daggers at Larry, is Eva. The godparents were Mercia Relph, Sybil Thorndike, Noël Coward and Ralph Richardson who had once said: 'Laurence has the most splendid fury.' So had Eva.

Alexander Korda was assured of the success of Vivien and Larry in 'Fire Over England' and he brought them together again to star in 'The First and the Last', a screenplay by Graham Greene based on the John Galsworthy book. As a film it did not succeed, but it provided time and place for their romance to mature. It kept Jill at arm's length. It became obvious to all that the affair was overpowering.

During the run of 'Romeo and Juliet', Tyrone Guthrie had been a guest at Apple Porch, and had told Larry that he wished to produce him in a season of Shakespeare at the Old Vic. 'Hamlet' opened early in 1937 and was hailed as pulsating with vitality, but vilified as manic rather than introspective. Alec Guinness said that as a performance it laid the foundations for Larry's future greatness as an actor. It was a full length Hamlet, which Larry said made it less exhausting: there were a few scenes without him when he could rest off-stage, scenes which are cut in any abbreviated version.

At one performance the most 'dweadful' thing happened during the duel. Laertes fell splendidly on his back, legs akimbo, but his cod-piece burst open. He raised a downstage knee to hide his manhood from the audience and the play continued. The problem was next evening's performance: the very first scene on the battlements of Elsinor, when the soldiers were expecting the ghost to appear.

'What,' Marcellus asked, 'Has this *thing* appeared again tonight?' It was no good. The actors' convulsed laughter brought the curtain down, long before the 'Crowing of the cock'.

Larry suggested to Tony Guthrie that before embarking upon 'Henry V' it might be a good idea, as a refresher, if he were to play a buffoon, lest he be type-cast as an heroic youth. He wanted to cultivate the variety which theatre audiences so relish, whenever there is an actor who can present it.

Falstaff? No. He regarded that as the exclusive preserve of his friend and mentor Ralph Richardson. He suggested Sir Toby Belch in 'Twelfth Night'. For this he stuck more make-up on his face, and into his mouth, than was believable; a nose like a fist, eyebags as if to push them would make whisky pour out. He gargantuanly o'erstepped modesty. He mistimed the pentameters, misplaced the commas, romped, huffed and minced, and scored a buffoon's hit. Alec Guinness played the most pained Aguecheek, Jill: Olivia, and Jessica Tandy: Viola.

His performance was a watershed, a kind of ha-ha between the neat lawns of his conditioning and the more fertile unmown grasses, where his own nature grew high. Wildness in the Shakespearian young male Mercutio is to be expected, and he had found more besides; after Sir Toby his inventiveness seemed boundless.

Curiously his Henry V was not his own creation. Like some of the greatest generals of this century he hated war, equated it only with ignominy, inhumanity and death. In his reading he found King Hal shallow, a sort of bully. He imagined that he could discover depth by slowing the pace for introversion, most tellingly of concern for his soldiers.

His director, the improbably tall Tyrone Guthrie, had persuaded him to take on the part, knowing of his fire and brimstone; now he was confronted with a wimp. Tony's limbs were immensely long. So were his fingers. When he could take no longer the molasses pace which Larry was mixing into a paste, he broke the rules which he knew the Esmonds and now Larry held so dear. He interrupted. He flicked his ruler-long fingers with an angry snap.

Then, certainly not for the last time in his life, Tony said, with the accented note liltingly lower: 'Rise a*bove* it.' He coaxed out of Larry the passion which was seven years later to be recorded for ever in the film. He awakened his nationalism, made him feel Henry simply had to be in the front line, scorning those who would think themselves accursed they were not there. With such a ball passed to him upon such a playing field Larry took it up, to run, and run and run, and found the silver trumpet in his voice to cry out the glory of England.

Day by day the love between him and Vivien blotted out all other love. It destroyed their most firmly held beliefs in the sanctity of marriage, outshone their religious upbringings, and replaced these with a new belief for each of them, only in each other, a kind of idolatry. They met in secret places. Some of their friends found it moving, exciting, desperately romantic, some found it a perfume-soaked game of let's pretend, the posies exchanged, the babyish endearments.

The Danish Government invited the Old Vic Company to perform 'Hamlet' in front of the Danish Royal Family at Kronberg Castle, a baroque pile with pointed copper roofs on the site of Elsinore. Larry persuaded a reluctant Tony Guthrie to recast the role of Ophelia with Vivien. Despite unseasonal storms and having last-minute changes of auditorium their romance made the piece become a *succès de folie sexuale* even during rehearsals.

Jill, as his wife for this Court occasion, had to accompany him to Denmark. It was a dreadful humiliation. Kindly actors in the company tried to keep her company. Alec Guinness who played Osric told me he took her rowing on the lake so as to get her away from it all, but it was a wretched time. Even the audience was gurgling, or however the glottal Danish buzz can be described, with the gossip.

On their return to London, Larry and Vivien told their respective spouses that they could no longer live without one another. Jill sought the advice of Noël Coward. He went to see Larry for a fuller picture and, having mulled things over, advised Jill, whom he had known the longest, that the best thing would be to escape to the South of France: 'Sail away'. He was thoughtful and fair-minded. He was also excited at witnessing in Larry such passion as he had never seen. Jill sensed this. She was not wholly convinced of his wisdom. George and Mercia told her she must stay, but Noël's advice carried greater weight.

She left the bottle-feeding to a Norland Nanny and set off for Antibes, accompanied by her fond but neuter stockbroker Donald Krolik – and Mercia. They stayed at the Hotel du Cap and swam and had wonderful food and wine and were determined that Larry would, when his filming with Vivien was over, see the error of his ways, be true to his real self, and return to be the good husband and father he had always believed in. Other friends were there – Jessie Winter, Cicely Courtnedge, quite a few theatre people and they all did what they could to make Jill forget that her heart had been sliced.

Larry and Vivien moved out of their houses and immediately created a love nest of their own in London.

The sad little party returned to England and found out.

7

The Bad Time

The Norland Nanny was alone in Cheyne Walk, the milk wrist-tested, the bottle full, a basket of fresh nappies ready to take upstairs. She was concerned to find the nursery door unlocked. She pushed it open with caution. The curtains were drawn and the light was dim. To her horror she saw that Tony was inside the cot, tail fluffed out, eyes like lasers burning with hatred.

After agonised discussions which brought them together for a while, Jill and Larry agreed that Tony had to go. They found him a home in the London Zoo where there was a female ring-tailed lemur, who they hoped would comfort him. But Tony never settled down. The female bullied him. Jill visited him, so did Larry, but his delight at their arrival and his increasingly agonised screams at each departure only added to his torture. He died.

Jill left Cheyne Walk and settled for a lease on a sizeable house, 31 Queen's Grove, St John's Wood, miles away. There was a pond in the front and a tiny lawn, and the back garden was large and featureless except for a plane tree with a branch cascading to the ground.

She took most of the furniture and engaged a healthy eighteen-year-old governess called Joan Coxell. She couldn't bear any kind of tenderness. The only records she could listen to were Stravinsky, cruel music. Sweet sounds made her break down completely. These years she was to refer to as her 'Bad Time'.

Joan was calm and caring. She took photographs, tucked wedges over the corners and stuck them into albums with black pages, the date and subject written underneath in white ink. Almost all the ones with Jill have her pacing in the background, restless in slacks, smoking.

Jill developed a rash on her face. In St John's Wood High Street the chemist drew back from her as he handed over the prescription. People stared as she walked back up Ordnance Hill, past the Royal Horse Artillery Barracks. She would stand in the drawing room at the bay window, lean against it and gaze at the plane tree. She took up gardening.

George and Mercia and others used to arrive unannounced so as to avoid her putting them off on the telephone, and take her to the cinema. Work in the theatre continued. Staunchly professional, Jill got the part of Principal Boy, Prince Hal in 'Beauty and the Beast', and the photographs show her made up as a splendid youth with his whole future before him.

Visits to Apple Porch were hard work. Joan loved the place but Eva could not contain her hatred of Larry. The head gardener Anderson's wife took a shine to the baby. Toddling became a long distance threat and one morning he went missing. Jill, Eva and Joan looked everywhere. They co-opted Mrs Anderson who said: 'Oh I know 'e do.' Country people generally do know. It was she who found the problem – standing beneath a pergola, crucified in open space, arms outstretched, adhering petrified to a spider's web.

Jill worked hard to keep herself together: April 1938 in 'Good and Proper'; October 'Tree of Eden'; March 1939 'We at the Crossroads'; November 'Judgment Day'.

After Romeo, Hamlet and Henry V, Larry took on the role of Macbeth, the play he and Jill had been working on when he decided to have a son. Whatever they had imagined for characterisation was buried under make-up almost as heavy as Sir Toby Belch's. The head-pieces brooded like thunder. Jill thought it overdone. Larry became persuaded it was a disaster when it gave Noël Coward the giggles.

Vivien played Titania in 'A Midsummer Night's Dream' with Robert Helpmann as Oberon. He had been a supreme ballet dancer and choreographer, but as his leaps diminished he decided to change careers and tread the boards rather than spring from them. His friendship with Vivien brought her more laughter than anyone else but Larry.

Larry next played Iago to Ralph Richardson's Othello, then Coriolanus with my godmother Sybil Thorndike as his mother. The dancing years seemed then to bless him and Vivien. Her aim was the same as Jill's had been – to nourish his acting career into greatness. At that time she must have felt that this was happening, and sooner than even she had hoped. Increasing admiration was expressed for the immensity of his energy, undertaking one after the other of the most demanding Shakespearian roles, in different productions, with different directors, and always an entirely original interpretation, all of which he had been discussing for years when he was with Jill.

He was indeed tapped into some source. Acting for him was like religion still is in the Middle East, the very air he breathed, the faith of which he had written to Jill in 1929: 'It is my only hope of being of use to God and the world and I think everybody should try to be that.'

He and Vivien settled in Chelsea at 4 Christchurch Street: Durham Cottage, hidden behind yellow gates with a walled garden, tucked between the high windowless walls of apartments. It was of brick painted white, the front door opened awkwardly into a dining alcove and the tiny interiors were a menagerie of Battersea candlesticks, snuff boxes and the fragilities Vivien was forever discovering and buying: her hobby of serendipity.

She had the gift of making him proud of her, in a way Jill had never been able to do, with her femininity, little flower arrangements or presents for a friend or some kindness. She always looked frail and beautiful: even if she had worn undercarpet and chains, her long pliant neck and the poise of her movement would have made her yet more regal.

She and Larry drove through the fields and vineyards of France to the Midi. They bumped into friends with similar itineraries which was embarrassing: no one was supposed to admit publicly to their living in sin, when neither Jill nor Leigh had agreed to more than a trial separation. Their children's future with single parents was not a happy thought. But the picnics were wonderful, the white Burgundy the best, and the eventual sea was the Mediterranean.

More and more it seemed that Larry's letter to Jill from on board ship had been a premonition; 'I suppose our happiest moment has just the faintest shadow lurking somewhere near it, some doubt, or fear – fear perhaps of hurting something, some ideal . . .'

Several times they found they were staying in the same hotel as Jill and a couple of her friends: the last thing anyone wished for. Jill had been persuaded to revitalise herself and get out of St John's Wood in order to have a better chance of winning Larry back by confronting him with his baby, family and domestic future. Instead she was haunted by his look of hate when they so unexpectedly met. She could not ask where he and Vivien were going next as that would have sounded like spying.

Larry's chance of a lifetime was to play Heathcliff in the film 'Wuthering Heights'. The director was William Wyler, who was to become acknowledged as one of the greatest directors of all time. He had observed Larry's earlier films, the hollow good looks, and knew of the animal passion and presence of his stage performances, especially as Romeo. 'Fire Over England' had not yet been released, but he had made up his mind.

He was soft-spoken but had great will-power. He it was who would douse Larry's excess of fire which blinded the camera's lenses, and fill up the hollowness which was merely perceived as false, not reflecting the inside mood. He bore down on Larry's flamboyance, and became the anvil required to break him in to the intimate medium of film. He was also extraordinarily inarticulate. 'Just be better' was about the only advice he ever gave, even after dozens of takes.

The producer, Sam Goldwyn, was noisier, more of a wide boy, and attacked Larry's short-comings. Larry had a steadfast respect for Wyler, but not for Goldwyn. At the very end of the film there is a treacly scene of the Yorkshire moors and the young Heathcliff and Cathy wandering away, hand in hand, for ever – terrible stuff, inserted with extras after the stars had gone home.

'There you see,' Larry told me. 'Shows what happens when a great director is over-ruled by a not-so-good producer with final cut.'

Working with Wyler convinced him of the possibilities of the screen. His hollowness had been banished, as had the seemingly random flamboyance. Another influence should also be remembered: Vivien. Because of her he knew in some ways what Heathcliff knew and felt: stupendous passion, forbidden love, becoming therefore an outcast, suffering the agonies of separation. For she was in London as the divine Titania. This passion of a lifetime was the making of his Heathcliff.

Vivien's pangs at the separation made her sail to New York and fly on to California to be with him if only for a few days. She had also long determined to be Scarlett O'Hara, which David Selznick was still trying to cast for 'Gone with the Wind'. How she and Larry contrived this is the best of all Hollywood legends and long may it remain so. She had set sail on 5 November, her birthday, and was given the part on Christmas Day. Her London producer kindly let her go and gave the role of Titania to Dorothy Hyson.

Larry's Heathcliff was Oscar material, while Vivien had landed the greatest female role in history against the competition of every American actress. Selznick insisted that Larry keep away from her lest the morbid and hypocritical public of the time denounce the scandalous affair and compromise his epic. Larry was offered the lead on Broadway in 'No Time for Comedy' opposite Katherine Cornell.

There, after the release of 'Wuthering Heights', and while he was also starring in the theatre with the actress who was the nation's darling, his life ceased to be his own. It was impossible for him to walk outside without being pointed at and crowded. He and Jill had hated the screaming fans of others at a Hollywood opening. Now he was the target even in the street, and was sickened and sometimes frightened by it. Once, when trying to close the car door, he gently eased someone to give room: 'Thank-you. How nice. Do you mind? How lovely.' And the girl screamed: 'You see that? He hit me!' He just managed to get away with the outside of the car being kicked.

Then he learned of his father's death. The ocean made it impossible to attend the funeral. His dejection at the peak of his fame was utter. Nonetheless, the adulation of New Yorkers was for him, even if he was lampooned by the press for seeming spoilt and miserable. He could not tell them of his illicit love, his desertion of his wife and baby, that his fame was an excruciating entrapment. When he returned to England and Durham Cottage to be with Vivien again he was a changed man.

He went to St John's Wood and asked once more for a divorce. Jill saw that he was a stranger to their baby. A three-year-old cannot pretend love. She could see that their family was broken and agreed to petition on the grounds of his adultery with Vivien. Leigh Holman could hardly believe the change in Vivien, who was almost unrecognisable from the exhaustion of the longest role ever filmed. Her stardom on stage and screen and the passion she had with Larry were things he could not handle. He also agreed to petition.

When they returned to the United States, Vivien had hoped to play opposite Larry in 'Rebecca'. After the ravages of Scarlett O'Hara, the screen-tests showed her inappropriate for the undented innocence of the girl eventually played by Joan Fontaine. Besides, Selznick remained adamant that they should not be seen together until their divorces came through. Further, to keep them apart, he cast Robert Taylor opposite her in 'Waterloo Bridge'. It was brave of him to allow Larry even in the background when 'Gone with the Wind' opened to the tumultuous welcome of Atlanta.

In England, Jill took a house on the coast at Shoreham for the Indian summer of 1939. Eva came to stay, so did George and Mercia, and Larry's widowed stepmother Ibo. Joan Coxell was there to look after the toddler. My very first memory is of Ibo trying to keep cool, lying on her bed stark naked. Joan pulled me out of the room.

It was a strange time. The year before, Neville Chamberlain had made his nauseous speech after meeting the Führer at Berchtesgarten. People then had felt relief at putting off the inevitable, but they were ashamed. Leaflets now explained what to do in the event of a German invasion: 'Stay inside your homes and on no account try to get away. The roads must be kept clear for our soldiers and tanks to move rapidly against the aggressor.' Notices were put in theatre programmes commending fortitude and valour, and some managements could not resist printing their own admonishments – 'With courage and the strength of the Island Race, you should find it possible to last until the end of the play.'

Jill's home movies show everyone laughing too loud, being over-jolly, running along the beach in swim suits with gasmasks slung from their shoulders. As the German armoured divisions swept over Poland the English sun was reflected by wet sand at low tide, and everyone was manic and frightened and determined to be gay: they knew it was for the last time.

A German aeroplane flew slowly along the shore. People stopped romping in the waves. They looked up from their sand castles. In silence they watched it approach and fly over their heads. Above the roar George Relph shouted: 'What the hell can we do?'

'Fuck all, dear boy!' Jill shouted back, 'Fuck all!' And they howled with laughter and hugged each other.

On 27 September Warsaw fell. They sat in the drawing room in shock, listening to wireless bulletins. An admirer had sent Eva a cartwheel-sized box of liqueur chocolates. These she opened and spread on the table. After she had taken two or three – Rum, Curaçao, Drambuie – she started to complain.

'These liqueur chocolates taste of nothing at all. Now let me see.' She leant over them again with finger and thumb ready to peck. She got hiccups.

'Tastes of nothing at all. I'll have another one. None for you? Ooh, that's better. Now what sort was that?'

As the full horror of the news soaked into them, the feeling that there was now no earthly purpose in hoping anything would ever turn back, she said: 'Poor Warsaw. Taste of nothing. I'll have . . .' That became one of the family's landmark phrases: 'Poor Warsaw'.

For the winter season Jill was in a play called 'Final Judgement'. She had taken a minuscule cottage near Pulborough. It was only twice the length of the little black Ford we had, FLD 835: the drawing room was damp, there was a cupboard for a kitchen, and two tiny bedrooms upstairs. It was called 'Keeper's Cottage' and stood by some woods. People were being encouraged to move away from London for safety from the Blitz.

There then occurred an illness which was to change my life, and consequently my mother's and Joan's. She wrote to Larry about it. The rough draft of her letter to New York is undated.

T. I think please God is going to be alright. From your cables I gather you are interested so I will tell you the whole story.

Eva had come to stay. To make room for her, Joan had gone home for a while.

T. was peevish and had an awful night Friday, no sleep at all, kept crying for Joan, going to sleep, then a moment later waking up with a start. At about five he said he wanted some water, tried to sit up to drink and said he couldn't he was too tired. He dropped off to sleep at six.

I was up at seven to do the fires (We have no maid) and clean up. 7.30 he woke up crying, and saying he had a pain in his neck and he wanted a drink. But when I tried to lift his head for him to drink he screamed. I took his temperature. 101. Not very high but I thought I had better get a doctor.

I have no telephone or garage. I keep the car at a neighbour's house nearly half a mile away. There were eight inches of snow, drifts of more than two feet. I telephoned. Of course all the doctors are in the Army. But eventually I found one who said he would come.

Then back to the cottage, this time in the car. Mummy thank God was with him. If she hadn't been I don't know what I should have done as it would have meant leaving him alone. He couldn't move and didn't move all day, just lay there whimpering and saying 'I'm tired'. He wanted Joan and kept calling for her.

Paralysis drew his head back, twisted the spine, and his skin went black.

The doctor came at five that afternoon. Meanwhile I had been on to a child specialist in London as I felt something was really wrong and he said he would come down the following day. The local doctor said nothing but that he would come again next day.

He gave me a prescription for a sleeping draught and that was all. I drove to Pulborough and got the medicine. In undoing the parcel, Mummy dropped the bottle.

Jill saw her mother standing stock still, the broken medicine bottle spilt at her feet, tears pouring down her face.

So I had to go all the way back. By this time, 6.30, he couldn't move his head at all and had had nothing to eat or drink since tea on Friday. He kept licking his lips with a very dry tongue. It was very difficult to get him to take his sleeping draught. We had to force it down his throat like you do with a dog.

He slept for an hour and a half. I had phoned up Joan and she came back at 11.30 that night. I met her, in some places having difficulty driving through the snow. When she arrived he seemed calmer. I have seen so little of him during these past few months, only weekends. I think that's why he trusts Joan more than me. He slept more that night.

Sunday he couldn't move. If you moved him he screamed, and always said the same thing: 'My neck hurts', and 'I'm tired'. At 4.30 the doctor came and said he thought it was meningitis – and that we must get a child specialist as there wasn't a moment to lose as a spinal puncture had to be performed.

He rushed off and was back in an hour with Dr Morley Fletcher, a Barts man now retired, but a very big specialist who lives in the neighbourhood. He said he thought it was meningitis and didn't want to do a spinal puncture with a local anaesthetic as it is a very tricky business. He said he thought he was very ill but there was nothing to be done, we must wait.

At 8.30 that night I met the specialist I had phoned in London and he was convinced it was meningitis but couldn't say what form. He said T. had a 3 : 1 chance of living, and was very gloomy about the after effects: insanity, blindness or deafness.

He stayed the night with the neighbours. The car by this time was behaving badly, stopped twice and wouldn't go. In the morning T. was a bit better. His head wasn't forced so far back. I got him to Petworth Hospital in a big car. He hated being moved, screamed with pain but it had to be. On Monday, Morley Fletcher came again and did the lumbar puncture. Fluid did not spurt out which was a good sign.

They gave him 'M & B 936' every four hours. It's a wonderful

My mother, the actress Jill Esmond (*Fayer of London*)

Jill's father, Henry Vernon Esmond, leading actor, director and playwright of thirty plays

Jill's mother, Eva Moore, star of her era

Jill with her parents outside Apple Porch, their house overlooking Temple Golf Course, near Maidenhead

Larry's parents, Agnes and the Revd Gerard Kerr Olivier outside their house in Dorking (*Felix Barker's collection*)

Larry aged nineteen as Richard Coaker in 'The Farmer's Wife' (*Theatre Museum*)

Larry and Jill's wedding on 25 July 1930, at Eva's London house, 21 Whiteheads Grove

Larry as the matinée idol (*Kobal Collection*)

Jill as a star (*Anthony Roger*)

The Nassau party

Noël Coward the Master

Noël the critic

Jill and Noël in a boat

Larry with the 16mm cine camera

The swallow dive – preparation eighteen years before the film 'Hamlet' and the cry: 'Venom to thy work'

Happy as Larry

Wrestling with Douglas Fairbanks Jnr

Exercising the little wires which hung from his shoulders (*Robert W. Coburn, Radio Pictures*)

Larry and Jill in their garden overlooking Hollywood (*Robert W. Coburn, Radio Pictures*)

Sailing back to England

'No Funny Business' or 'Professional Co-respondents'. Two illustrations of Jill's sharp focus on screen, and Larry's characterisation as merely hollow (*United Artists*)

'Hamlet'. The full-length production by Tony Guthrie, set apart from any other play, 'because with Hamlet you cannot cheat. You have to give your complete self, no role-playing, no defence' – the difference between being a husband and a lover (*Angus McBean*)

'Romeo'. The role which he had worked on for years with Jill, hoping to have her as his Juliet, played by Peggy Ashcroft in John Gielgud's production. Sir Kenneth Clark said: 'If you can't look like that, don't play Romeo.' (*Portrait by Harold Knight, courtesy Royal National Theatre*)

'Fire over England'. Alexander Korda's production at Denham, during Jill's
pregnancy, when Vivien and Larry were overtaken by their passion for each other
(*United Artists*)

My christening, much delayed, outside Chelsea Old Church. Larry improperly dressed and looking as if he has arrived late, Jill weighed down by a three and a half month old baby, the Revd Gerard Kerr Olivier's profile unaware of his son's affair with Vivien, and Eva aware of everything (*Portman Press Bureau*)

Jill with all she had left (*Dorothy Wilding, courtesy Tom Hustler*)

Larry as co-respondent with Ronald Colman moustache

Larry as Nelson, with Vivien as Lady Hamilton (*The Korda Collection, Central Television Enterprises Ltd*)

Jill, Gregory Peck and Gladys Cooper in Broadway production of 'Morning Star' (*Vandamm Studio*)

Me in Hollywood, opposite C. Aubrey Smith in 'Scotland Yard Investigates', old Eva in the background

'God for Harry, England and Saint George!' (*Rank Organisation plc, from 'Henry V'*)

Medieval London, from the Globe Theatre to the Tower (*Rank Organisation plc, from 'Henry V'*)

new drug used a lot for meningitis. The tests were negative. The doctor said that if it wasn't meningitis it must be Infantile Paralysis and that he didn't see much chance of him ever moving again and we must watch very carefully for paralysis getting in his limbs as well as his neck.

T. was about the same but more cheerful in himself. On Wednesday he woke up and said he wanted some bacon. Thursday he ate some jelly, his first food for six days, drank a lot and was a changed person. He would not move his head but said he had no pain. Friday he moved his head. Saturday it was difficult to keep him in bed. Sunday he got up for a bit, but his legs were so weak he couldn't stand.

That week gave her a curious sense of invincibility. She knew that, whatever happened, nothing could ever be worse.

Seven days before her play, aptly called 'Final Judgement', closed. And in the same letter she described the divorce case: ·

. . . which was over-produced by the weather: London had never seen so much snow. If the press hadn't called at my house I should never have been able to fight my way through the snow in the car.

The whole proceeding took place in a very poor set. Perfect but dull casting, for Judge and Council. The only light touch was when I was handed a photo of you for me to identify. It was a horrible film still of any co-respondent. The Judge had a look at the picture, looked at me with surprise and then gave me a Decree Nisi straight away.

Jacky [her brother] is off to France tomorrow, Glen [Byam Shaw] too very soon, more and more people seem to disappear into the Army or Navy . . .

But to me, everything is filled with great thankfulness to God. T. is well. All love Jill.

After Holland and Belgium had been overwhelmed by German forces, and the French 1st Army had been outflanked, the British Expeditionary Force withdrew. We drove down to Southampton to collect Jacky. Mummy and me, and Eva. Jacky had been in Tanks in the First World War. At the start of the second he was in the Royal Army Service Corps – a choice of regiment which did not quite reflect his style with racing cars at Brooklands.

We were told to wait for him in a field overlooking the harbour. Many soldiers were there, exhausted, bedraggled, looking for their people to collect them, collecting vouchers for train journeys, getting into buses.

An RASC sergeant said Mr Esmond wouldn't be much longer, he was just signing some papers. Then he saw me, half-paralysed, running knock-kneed and on tip-toe. To cover his embarrassment he said: 'Only yesterday in France, beside a school, we were attacked by Stukas. Dive-bombed. We soldiers hit the ground of course. But all those kids . . .' Then he dug his fingers roughly into my hair and squeezed them together, hid his face, and turned away.

Mummy was driving. Jacky sat in the back of the Ford with Eva. With the relief of being back in England, after withdrawing his troop-filled trucks in a convoy stretching dozens of miles across France, being strafed and dive-bombed, trying to improvise mechanical repairs, with a civilian population that was hostile and fatalistic, and the accumulation of exhaustion, he broke down and sobbed into Eva's bosom, deep uncontrollable worn out sobs.

It was a long hot drive and I needed to relieve myself. Mummy stopped the car and I got out. The grass verge was clear so I wandered off for privacy into the wild flowers, tall daisies bobbing their heads in the breeze. I leant forward awkwardly, balancing on tip-toe, heels locked by shrunken Achilles tendons, wearing prescribed shoes with steel soles. 'Come on, darling.'

'I can't,' I said. 'The flowers are looking at me.'

8

Evacuation

During the summer of 1940 Hitler's air raids intensified over England. The U-boats torpedoed our convoys of supply ships with increasing deadliness. Evacuation of families and children from the towns to the countryside was supplemented by the government's encouragement, for those who could, to leave the country altogether for safety's sake and reduce the number of mouths to be fed. Larry, filming in America, agreed by telegrams across the Atlantic that the after-effects of meningitis made such a move essential for us.

Britain had introduced total censorship on inward and outgoing mail. All Jill's letters to Eva were opened, read, and clumsily resealed with a gummed sticker numbered P.C.90, printed in thick black letterpress with the words 'OPENED BY EXAMINER 4122' or some other identifying number, even while still in harbour.

26 June 1940. Cunard White Star. *Scythia*

We are still sitting in Liverpool and have no idea when we sail. T. is having a lively time rushing all over the place, very nice people on board and lots of children, and thousands of Jews from all countries.

On the same ship were Vivien's eight-year-old daughter Suzanne whom we liked, and her old mother Gertrude who understandably remained aloof. They were going to stay in Vancouver with Vivien's aunt. Jill's plan was to earn enough money in New York to set off for California and take up her film career. Funds were low: a £10 limit each for her and Joan, and £5 for me: all anyone could take out of Britain.

Our convoy was under constant threat from German submarines and we were routed to Halifax via Iceland and Newfoundland in an effort to avoid them. Luckily the wind was howling and the seas were mountainous.

We would all rather feel ill than be torpedoed. We were told to sleep in our clothes for the first 48 hours and always have to carry our life-jackets; lots of life-boat drill.

The *Scythia* arrived safely at Halifax. The very next liner, carrying civilians away from the war zones to safety, was torpedoed, sunk, and almost all were drowned. Once landed on the other side of the Atlantic, Jill spoke to Larry on the telephone. He suggested that he buy a farm for us near Toronto, a good place for a child to grow up.

The crisis of our evacuation brought out the best in him, despite an extraordinary six months. He and Vivien had still to appear to live apart from each other for Hollywood's prurient sake. They had both been nominated for Oscars: as Scarlett and Heathcliff. She was given the award, he was not, and his fury gave rise to a number of apocryphal stories. He told me that his rage reached its height after their separate limos had decanted them secretly into their own car and they were alone together. On their way home he grabbed her Oscar and 'It was all I could do to restrain myself from hitting her with it. I was insane with jealousy.'

Award or no, he received a further nomination for Max de Winter in 'Rebecca'. She resented not being cast opposite him. Her motivation was to support him to every height. Although they were both overwhelmed with their separate successes, they were frustrated at being kept apart professionally. They decided that as soon as the Decrees Absolute established their divorces, they would present themselves together in 'Romeo and Juliet' on Broadway.

They invested their own money in the show and received substantial funding from Warners. Lavish designs were done by the Motleys. The nurse was played by Eva's old friend May Whitty. After touring in San Francisco and Chicago they opened in the 51st Street Theatre on Larry's birthday, 22 May 1940. The New Yorkers took against the two lovers flaunting their success, and felt put upon by Britishers, who were so adored by Hollywood, having such patronising expectations of being adored by them. The show closed almost at once after queues of people lined up to get their money back.

The flop cost them all their savings. Yet their supreme fame made it impossible for them to walk down the avenues of New York without being mobbed by crowds that erupted around them from every doorway and side street. The Larry who presented himself to Jill at the Windsor Arms, St Thomas and Sultan Streets, Toronto, was distraught.

He and Jill drove round a number of farms but they looked gloomy and the neighbourhood provincial, so they dropped the idea. Jill had received a tentative offer for a play in New York. Emlyn Williams's wife Molly was there too trying to interest Broadway in Emlyn's plays and she wanted Jill to act in one of them.

22 July 1940

Larry is arranging for me to take a little house just outside New York where Molly and I could be together. Both Larry and Vivien were up here last weekend for a film gala and I saw quite a lot of him. He is quite the film-star now and suffering from a persecution complex, terrified of being recognised and distrusts everybody. Some of the times I saw him he was very charming but others he was bad tempered and scowling and talked a great deal of very hot air.

He got on well with T. but didn't seem really interested and never asked about his illness. He wanted me to go out with him and Vivien but I said No.

Vivien's photographs as Scarlett had filled magazines and newspapers. They were plastered across massive hoardings, so when I met her I was amazed. Larry introduced her to me as Bibs. Bed-time came and Joan my governess took me away. When I was pyjama'd and tucked up they sat on my bed and chatted. Larry hugged me and from the door they both blew me a kiss.

'I want to kiss Bibs.' She smiled and approached. She leant down, kissed my forehead and I was enveloped in her perfume.

'On the mouth.' This embarrassed everyone. I was left with the vision of her lips above my eyes.

On their departure from Toronto railway station Larry decided to take me firmly in hand and show what an important fellow he was. He went to the Canadian Pacific Railroad management and insisted that I be allowed to drive a train. They thought he was mad. They all recognised and admired him and were touched to see him holding a little boy's hand, but this was ridiculous.

He took me down the platform to an enormous, steam-hissing engine; he shouted up at the driver who said there might be an unhitched engine along the track. So we went out into the dark, the rails shining under bright lights, my steel-soled shoes clumping on the gravel and sleepers. Vast shapes moved in the middle distance and we were blinded by a head-lamp. I got leg-ache so we returned.

Jill wrote that it had been interesting seeing him, and proved that she had got over her bad time, even though she was still upset by his presence and charm and felt happier when he was away.

He left for a five-week holiday to be followed by another film, which would delay any departure for England by four months. He had been trying to be called up by the Fleet Air Arm, keen to play his part, preferably a warlike one, in Britain's fight against the Nazis. Ralph Richardson had been allowed to join but he already had a pilot's licence. So for many weeks Larry accumulated the solo flying hours required: even during filming, when he flew before dawn. This was an outpouring of energy which really does mark him out as different from most people.

> I could tell you masses about Larry. I know that as long as he is in USA I need have no real fear of money. He may not be very generous but I think he will always look after us financially so long as he is here.

With his support Jill was able to obtain the English Court's permission to take me to the United States, outside its jurisdiction which did extend to Canada. To pave the way she went on her own to New York, where she had been offered a part in a play with Jessica Tandy. The last time they had played together was in 'Twelfth Night'.

American Equity only allowed aliens to do one play every six months, so a long wait threatened after any failure. She hated turning down the part, but felt that it was unwise to play the role of an unpleasant spurned wife at precisely the time her own divorce was being so publicised.

> Larry phoned up and asked me to see him so I went to his flat as I didn't want him in the hotel. We chatted about nothing, then Vivien came in. She is more beautiful than ever, but her face is just a mask and her eyes hard and cruel. We were *so* charming to each other and so insincere. They both flew to Hollywood that night so I shan't see them again.

New York had spurned their romance and spat them out.

Molly Williams wrote to say that their old friend, Robert Montgomery, had lent her his house in Connecticut, rent-free plus servants for as long as she wished. She wanted us to share it with her and her sons Alan, aged five, and Brook, two and a half. I was four. It was a beautiful place with a garden, swimming pool and lake, and the night sounds of crickets and far-off trains. I enjoyed sharing toys with Alan, even if we were sabotaged by Brook.

A month later:

> It was splashed all over the front pages when Larry got married. Well, I hope he finds happiness but I very much doubt it. He has become nervous and frightened of everything. He says he has lost all his money on 'Romeo and Juliet'. The production cost $90,000 and he lost $40,000 and has only a few thousand left. Vivien did *not* put one penny of *her* money into it. She has more sense. Of course it is very difficult under these circumstances to get my maintenance finally arranged.

This statement about Vivien's non-investment is contrary to all previously published accounts which say that they *both* lost. I suspect Larry lied to Jill, to hide his shame at Vivien's loss. His voluntary maintenance was a generous $800 a month, now that he was filming with Vivien in 'Lady Hamilton'.

We moved to New York and shared a tiny apartment with Jessica Tandy in the Hotel Franconia, 20 West 72nd Street. A poor address; consequently many 'friends' eschewed her, but not the real ones: 'Jessica and I share a room but as we don't snore and both sleep like tops it's rather fun.'

The pace of life accelerated. They both competed for the same part and both lost. Jessica returned smiling, arms filled with flowers. Jill dined with Lynn Fontanne and Alfred Lunt. Charlie Chaplin was also there. She was given a radio part as Emily Brontë in 'Wuthering Heights'; she did not say who played Heathcliff.

Jessica was good for Jill and bullied her about her looks. During the 'Bad Time' Jill's hair had gone completely white, which Jessica pointed out put a fearsome limit on the parts she might be given. They decided that dye was essential. Restoring it to its original dark colour made the hairline around her brow too hard and schoolmistressy, and within days the roots began to show white. They tried auburn and this succeeded; the hairline was less stark. Physically and mentally she became a redhead, which suited her. She bought new clothes to establish her new style.

She found a school for me 'where the children are not allowed to be rough and rude like most American children'. If I shouted she would say: 'I don't live at Putney' – which left me wondering where on earth that was. In the evenings she would step further back into her reveries of England and the two actresses would play six-pack Bezique.

The news was of Apple Porch filled with people wanting to live away from the Blitz and Eva becoming exhausted. Jill and Jessica went to a newsreel.

9 November 1940

'London can take it' upset me terribly – pictures of Oxford Street bombed, the City and places we love. There was a shot of Wilton Crescent and people being dug out. The news of Coventry has just come through. The suffering and terror must be terrible. I hope it's true that we have sunk half the Italian fleet.

Raids on the Berlin civilian population means only more death and damnation. It doesn't help our war effort but just causes more suffering and stiffens their morale, because I am sure that their people are made of stern stuff and love Germany as we love England.

She besought Eva to leave England and join us, or indeed go to Hollywood where she was sure to get work.

Jessica's daughter Susan arrived. She was a year older than I, had lovely brown eyes and hair, looked serious but was fun. We went skating together and for fancy dress parties we wore each other's clothes. Christmas was a tangle of paper chains, parties, presents, and a number of visits from Larry who gave me a tricycle.

26 December 1940

T. was very pleased to see him and Larry was charming, quite his old self. He came at about 4.30 and stayed till seven. He has done over 200 hours of solo flying. He seems to have lost his pomposity and for the first time I felt really at ease with him. As he and Vivien had to do a broadcast and rehearse there was not much time. I think he has done all he can with money for me. He won't be able to send me any more as he will be in England but I have no need to worry for at least two years.

Besides, she was making money from two radio broadcasts each day.

When he came to our apartment to say good-bye Jill asked him to take me to the loo and let me see what a grown man looked like. So I stood at his side there, on tiptoe to aim from higher than the edge, while he fired accurately down from my eye-level. Later, after he had gone and I was in bed with the light out, Jill heard me sobbing. She thought I was missing him. I was inconsolable. She turned on the light and eventually I calmed down enough to explain: 'Daddy has male organs, and I only have flies.'

On 28 December Joan took me to the docks to see him and Vivien off. Jill stayed behind so as not to risk photographs of him together 'with his two wives'. I remember the white ship's rails far above, and Daddy and Vivien waving.

After docking at Lisbon they flew to England. The plane's engine caught fire and they prepared to crash-land. Vivien told me much later that she looked round at the others, all knowing they had little chance of survival. Their faces had completely changed: cheeks sunken, temples collapsed inwards, making them look like skeletons. Larry's was the same. With a great effort she raised her hands and realised that hers was too.

My uncle Jack's house had been bombed. Cheyne Walk studios had been flattened by a land mine and Chelsea Old Church badly damaged. Queen's Grove had been bombed as well, but most of the damage was on the other side of the road.

The censors in England did a thorough job –

January 19 1941

I enclose a specimen page to show what care they take – cut to ribbons – very like the paper patterns cut out by men outside theatre queues. They obviously take great trouble. Page 1 cut out telling me where the bomb dropped. Page 2 half cut out with a bit off the end of page one. Page 5 just isn't there. I do think it's awfully kind of them.

There was talk of plays, but none materialised. Jill had her radio work, but poor Jessica had to get a job as a clerk in the British Consulate. There were only occasional weekends at Towners, the two of them, Joan, Susan and I going to stay with Molly and her boys. In our tiny flat that winter we were on top of each other.

22 March 1941

There is chaos going on all round. Two children. T. shouting, Jessica doing the ironing, Joan setting the lunch ready and the maid trying to clean. All in the same room. A nice peaceful Sunday morning.

I had dinner with May Whitty who is in New York for a few weeks doing 'The Trojan Women' for Peggy Webster. She is a very interesting but wicked old lady. She wants to know everything and tried to pump me about Larry. I think she envies you and Apple Porch. But I enjoyed myself with her; her brain is quick and to the point.

26 April 1941

I went to a lovely party Kathrine Cornell and Guthrie McClintic gave. It was the sort of party Larry and I used to give and it was lovely to be with real theatre people again. I did so love our 'After the Theatre parties' at Cheyne Walk. I had a lovely evening and got home at five in the morning.

One fine day she took me to the Zoo in Central Park. On our way back we sat on a big rock. I pretended it was a ship, and went round the back to do something about the funnel.

He was out of sight for about one minute and when I called him back there was no answer. I shouted. No answer. I looked all over the place, but didn't want to leave in case he returned to it. Then a boy who was in a tree said he saw him run in the opposite direction. I found a policeman.

'The boy's name, ma'am?'
     She told him.
     'Like Laurence?'
     'Yes. It's his son.' The pitying look of an Irish American cop: 'Lady. You've got a kidnap on your hands. When they phone, don't pay, just call us.'
     She went home.

T. was playing with the lift boy. He said he wanted to go home alone. He was very pleased with himself, had had to cross most of the park, the road in the park where cars rush by, and Central Park West which is like crossing Fifth Avenue. When I asked him how he crossed over he looked at me with great contempt and said: 'Waited for the lights!'

As the hot summer approached and the New York theatres were about to wilt into emptiness, Robert Donat's wife Ella wrote from Hollywood inviting us to stay, 'Just for the holidays' – a disguise which would enable Jill to whip round the studios without seeming to tout for work. David Selznick said he could keep her busy in films. She shopped for smart dresses and wired Harrods in London to take her white ermine jacket out of storage and send it to her. Then she learned that war-time regulations required a permit for its export which would take three months to obtain.

The journey took five days, puffing across the face of America. We were met at Pasadena by the Selznick Agency and taken to Ella Donat's house, where we met her two ruffian sons and breathed freely in her commodious garden. One of the agents was Harry Ham, an Englishman who had teamed up with Jill's brother Jacky as a young racing driver. Jill re-established her contacts with MGM, RKO, and Columbia on her first full day there. Then she had her hair done, got a driving licence and went to the bank which still had $5.40 left from eight years before. She visited other studios, and a number of directors including George Cukor (the first of three 'Gone with the Wind' directors).

Ella was a fine pianist and gave music parties to raise money for British War Relief. The English Colony of Hollywood clung together like an expatriate tribe and gave me my first exposure to cliques, snobs and moral fibre. I was proud of being English, of course, but resented being told that it made me different from Americans. Jill wrote: 'They seem more depressed by things here than people back home. I expect it's because they've nothing to do, content with California and themselves.'

She found a bright and cheerful house at 424 South Cliffwood Avenue. It was next to an empty lot and had a huge garden with fruit trees. The owners had filled the rooms with flowers and left behind their collie bitch to look after us. We had a Japanese gardener who gave me a box of chocolates when I had him in my room for tea. We also inherited a black maid called Ozelia who took exception to Jill's palest silk underwear and dyed it puce. Generous-heartedness found frequent expression.

Margaret Sullavan lived nearby, now married to Leland Hayward the leading Hollywood agent. They had two houses: the Barn for the children, the Other House for themselves, a huge garden, a swimming pool and three children. Brooke was dark, intense, wanton yet full of sunshine, and I was the boy she fell for. We were both four and a half. Unfortunately I fell for her younger sister, Bridget, a platinum blond with pointed features, deeply quiet, who didn't give a damn about me. So Maggie had much to cope with. Her youngest, Bill, had just learned to walk.

Next door lived Joan Crawford. Jill went there for dinner one Sunday –

2 July 1941

Her adopted daughter [Christina, who later wrote *Mommie Dearest*] is charming and Joan is very sweet with her. Joan had just got her adopted son, about seven weeks old. I gave him his bottle and it was lovely to hold a very tiny baby again. I wonder if she will get fed up with them.

The premonition came all too true, if Christina's book is to be believed – Joan's alcoholism, the shuttle of different men, the night raids into her children's bedroom, her having them strapped into their beds. As neighbours we knew none of this, but my recollection is of a goody two-shoes atmosphere, all pretend and prissy, like the plastic covers on their chintz cushions.

Apart from the children Joan seemed just the same. We discussed the latest films and talked of Greta Garbo, and after dinner saw a very poor film in her private theatre. Just the same dull routine as 8 years ago. [When Larry and Jill used to dine with her and Douglas Fairbanks.] She is still a bore and has no humour.

Then suddenly the news broke: Hitler's invasion of Russia. Within a few weeks there was better news from home. The horrors of the Blitz ceased, giving Britain a breathing space, some time to reorganise and regroup. The shipping convoys suffered fewer losses and the US stepped up its help. At home in South Cliffwood Avenue the preparation and dispatch of food parcels became a way of life, for family and friends, and for the one prisoner of war in Germany we knew: John Casson, Sybil Thorndike's son. These food parcels were Douglas Fairbanks's idea, and thanks to his guidance through an isolationist Congress. He was later given an honorary knighthood.

Jill gave a dinner party for May Whitty and her husband Ben Webster, the actor Alexander Knox whom I found impressive, and Percy Harris of the Motleys; then a cocktail party in the garden for Maggie Sullavan, Joan Crawford, Bob Montgomery, agents and a few directors.

At such parties it was inevitable that many would ask after my father, say how marvellous he was, how much I resembled him, obviously cut out to be an actor. Yet I had no image of him, except the once we had stood side by side at the loo. As for Vivien, I remembered her lips nearing my brow, her long throat, her scent. I can't remember having seen any of Larry's films. There was no photograph of him in our house. Once or twice, when I saw someone handsome and extroverted and perhaps over-acting I would ask: 'Is that Daddy?' Such was the dumbstruck silence, the overtones so heavy, that I stopped asking. I did want Jill to marry. 'Why not Alexander Knox?' I kept suggesting.

'Because he's a bore.'

'He's not. He has a racing car.'

2 August 1941

T's birthday soon. How I wish I had a daughter too. I wonder if I ever shall have one. I feel I have got over Larry, yet I can't even think of having a child without him being the father. I think I shall have to borrow him for a bit.

I sent him a lot of T's photographs and Mercia says he is thrilled with them.

I'm so glad.

His lack of acknowledgement, or messages of any kind, hurt.

I still think he is a nice person. He was just *very* weak and still is. Maybe the War will make him grow up.

Eva asked whether there was anyone else in her life.

Not yet. It's not very long since I have felt free of Larry and I never fell in love easily; but there is still time and I don't suffer

from loneliness except for all of you in England. I expect someone will turn up for me sometime and meanwhile T. is with me.

For my fifth birthday there was a crowd, mainly my age, including
Brooke and Bridget.

21 August 1941

Larry sent a cable. He signed it Lieut Olivier – he is getting on.
I'm glad he remembered. T. is a happy little boy. God knows
what will happen if we ever go back to NY. I shall need an
enormous apartment for his toys.

Jill's first job in Hollywood was a radio play 'Lost Horizon', with
Ronald Colman who had ten years earlier been Larry's role model
down to the trim moustache. She signed up the week before starting
and immediately took us off for a three hundred mile drive to
Yosemite. The mobility of life in America was wonderful. We rented
a bungalow for the night in the foothills, then drove up to a height of
ten thousand feet and took a log cabin for four days among the
redwoods.
    That evening she sat on the porch overlooking a valley and water-
fall, with the radio on.

There were recordings of the bombing of London, sirens, huge
explosions and things. It was quite terrifying. I found myself crying. It seems impossible that anybody could have lived through
it and remained cheerful.

Joan was making plans to return to England, either to help run a
home for evacuated children, or to join one of the services as a
woman driver. Jill was in full agreement with this and saw that it
would help make me more self-reliant.

I want a daughter so very badly. I do hope one day I shall have
one, but really we have in this world so very much to be thankful
for. You had and knew a real love for Harry. I had the same
thing for Larry. They were very alike in many ways. Do you
remember how you used to call Larry 'Harry' by mistake?
    Both our loves had faults and gave us great pain in different
ways, but at least we had a hell of a good time while it lasted and

we both had a completeness of body and soul that comes to very few. On top of that we have children – you two and me one – and they mean so very much. We have been very lucky, in lovely surroundings amongst good friends. I hope that I may find a companion and have my daughter but I feel in my heart I shall never find Larry or his equivalent again. We belonged to each other as you did to Harry and that doesn't come twice.

With her decision to stay on in Hollywood I was sent to a co-educational day school: Brentwood Town and Country School, off San Vicente Boulevard. There was the daily instilment of patriotism. The entire school, of sixty, aged from four to nine years, stood in ranks and Pledged Allegiance, hand on heart, facing the Stars and Stripes. It was difficult to follow: 'The red is the brave, the blue is troo and the white is peeyoratee.' (Purity). Then came the 'Eggsortation to the dahn'. (Dawn, but what we exhorted it to do escapes me.)

Jill's first film was a small part in 'The Sunny Side of the Street', about an evacuee English child and his life with an American family. She played the mother in England. There was a moving scene in which she spoke to the child over the radio. Only two days' work at Fox studios, where she was lobbying for an important part in another film.

She took me to 'The Wizard of Oz', the first full length film I had seen. I fell in love with Judy Garland. As Jill was in constant touch with MGM I sent flowers to Judy who worked there. By return I received a signed photograph and was convinced that the wide-eyed puckish face was one of the most beautiful in the world. Then MGM asked to see me for a screen-test because they wanted a boy with an English accent. Jill was doubtful, then realised it might give Larry a chance to see me, if only on screen.

Suddenly, from out of the blue, came a deed so explosively shocking that America felt as if its feet had been cut off. The nation heard over the radio that its entire fleet at Pearl Harbor had been sunk, without a declaration of war, by the Japanese. Californians in particular were shaken because they felt that the Pacific Coast was the front line. They had to look out at the sea as a source of attack on them. Their young soldiers had indeed fought before with conspicuous gallantry overseas, but this was the first time they were threatened by a foreign attack on their homes.

Misleading instructions were given about black-outs. There were two or three false alarms. The rule was: at an air raid warning, no one was allowed on the streets and all cars must stop. Fairly soon people sorted themselves out. Studios started earlier and most shops and offices closed at 5.30 p.m. so that people would be safely home before dark. The news that they might be bombed, perhaps by planes from Japanese aircraft carriers, led to women starting Red Cross Corps and organising for various emergencies, while the men started voluntarily to enlist now that the Neutrality Act had been rescinded.

Ridiculousnesses abounded, as they had at the outset of the war in England. The air raid sirens were faint as a whisper. Instructions were printed in the morning papers which were countermanded the same evening. Sugar was 'rationed': 10 lb per person, per shop, per day. The only real upset for us was the loss of a friend: our Japanese gardener. He had been born in America, was a US citizen, but was interned as a potential fifth-column threat.

MGM signed me up for the film 'Eagle Squadron', with Robert Stack as leading man. It was about the dedicated US airmen who volunteered to go to England and join the battle even though war had still to be declared by the United States: propaganda in keeping with FDR's aims. I played a beastly little boy who had to stand terrified on a hill with bombs raining down all round. Robert Stack had to grab me and I had to hit him in the face and scream: 'I hate you, I hate you. Brbrbr!' – The most memorable line I ever had.

> Maggie Sullavan's daughter Brooke phoned him up and said how she missed him at school. She is four. He said 'I'm awfully sorry I haven't been able to see you but you see I have to work.' At the end of the day I get home exhausted. Tomorrow he does a tiny scene with Gladys Cooper.

Anti-British sentiment was fanned by the Randolph Hearst newspapers, prompted by bitterness after Pearl Harbor. The Royal Navy lost many ships in the Battle of the Java Sea, yet his reports claimed that our navy had stayed at home and left all the fighting to American ships. Jill received news of our losses during her rehearsal for a radio defence programme. She had to speak about England through the strains of 'God Save the King' and had difficulty fighting back the tears.

Her friendship developed with Gladys Cooper, fifteen years her senior, who had in earlier years been down to visit Harry and Eva at Apple Porch. Her daughter Sally was ten, and the following spring the four of us went for a walk far into the hills with our collie and

Gladys's red setter. We came across a valley spread with blue lupins. For the two Englishwomen it was an escape – from all the terrible news, and from the failure of so many close to them to comprehend their feelings, to sit among lupins, watching their dogs running wild.

In the autumn of 1942 Jill went to New York to play in 'Morning Star' with Gregory Peck and Gladys Cooper. Despite wonderful rehearsals and loving the play and the director Guthrie McClintic, they closed after three weeks, heart-broken. Business had been terrible: $7,000 the first week, then $6,000, then $5,000, and they knew it had little chance of building into a success. Larry wrote –

> It was miserable luck about the play. I was a bit disappointed in it in London, though it was extremely well cast and mostly well played. One did so desperately want a *great* play about the war, and it was a bit too slick with too sentimental an eye on public reaction for that. We found it very clever in parts but a bit too artful on the whole.

On her return to LA the good news was that Jessica had arrived with Susan and her new husband, the Canadian actor Hume Cronin. Jill described him to Eva as 'Such a pleasant fellow but I shouldn't have thought that he was Jessica's cup of tea.' Well, fifty years later they were still married and working together, the Lunts of their era, and Jessica with an Oscar for 'Driving Miss Daisy'.

Boyhood in California was timeless and the warmth, peace and plenty have blunted all memory of the sharp edges of growing up. The Los Angeles reviews of 'Eagle Squadron' had one or two photographs of me but no mention. Undaunted, Jill went to Universal Studios and found there was unwarranted praise in the *San Francisco Times* which said I was the best thing in the picture, which she pooh-poohed as fatuous as I was only on screen for five minutes. The best parts of the film were of the Battle of Britain. They had used footage of the actual RAF and Luftwaffe dogfights over England.

A number of mainly English actors started a group at the Little Theatre, where it was hoped that most of the hundred seats would be taken up by soldiers. There were twenty-five thousand of them nearby.

> We are building our own scenery on the tiny stage, Hume and Jessica, Philip Dorn, a grand actor and also a good carpenter,

Philip Merivale, a bad carpenter and Gladys perched on an old box sewing the rings on the curtain and doing odd jobs. I would have loved the London Theatre to see the great Gladys Cooper in her slacks with her glasses on the end of her nose being very serious as to whether the canvas was straight. In the middle of it all we got into a serious political discussion and sat on the stage in the sawdust, waving hammers and having a heated argument.

Yesterday I found Gladys scrubbing the stage. We have made the scenery, done the lights, painted signs, got props, sold tickets.

The American screen actors proved amateur on stage and were not much help in getting everything together.

God help us from the American film star, they haven't done a damn thing except complain and get in the way. The other Americans, the helpers and technical crew are grand. The film people backed out as soon as they realised it meant a lot of dull work.

Every few nights, Jill would put the scales on the floor and weigh six pounds of things such as butter, soft loo paper, nylons and suspenders, razor-blades and hair-pins, and pack them into cardboard boxes for family and friends. This all created a vivid impression of England's isolation and struggle, and how far away we were.

He can't understand why we are over here. He is very proud of being English and wants to go back – he says he wouldn't mind the bombs.

My likeness to Larry often took her by surprise. I would put on an act when telling a story, indulge in mimicry, react incongruously to something I did not want to do and she would tell me to stop imitating my father, whom I no longer remembered.

Plans were finalised for Eva to come to us. US permission was granted on the grounds of a consultancy contract drawn up by Universal – keen to have her on tap for any fine old lady's role. They remembered her from her visit in 1934 to Larry and Jill and her success as the harridan in 'The Old Dark House'.

She came to the sun of California, mainly as therapy from the immense strain of wartime England. One part she did play was of an

old peasant woman in 'Bandit of Sherwood Forest', in which Jill
played the Queen of England. They wanted me to play the heir to the
throne but the dentist said my teeth had to be kept in their braces;
otherwise we three generations would have acted in the same film.

There is an undated letter Eva wrote prior to her departure from
England – apparently addressed as a codicil to her Will.

Eva Moore
Apple Porch
Maidenhead

. . . give things, dresses, shoes, wigs, etc, to the Actors Church
Union and Theatrical Ladies' Guild.

Various provisions were made for Mrs Anderson if still in her service,
Donald Krolik and Mr and Mrs Aubrey Smith, then –

Laurence Olivier wanted all my glass pictures. I meant he
should have them. But *not now*: he broke my heart.

Within a profession that recreates human emotion are those who
shoot down any appearance of the real thing. Emlyn Williams was
told the sad news that Eva Moore had been knocked down by a
bicycle and was still in considerable pain. Like a laser through a prism
bounced his wit: 'I didn't know Larry had a bicycle'.

9

Larry and Viv

Larry's fervour in qualifying as a pilot, at his own expense and while filming in America, brought him into the dreariest doldrums of his entire working life. He had become a sub-lieutenant in the Fleet Air Arm, but as a flying teacher, a pilot of planes for gunners' target practice, the ultimate non-achiever, never to fire a shot in anger.

He was horrified at the destruction of the Blitz, and deeply impressed by everyone's fortitude and sense of being part of the Island Race and proud of it. The optimism and sheer brassy guts that flew in the face of any factual analysis were personified by Vivien's lovely old Yorkshire father, Ernest.

Larry had been flying along the south coast: 'Ernest, old cock, I tell you there's nothing there. Bloody well nothing. A few, very few strands of rusting barbed wire. Occasional hunks of concrete in a line as tank traps which could easily be driven round. I tell you honestly, there is nothing to stop them at all, nothing.'

'Ooh Lurry,' Earnest drawled hummingly. 'They won't invade. They won't. Oh Noo . . . und even if they *dooo* . . .'

Larry felt out of place in his unit near Winchester. He was a film star and could never convince his men otherwise. He could never be one of the boys with his brother officers, even if he had wanted to. He did not. So many of them were selfish, ignorant and self-important. He role-played to keep something between himself and the meanness of spirit he perceived. His mimicked description of this shows how he felt.

He had arrived late (pron. 'leyet') before his commander to put in a plea for one of his men. After saluting he said: 'I do realise, Sir, there is a small stain on my sleeve. I was held up, you see, by my duties as Officer of the Day and so I thought, rather than delay a second, I should come directly.'

'Gooood thinking' said the commander. Papa's impersonations were spikily detailed. 'Ayund, this man? Applying for compassionate leave to go to Eire?'

'That's right, Sir. His mother is dying and he has to find someone to care for the little ones. His wife left.'

'Eire? . . . Thought you said he lived in Ireland.'

Larry, not wishing to point out the obvious, said: 'That's right, Sir.' The commander's ignorance exposed, his expression hardened and he decided to exercise his power. He said: 'Neaow. Refused.'

'Thank you, Sir.'

The hierarchy was delineated by stripes, and the number of stripes ill reflected the quality of the men wearing them. There was one officer who had a half stripe over Larry – a worm and no man, for whom Larry's loathing became obsessive. 'And how is our film star today?' This creature had a charming wife and Larry seriously wondered if that were the way to hurt him . . . to be found talking to her closely one evening when wives were present, and turn too suddenly at the husband's approach, call her 'darling' by the merest slip of the tongue . . . then he realised with self-disgust he had become IAGO . . .

It was a feckless existence. Vivien also found it difficult to settle down in wartime England. The pair of them were too glamorous to be accepted the way they wanted to be, like ordinary people buckling down in a shared national effort to defeat Nazism. He wrote to Jill –

14 May 1942

Headlands
Near Winchester, Hants

Darling Jilli

It is on the late side and I am just *ever* so tired, but always it is the same. I am tired and cannot do justice to foreign mail (Always somehow more demanding special mood and address) and so I dash off all the routine stuff and then I really am tired and cannot cope. Always in the hope that one night there shall be no routine stuff and I shall not be feeling fagged.

Bless you Jilli darling for the BEAUTIFUL sweater you knitted and heaven-sent parcel. If I don't say at least just that, then I never shall. For I have been kicking myself for not having written and said, if only that, for I don't know how long.

You are a sweet girl for sending such lovely things and for the pictures of Tarquin which I love. And what's more I hear you've signed up with 20th Century Fox. I *do* hope that is as splendid as it sounds. Many congratulations.

Life is just about the same and therefore a bit harder to cope with all the time – stiffer restrictions all very necessary – slightly less of this (nice) slightly more of that (nasty). People abroad don't seem to grasp the *cumulative* effect of what's been going on all this time. It's like a dentist's drill – suddenly for a time it gets on a nerve, and there's bleeding murder for a bit, then the terrible part stops, and there's no pain particularly, but the *drill* goes on and on and on and just the same.

It's the way the chaps are standing up against *that*, that I think is so marvellous, even more remarkable than the way they stood up to all that heavy dramatic stuff, when there was a strong sense of gallantry etc to keep them going.

I am still doing the same job, tho' it's developed into about five jobs lately. One of them has to do with Ralphie [Richardson] who came to see me today. He often asks after you. I'm always filled with the most affectionate admiration for the 'lads', tho' many officers I don't think much of.

Sometimes I have to go outside to make 'Warship Weeks' speeches etc. Last week I was at the Albert Hall, – 'Chrystallising the fighting spirit of the Empire' or something – or maybe it was 'epitomising' something – anyway the *Daily Express* knew what it was. And dear Esmond Knight was there [who had one quarter vision remaining in one eye only] being incredibly moving and wonderful – reciting Bunyan's 'Bells'. We sat together in a box and it's most wonderful to be with him and describe things to him.

Churchill was there and 10,000 people, an Empire hook-up and news reels. The perfect moment to dry up. Which of course I did, but only friends noticed.

He then lambasted Eva's sister Decima, who had read of Jill's renascent career in Hollywood, sent her a white feather and accused her of being a renegade. She had done the same to her son, who had been a naval commander in the First World War, but was now being retained at home for his management expertise required by industry.

Mercia and George are very well and are coming down this weekend. We are very happy here in our bungalow, with its own furniture, but our pictures.

Viv comes down 3 times a week, her play still goes beautifully ['Doctor's Dilemma'] and really I am quite wonderfully lucky compared with so many others. Glennie [Byam Shaw] went abroad 3 or 4 weeks ago. We see quite a lot of Angela [Baddeley, his wife, much later the famed Mrs Bridges in 'Upstairs Downstairs'], and now poor Sophie [George Devine's wife] will be so wretchedly worried – she's expecting a child in a very few months.

Everyone one knows practically has gone. Roger [Livesey] is in a factory in Leicester, Ursula [his wife] on tour in 'Blithe Spirit' with Ronnie Squire and Irene Browne. Noëlie is making his picture 'In Which We Serve' which we hear is excellent. Johnnie [Gielgud] on tour in Macbeth with Gwen [Ffrangcon-Davies], Michael Redgrave out of the navy for the time being making movies. Bobbie Newton invalided out and fabulously successful in movies, he and Ann are now living in Durham Cottage. Johnnie Mills invalided out in Noël's picture and almost every picture you see in fact. He and Mary have a beautiful baby Juliet.

Ever with love to you both and to all beloved friends there, Gladys, Websters and Motleys particularly.

Larry.

His declamation at the Albert Hall in the news clips now seems overblown: 'We will attack! We will smite our foes! We will conquer!' His gestures were histrionic, but he filled the place with his glorious silver trumpet of a voice and sent shivers down every spine.

His frustration with the Fleet Air Arm worsened. He wondered whether it would have been better for the war effort if he had stayed in Hollywood and made more propaganda movies to bestir America into further practical assistance for Britain. After all, the studios had tried to entice him to remain with them, offering first to pay for a new Spitfire for the RAF, and when he refused offering a bomber. He might have been able to hold out for a fighter *and* a bomber. But as an Englishman he had wanted to play an active part. This was denied him.

He counted himself a good pilot, after a learning process in America that had indeed been alarming. Apart from being an instructor he gave demonstrations and it was appalling luck, and not his fault, that on one of these he was involved in an accident even before take-off. His plane was line-abreast, wing tip to wing tip, and he started the engine. The groundsman stood in front and signalled that the chocks had been pulled aside from the wheels, which were hidden from Larry's view, under the wings. So it was the groundsman's fault that one of the chocks remained, causing the revving plane on release of its brakes to swing round and chop through its neighbour.

That is how he told the story to me, later corroborated by one of the men there, Mr George Tookey, whom I knew in the Birmingham Mint many years later. The laughter directed against Larry was unfair.

For Vivien things were better now that she had started in 'Doctor's Dilemma'. Theatre was quite rightly considered good for morale; the attitude that 'We never closed'. Had she not been acting, she, as so many other women, might have had to work in a munitions factory. Like everyone else she knitted for soldiers.

Larry was given a reprieve from his shuttling pilotry, amateur dramatics and occasional stirring patriotic broadcasts; hence the following address where he had been working for a couple of months.

12 March 1943

Denham Studios, Middlesex.

Darling Jilli

You and Tarkie will by now have given up all hope of hearing from me . . . I have been endeavouring to see 'Eagle Squadron' before I wrote so that I could write my raptures, but it never came to my station when it was released . . . Anyway I hear from all who saw it that Tarkie was quite enchanting. I caught you in 'Random Harvest' and thought you were absolutely first-rate – so real and true and good. I do congratulate you. I hope more and better are coming along, they certainly should be.

Well, as you may have heard from friends, I have been given leave temporarily to do two pictures, one 'Demi-Paradise', a Russian-Anglo propaganda picture.

The producer was Filippo Del Giudice, whom Larry was to refer to ever after with an almost mystical admiration as 'Del'. He was an

Italian lawyer who chewed a big cigar, wore dark glasses and made his first success in England financing Terence Rattigan's 'French without Tears'. Because Italy was an Axis Power alongside Nazi Germany he was interned on the Isle of Wight. Four months later he was released. It was he who suggested to Noël Coward the idea for 'In Which we Serve'.

While William Wyler was the single greatest influence in developing Larry's artistic understanding of the screen, it was Del's foresight and tenacity that gave rise to an image of glory and greatness for all time with the film of 'Henry V'. He had heard Larry's broadcasts, the Crispin's Day speech and other excerpts from the play, and he had been overwhelmed by 'Wuthering Heights'. In practical terms the making of 'Henry' was immeasurably eased by retaining many of the key creative technicians whom he had made into the team for 'Demi-Paradise'.

. . . and the other – 'Henry V' which I am to produce myself. It's all a great change. Very welcome indeed is the feeling that I am doing something I feel I know something about, and over which I have some control. The job I had was beginning to get me down slightly owing to all sorts of circumstances, and I shall feel better when I get back that I shall have had a whack at serving in every way, and that I shall not have entirely wasted what talents I've got.

Thank you for your Christmas letter and the pictures which are quite lovely. Mercia tells me that Tarkie would like a picture of me in uniform. Well, the ones I had taken when I first joined up had such a goddam sacrificial expression that I really never liked to show them to anybody. But I'm going to get the Stills Department to take a few on this picture and if any look like a father he needn't be too ashamed of I will of course send him one of them.

I think I really look about the same (younger every day of course). I got frightfully fat in the Navy, but I took up smoking again and I've since carved some off. There are one or two delightful gleams of 'silver mingled with the gold' above the ears – which are going to make me look ever so distinguished one day.

Now to hell with *me* . . . Paul Sheriff and Carmen Dillon who are the designers both for 'Demi-Paradise' and 'Henry' are coming in now, and I must stop for a confab. I'll return to this later if I can.

* * *

22nd March

Well here it is, ten days later, and this as 'Nym' would say seems to be 'the humour of it'. So I will get what there is of this off, so that you get *something* with no more buggering about.

I have to go to Eire at the end of this week to look out locations for Henry V. We'll probably be doing certain chunks of the picture there some time in May. At about that time Viv goes to Malta, Gibraltar and Algiers to entertain. It'll be very strange and rather worrying to be separated in two such odd places.

We have been living in a house of Noël's for the last 3 months, and are moving to another nearby in Fulmer, this week. With any luck we shall kiss good-bye to 'Demi-Paradise' this week after 16 weeks!

Such are the conditions of work at this time. It's been a sod of a task doing that and trying to wrestle with Henry at the same time, as well as O lots of other things.

Take care of each other. Pray God this bloody business stops before we're all too old to realise it.

Love ever, Larry.

For investment in 'Henry V' Del had had to persuade Rank, a civilised man who wanted to understand more about the concept of the film. Del, with his spikily Italian accent, pointed to the absolute relevance of the story to their own moment in history: 'Just imagine the English army landing on the French bitches.'

The other key activist was Dallas Bower, who had produced Larry's patriotic outpourings for the BBC and knew that Churchill himself thought that 'Henry V' would be a rousing film for the country. He cut through red tape, and had the idea of doing the exteriors in Ireland – the country was neutral, had no vapour trails in the sky, did have men available for hire, farmers and others whose careers were not to be enquired into, and horses.

Larry explained the kinds of impossibilities that were daily fare. They needed horse-shoe nails. There were none left in Ireland. A care-worn assistant had to go to the London Ministry of Information to be met by a paroxysm of unco-operativeness from an ill-willed official: '*Horse-shoe nails?* Are you mad? *Horse-shoe nails?* For a *film?* Don't you know there's a war on . . .'

It was a miracle the film was made at all.

They filmed at Enniskerry, the estate of Lord Powerscourt, thirty miles south of Dublin. The Irish were loyal and stalwart extras, but some were not quite 'switched on'. They did tend to run into battle holding their trousers up with one hand and their helmets on with the other, which was close to the historical truth because the English soldiers suffered from such dysentery in medieval France that they had fought trouserless. But this was to be a tale of glory, not a realistic account. Bit by bit the Irishmen rose to events. Despite shortage of armour and clothing for men and horses alike, they managed to ensure that whatever they had was worn on the side that faced the camera.

Lack of film was the main constraint: there was only enough for two takes of 'Once more unto the breach'. Rehearsals prepared the way but there were many faces reacting, many expressions straining to understand the King. On the first take, with the extra sharp nervous energy in the King's voice: 'I see you stand like greyhounds in the slips . . .' one forlorn soldier nudged the other and both gasped.

The tapestry-like clarity and colour were to uplift Britons who knew too much of the realism of war, the mud, the blood, the sickly mist, the exhaustion of those surviving death. It was a film with hardly a drop of blood, an anthem to the glory of the human spirit, addressed to its own generation and not intended as a standard against which future remakes should be measured.

Larry was the only actual actor on location in Ireland. The Irish extra selected to play Leo Genn as the fully armoured Constable of France was chosen simply because he had the grandest horse. Larry took one or two tiny roles which even in backview demanded some finesse: for example, he is the messenger who scurries from knight to knight before the fully armoured French Lord is lowered squeakingly into the saddle. Once, when watching it together on video, he pointed himself out to me in another part as well. Otherwise everyone on screen was Irish, proudly, and they all were caught up by his excitement and leadership.

Early budget over-runs alarmed J. Arthur Rank, who threatened to pull the plug on the whole project. Del came to Ireland in crisis of spirit, but proved a balm of comfort to Larry. He beheld 'So great an object', was awed by the splendour, and reassured Larry in his gruff Italian voice that it was a masterpiece and he was not to worry about 'teeny-weeny' financial problems.

Towards the end of the location shots Larry sought out the best way to suggest the aftermath of a medieval battle, the clotted remains of a mighty French army. On his grey he rode round the estate of Enniskerry. He came across a newly planted coppice on a hill, freshly fenced. He dismounted. There was a wicket gate with the name 'St Molin's Wood'. Inside, the saplings were hardly visible in the long grass. The view was all he had wished.

He approached Lord Powerscourt. 'What?' the old Irish peer riposted. 'You mean you've been to St Molin's Wood? I hate your cameras and your machines and your railway lines and all your horrible tents and mess.' Somehow Larry persuaded him to come to the coppice with him. Hardly had they closed the gate behind them than they came across a foot high twig veering five degrees from the vertical.

'Look at *that*! See that! Awful! My poor St Molin's Wood. Where shall I be buried now?'

Seeing that he had the poet's eye of the Irish, Larry was able to show him, almost as Satan had done from a high place, the glory of his estate, the panoramic slopes where riderless horses could canter exhaustedly, trailing emblazoned shreds of heraldry, the wrecked English encampment, the dying soldiers. He could see it all in his mind's eye, a worthy farewell to the battle and the estate. And it was so.

When he returned to England he wrote his first full letter to me.

1st August 1943

Old Prestwick,
Gerrard's Cross, Bucks.

My dearest Tarkie,

I am writing this in the hope that it will get to you in time to wish you many, *very* many Happy Returns of the Day. I hope that you will have a lovely day. I hope that you will always have lovely days, dear boy, as lovely as possible *particularly* on your birthdays because they should be fine days. Old as I am I still remember most of mine.

The last I heard from Joan Coxell was that all was well. I was sent a form to fill in to recommend her for the WRENS. I know she is just the type they are looking for.

I am at present in the middle of a film of 'Henry V', having just returned last week from Ireland where the exteriors were made. I hope you will like King Harry. I think of you often while I am trying to play him, he was a fine lad in many ways who always managed to be inspiring at the right moment, particularly in Shakespeare's play.

I expect you will get to know a lot about Shakespeare before you're much older. We are starting on the interiors now. It's quite a tough job for me as I am producing and directing as well as playing. (An experienced actor like yourself can judge what that entails.) So it'll all be my fault if it's no good. I'm afraid I've made rather a mess of a good many things in my time; let's hope this will be an exception.

I do wonder what sort of things you are interested in and what you are thinking about doing in life. I dare say life for you and your friends may be a bit hard to handle after this blessed war, but with courage, strength and good will you will be able to cope with it alright. How is your swimming? And diving and boxing? Can you turn a cartwheel? I'm ashamed to say I've never been able to. Can you read and write *well* now? Go on with you you're *seven* you ought to be able to. If you can read this and write me an answer, then I shall be reassured on two points!

Bibs has been away now for nearly 3 months, entertaining all our boys in Gibraltar, Tunisia, Algeria and Tripoli – also Egypt where they've been fighting and still are fighting. It's rather worrying her being so far away but she's right to go and try and cheer them up a bit. Perhaps you don't remember Bibs, it's a long time since you saw us off on the boat in New York. It seems a long time to me, I know.

I am sending you a silly snapshot of me in Ireland while working on the picture; that lovely white horse is 'Blaunche Kyng', King Henry's horse, the fellow on the other horse behind me is more or less what all the soldiers in the film have to look like. Except that most of them wear more armour than that – and I am simply covered in it!

I found Ireland to be the most beautiful place and mixing with the fine men who belong to it is a pleasure that will come to you one day I hope. I have got a peculiar haircut, haven't I! It's all for the rather peculiar make-up I have to have; in fact altogether it's a rather peculiar little photograph, but it's just in lieu of the one I promised I would send all dolled up in my uniform as a

Naval Officer. I ordered it before I went away and it ought to be through soon but things take time these days.

Be as good as you reasonably can be, dear boy, and at all times be better than good to your Mummy, and give her my love.

Your loving father.

Larry ('Olivier' follows, is crossed out, then the words 'well well well').

Vivien's tour of North Africa lasted more than three sweltering months, sometimes three shows a day, with John Gielgud, Dorothy Dickson, Beatrice Lillie and others, playing to the Desert Rats and other Allied troops. She was pale beneath a picture hat, in a diaphanous dress: every soldier's dream, her frail self come to visit him. She recited poems sometimes to an entire division of men, and must have looked almost invisible from such a distance.

They performed before General Eisenhower, and then General Montgomery. In Tunis she was presented to King George VI in whose name all the British and Commonwealth men were fighting; and he wished to be there among them. He asked her to add 'The White Cliffs of Dover' to her repertoire. This was a strange co-incidence: it was the name of the film Jill was making at the time. I was staying at Gladys Cooper's house, together with Philip Merivale, the father of Jack, who became Vivien's end-of-life companion.

Vivien rose to every occasion, but there were long silences from Larry who was dedicated to 'Henry V' for a year and a half. She lost fourteen pounds in weight and the strain of torrid heat, desert winds and blinding sun, poor food and dreadful rooms was certainly far greater than the making of 'Gone with the Wind'. In addition, there were many heart-searing visits to the wounded, and the knowledge that many men before whom she gave her performance might never again see their homes.

Vivien's exhaustion was manifested by a kind of superficial energy. She did not have the physical strength to shake off a cough she had caught in the desert, and carried it with her all through the English winter.

As spring led to summer both she and Larry began to realise the full scope of Henry, its unprecedented scale and its glory. And as they heard the music composed by William Walton, which uplifted them from the very first choral cadences whipped with brass into a swirling majesty, their love was crowned by her conceiving Larry's child.

The timing was not ideal. She had signed up to play Cleopatra in Pascal's film, opposite Claude Rains's Caesar. There was madness in the air in the months preceding the Allied invasion of Normandy. Despite her exhaustion she wanted to do everything, have the baby, maybe to be born after the war had been won, and make the film to broaden her scope as a film actress. Their wish had long been for a baby to set the seal on their marriage. They should have devoted a year of her life to its fulfilment. But she knew that Cleopatra was meant for her, and she took the part.

Shooting started in July, a month after the Normandy Invasion. As a film it did not really work, but as a portrayal of Vivien's life-giving brightness it is a marvel. The sheer sexiness of her voice and looks, winsome and delectable, when she says to Caesar: 'You sit on the other paw' evokes the most delicious desires.

While she was filming, and Larry was bringing the work on Henry to completion, he was approached by Ralph Richardson who wanted to revive the Old Vic Company, not in its original home at Waterloo which had been bombed, but in the West End's New Theatre, now called the Albery. The third partner was to be John Burrell, a BBC producer who had learned his craft under Michel Saint-Denis. This was a signal opportunity for Larry to re-establish himself in the public mind as its leading theatre actor, after five years in uniform or in films.

His next letter to Jill is undated, but was written two weeks after 'Henry V' opened at the Carlton Cinema, Haymarket, in November 1944. The Russians had broken the German Armies in the East and had advanced irresistibly from Stalingrad, taken Finland, Czechoslovakia, the Baltic States and Yugoslavia. The Nazi attempt to wipe out London for ever with V1 flying bombs and V2 rockets once again forced Londoners into air-raid shelters and the Underground for protection, even as the Allies were over-running the launching sites on the continent.

The printed letterhead 'Old Prestwick, Gerrards Cross, Bucks' is crossed out, and 'New Theatre, St Martin's Lane, WC2' written in.

Jilli Dear,

I must have seemed to be most remiss, most horrid, most unthoughtful in being so silent for such an age. I have had one hell of a year, and so much, so very much to do and worry about, and the settling down to write letters abroad always seems to require more calm and opportunity than other letters, for no known reason.

It is splendid news that you may be coming back soon. (As I wrote that the siren started just to remind me that of course life isn't too comfortable yet and won't be for years to come, I fear.) London is quite filthy and all the restrictions begin to get more and more on the poor old nerves.

Suzanne [Viv's daughter] is just back from Canada and seems to be fairly happy so far. We have been so worried lately as to how the kids are going to take their own country: she from a life of winter sports and Tarquin from one of swimming and sun. One can't help feeling frightened that they'll find England on the dingy side and the way of life extraordinarily old-fashioned.

Thank you ever so much for the lovely photographs of Tarquin, godfather Ralphie insisted on pinching the best of them and has it in his dressing room. It's quite absurd to send him these photos of me at this juncture just when he's coming home, but the poor things have been waiting so long I feel they might as well go.

I have had a vewy vewy exhausting time of it lately, for quite a time in fact. Straight out of 'Demi-Paradise' into Henry, and straight from that after 18 months solid into this maelstrom of work. I'm really more exhausted than I have ever been before.

The outpouring that follows, of condensed grief piled upon condensed triumph, the ferocious determination not only of him, but of Vivien too, immediately afterwards to throw every ounce of energy into their work and stamp out human emotion and biological need, makes one want to stand back, with Orson Welles, and ask: 'Why must the show go on?'

Poor Darling Viv lost her baby (3 months) on the first night of Peer Gynt. We were about to cable you asking if Tarkie's pram was still in existence as such things are unobtainable and if you'd mind if we borrowed it.

For Jill, to be asked by him to give so symbolic a thing as my pram to the baby of the woman who had taken him away from her, the sheer heartlessness was unimaginable.

Then 'Arms and the Man' and then 'Richard III' and the week before last 'Henry V' opened at the Carlton. Amazement upon amazement, all wonderful successes – quite unbelievable. Nothing like it has ever happened to me before.

Viv is still hard at it on Caesar and Cleopatra. She had to have 3 weeks off for obvious reasons and shouldn't really have worked so soon after. It was a horrid horrid disappointment. She's well but much too tired. Ralphie and Mu are expecting in January.

We are wondering ['We' being the Old Vic boys] if you would like it for Tarquin to play with me in 'Lancelot' our new Bridie play which goes into the bill in the middle of March. We are not quite sure about the law, with regard to one so young, but fancy that if parents consent is given and education guaranteed not interfered with it's OK with the law.

We are checking up on this and if it is alright you will have heard from us by cable by the time you get this. If not then we shan't bother you, and don't think any more of it. It's a very very dear little part of Galahad my son, plays in two scenes, would only be for 10 performances this season, 3 performances a week, only two nights, and every third week. That's the way all the plays go and of course theatre times are early now, and he could probably be home and in bed by 8.30 or nine at the latest. So I don't think it would be strenuous, it's just a question of whether you like the idea of him acting or not, or whether you thought it uncomfy (publicity-wise) to have him acting with me.

Darling I must start making up now. Gynt tonight. No, darling, I didn't direct it, I only wish I had. It's master T. Guthrie at his very best too. But I did direct Henry about which I am quite pleased with myself. He (Tony G.) and I are supposed to do Lancelot kind of together, but I expect he'll do it all when it comes to it.

Rehearsing Vanya every day now. Ralph Vanya, me Astrov. Wonderful play. We don't seem to be much good at it yet. It opens Jan 16.

Johnny Gielgud is at the same gag as we are, at the Haymarket with Hamlet, Love for Love and the Circle, only he doesn't alternate every night. Oh yes there's quite a little renaissance in the theatre and the public are responding beautifully and seem to like the friendly rivalry between us.

'Renaissance in the Theatre' would have been his answer to Orson Welles's question.

> The Lunts are on next week. I hear they are quite wonderful – 'Love in Idleness' by Terry Rattigan. Darling I don't think there's any more news and I am about to be called.
>
> Let me know if there is anything I can do to ease your home-coming, tho' I don't swear I shall be much use as I've really no time to do all I have to do. Donald Krolik has been finding out about your house (31 Queen's Grove) as none of us knew what the situation was. All love to you Jilli for Christmas and the New Year.
>
> Larry

The sheer volume of all that was happening to them must have sounded to Jill in California like a hurricane. There, 'back at the ranch', life had been free and easy.

Part Three

10

Home-coming

The *S.S. Franconia* was battleship grey, as was the entire convoy. The cargo ships and passenger liners were spaced far behind each other, while the destroyer escorts each side were out on the horizons. Our ship had taken part in target practice, firing its stern gun of about six inches calibre. One of the destroyers was stalked by a U-boat manned by fanatics, despite Hitler's suicide two months earlier and the Armistice signed by Admiral Doenitz on 7 May.

My exceptionally brief diary reads –

For five and a half years I was in America. I came back on 9th June 1945. It was a very great excitement in the dock, seeing how small everything looked, but I was ashamed that Liverpool was so dirty.

From the ship's rail was the most depressing sight I had ever seen: the inside walls of bombed-out houses, the remains of patterned wall-paper, the rising shapes of steps where the stairs had been, the coal black-mouths of fireplaces, on the ground the collapsed bricks, and from them the pinkish mauve haze of flowering Blitz Weed. Over the corrugated roofs of the cargo halls one or two damaged buildings were still standing, but the rest were gone.

The tug boats tooted and laid off their hawsers. The liner sidled the remaining few yards until we were made fast alongside. A railway siding led past the cargo shed. There were some wooden wagons, twelve feet long and with spoked wheels, tiny in comparison to American freight cars.

'What *are* those?' I asked my mother.

'Trains.'

'But they can't be. They're like toys.'

'They're the fastest,' she said bravely.

England smelt of coal. The people looked unwell, pallid, doggedly determined. Their frayed cuffs were stained with coal. The dust on every surface was black. Every nook and cranny was encrusted.

'These yours, lidy?' It was a porter in the cargo shed. He was hunched with a wheezing cold and mucus-soaked moustache.

'Yes, these four.' My mother, Eva and I wondered what he was going to do with them. They had locks of brass and were very bulky. I remembered the huge black porters in America struggling with them, two to each one, eyes bulging, their smiles flashing when they had placed them.

'Olivier?' He looked up from the Cunard White Star labels on our luggage.

'Yes.'

'Any relation?' He sniffed.

'Yes, he's his father.' She pointed at me.

Larry's films had made him world famous. In Los Angeles it had made no difference because everyone we were with knew us. On the train it was different. Strangers insisted I was Laurence Olivier's son and what a wonderful thing to be and how honoured they were to meet me. It was disconcerting. And was my mother Vivien Leigh? That put the wind up Eva who acidly referred to her as my father's new wife, my father whom I could not remember.

The porter bent forward, chest on case, fingers barely over each end, and rocked back with it. The immense burden rose and sat proud on top of him as he tottered down the cobbled platform.

'Can you manage?'

'Course Oi can, lidy. Oi've manidged biggerv'n vis.'

He made a strong impression, my first compatriot in England. My mother watched him stack the final 'Not Wanted on Voyage' trunk in the van then we went to our compartment. He put our suitcases up on the luggage racks. She was embarrassed as ever about money and over-tipped. He looked at her pityingly. 'Half that would do.'

'Keep it. You deserve it.'

'Ta then.'

He disappeared. We sat down. The windows were grimy, the frames of chipped stained wood, the one in the door had a curly leather tongue with holes in it. The ash-tray was full. A fat woman ~shed in and sat opposite with a bounce. She pulled an apple from
~g. ''ere you are, lovely. A beauty.'

My mother and Eva froze.

'Go on then.' She proffered it to me, leaning forward, knees spread open. I smiled and thanked her and held it.

The train started with much banging back and forth between the carriages before they steadied with the accelerating piston thrusts. It puffed and squeaked out of the station.

'How old is this train,' I asked, to break the ice. 'A hundred?'

'No, darling,' my mother said uncomfortably. 'I should think about fifteen.'

The fat woman went to relieve herself and they turned on me. They tried to explain that she was 'Not our class'. Eva thought she had had 'One over the Eight', a phrase I could not understand and therefore remembered. We were all travelling Third Class; it said so in huge gold letters on the door. The woman spoke in much the same way as many others on the boat, no more different from the way we spoke than American had been.

Eva went down to Apple Porch. My mother and I stayed with a cousin at 29 Clarendon Road, Holland Park, W11, in a terrace of what seemed minuscule houses, set above steps behind hefty but gateless posts. There was a brass knob in the wall which we pulled; it did not ring, it clanged, inside far below.

About half the house seemed taken up by corridors and stairs, each tiny room with its own bell pull. Alongside the stairs down to the kitchen were parallel steel wires, guided over pulley-wheels into a box faced with small windows for each room, to summon servants who no longer existed.

I slept on a sofa. After breakfast we did the washing-up at a wooden sink amid much fussy conversation about keeping up appearances. The atmosphere was strait-laced and mean. The garden was too small to play in. I went next door to say hello to the neighbours.

The door-bell clanged and I waited. An upstairs window opened.

'What do you want?' It was an old woman looking down at me.

'I came to say hello.'

'What?'

'We've just moved in next door.'

'So?'

'I wanted to . . .'

'Go away.'

Bang closed the window. It had brown tape across it to prevent the glass shattering from bombs. I turned back down the steps and saw three bigger boys sniggering at my blue jeans and sweat-shirt. Their faces were very white. I was brown. Their knees were grey, their wool socks collapsed round their ankles. I waved and said 'Hi' but they were unresponsive, so I let myself into our front door and closed it. Next morning a graffiti artist had scrawled 'SHIT' in indelible ink on the gatepost. The more we tried to erase it the brighter it became.

Several days elapsed before Larry could see us. We went to look at our own house, 31 Queen's Grove. Its occupants were Czech refugees who refused to move. We stood in the street and looked at the flakey stained walls, the filthy taped windows, the overgrown front lawn, the dislodged garden wall.

My mother showed me 74 Cheyne Walk where I had been born. The whole block had been blasted to smithereens. Weeds had taken hold and sycamore saplings had sprung up from the bricks. Chelsea Old Church was patched up with boards.

A woman told us that one night the fires in the City of London round St Paul's, two miles away, were raging so brightly she could read a newspaper. The night the land-mine hit Cheyne Walk, she and everyone else had hunkered down in an air raid shelter. In the morning they picked their way silently over the rubble, upset chiefly by the damage to the church. The huge brass lectern, an eagle with wings outstretched for the Holy Bible, had been blown out, and landed high in a tree, silhouetted, like the emblem of Nazism.

Jill tried to re-establish theatre contact but found it disheartening. It seemed that where there were openings the people took against her, as if she were foreign. House-hunting also occupied her because No. 29 was too small.

I made friends with our daily woman Alice. She had a loud and friendly cockney voice, was my mother's age – 37 – but she looked much older. She had no teeth, her face was sunken, pink lips pursed philosophically between pink gums, spectacles awry and cracked, a headscarf knotted on top.

Alice scrubbed the kitchen table and floor every week-day, singing. She told me about her husband Teddy, a carpenter, and her son John, who 'wasn't no Jesus Christ either, about your age, and 'as a Welsh granny in Swansea. Now 'e'd be good company, now 'e's back.' So it was arranged that I should stay with them, in principle just as I had stayed with Maggie Sullavan, for the company of other children.

Lorne Close was off Holland Park Avenue, opposite Royal Crescent, a cul-de-sac of three-storeyed council houses, windows taped up like packages, the nearby buildings flattened. Broken glass was set on top of a wall alongside an Army lorry park.

'We 'ad our own bomb,' Alice said. 'Ruddy thing came through our roof. Never went off though.' She pointed out a patch of new slates. We went inside. 'That's Teddy's demob suit,' she pointed to it on a clothes hanger under the stairs. 'John's 'ere.'

He was of heavy build, about a year older than I; his smile pushed his cheeks upwards and made his eyes disappear. He took my suitcase upstairs, showed me the two little beds and pulled back some wooden boards. There was a hole in the carpet and the floor. The bomb had missed him by two feet.

'Is it still there?'

'No fear. They evacuated all the 'ouses and came and defused it, carted it off.'

We went train-spotting. The railway lines ran past Olympia and we sat on a bridge and looked down, choked by coal smoke each time an engine steamed below us, and we recorded the number, class and wheel configurations in notebooks.

Bath-time was an adventure. Alice filled a zinc tub under the kitchen tap and with John's help lifted it down. He made me go first. I peeled off my blackened clothes, winced at the shock of cold water and began rubbing the Lifebuoy soap between my hands. It took forever to lather.

On Saturday morning we played cricket with a tennis ball in Lorne Close with the other boys. John told them I had come from America which was why I didn't know the rules. Then we went to the cinema at Marble Arch. The film had played for a long time. It was 'Henry V'.

'That's 'is Dad,' John said.

'Tisn't,' they chorused. I nodded and let it rest.

The cinema was alive with excitement. The manager made a speech in front of the curtain and introduced three young starlets who sang a patriotic song. An electric theatre organ rose from below stage in an oasis of geraniums with a cascade of roaring brass made hideous with *tremulo vibrati*. The lights dimmed and two spots blazed down upon the ice-cream girls in linen aprons.

The Pathé News Pictorial poured out black-and-white images of Allied success in Burma and the Pacific, the liberation of the world from the enemy, while the commentary in clipped 'Standard BBC English' tempered the military discipline of 'Your country needs you' with a sense of fair play and the 'done thing' and 'mustn't get involved'. At the end the Pathé Rooster stood flapping its wings on the weather-vane, which had the points of the compass spelling out 'NEWS', and gave a climactic Cock-a-doodle-doo against a sweeping orchestral score and the interfering clash of the theatre organ as it sunk from view.

There was silence. We were stilled, spell-bound as the screen went blue. The excitement of technicolour.

A Laurence Olivier Production

To the Commandos and Airborne Troops of Great Britain this film is dedicated, the spirit of whose ancestors it has been humbly attempted to recapture in some ensuing scenes.

The screen became a pure sky, lighting up our faces. A flash of white appeared in the distance while a flute played freely as a lark. The piece of paper swirled and unfurled out to fill the screen with the Titles, in Olde Englishe, to the sound of taut side-drums and trumpets, the urgency modulating into a heavenly base ground on 'cellos and double basses, with a wondrous view of the Elizabethan City of London, ships under sail on the placid Thames, in peace.

Was there ever such a time? Would the now flattened City ever be rebuilt? The chorus of singers built the melody into a languishing lament. That music's richness and pulsating energy swept away the wail of sirens for ever, the terrifying indiscriminate unfairness of the destruction of homes, and established a sense of wonder, glory and absolute belief in this Star of England, with the 'Few, we happy few, we band of brothers,' and their great achievements out there, somewhere.

> This story shall the good man teach his son,
> And Crispin Crispian shall n'er go by
> From this day to the ending of the world
> But we in it shall be remembered,
> We few, we happy few, we band of brothers.

When it was over I was pulled to pieces, heart bursting with pride, overwhelmed by the pain of abject unworthiness and riven with self-pity that this man, my father, I could not remember. I only really knew it was he because of the photograph of him on Blaunche Kyng – a mere photograph to hang on to.

Alice walked me home on Monday morning in a state of great tension. She tutted at the graffiti on the gatepost and opened the front door. She told me to take my suitcase upstairs and went straight into the drawing room to confront my mother, and say that I must never, ever, stay with her again. 'Miss Jill,' she said, 'moi foinal word.'

'I am sorry. What did he do wrong? Perhaps I should talk to him.'

'Ain't no talking to be done.'

'What's the matter then?'

'These few days and 'e's started talking loik us.'

Unlike an American accent which I could switch off at home, cockney was made of sterner stuff. It was weeks before my mother stamped out 'Oo?' for 'Who?', 'Pudd'n' for 'What did you say?' When Alice was satisfied with my progress I was allowed to stay again.

Jill had scant luck with agencies. No one wanted her. In retrospect she seems to have been too theatrical, over enthusiastic and easily frustrated, unsure of her roots.

We moved to Campden Hill Gardens, W8, a taller but equally thin house, 20 per cent devoted to flights of stairs, with linoleum floors and gas fires like old bones.

Larry came to see us one evening.

'Let me look at you,' she gazed up into his face. He smiled down obligingly.

'How did you get that?'

On his upper lip, running down from his nostril, was a concave scar. He described how when filming one of the battle scenes a horse had bumped the camera back into his lip and cut it almost through.

'Extraordinary how it changes your face.'

At her suggestion he and I dined together in a Hill Gate Village restaurant.

He picked up my hand and turned it over.

'How far back can you stretch your fingers?'

'Like that?'

'Marvellous.' He pushed his own finger-tips against each other and could not even reach the vertical. 'I have worked at this since I was a boy. You see, for an actor, to flash your fingers back, like you can, is a marvellous dramatic gesture. Keep that ability, in case you ever want to act.'

After dinner we had a pee, *sans exposition*, and it was pleasant standing side by side. 'I do love peeing,' he said. 'That warm feeling afterwards.'

As we strolled back to Campden Hill Gardens he delivered himself of his preoccupation. He was determined to be a good father, and for that to happen I ought to be free to say anything to him, raise any problem. I should never doubt his love for me. Whatever happened he would always love me. If I were to burn down the house, or commit murder or something, he would still love me. It was a key turning point in our relationship. I was troubled, but grateful.

'And there is one thing when you go to school. Don't give away that your name is Tarquin. They'll tease you mercilessly.'

How could he ask me to deny my name?

In my room I showed him my *Boys Own Annual*, the image of the young out-of-doors and how to make bows and arrows. There was a story with a picture of three naval officers who looked rather like him, in an open boat on the high seas with a torpedo bearing down on them. Conversation had become difficult so he read it to me. His voice was thrilling, and transported my imagination into actually being in the boat, at one with the officers and ducking as the torpedo roared out of a wave and flew over us to crash harmlessly back into the sea.

The house was freezing. I complained that the neighbours were exceedingly unfriendly. One had called me a 'nosey parker' when I had gone to introduce myself. He sympathised, saying there were huge differences from California. I said something which sounded churlish and he delivered a memorable riposte: 'There are two things I learned in life which you must learn too. The first is not to play "Macbeth". The second is don't even sound as if you are contradicting your father.'

We discussed further the problems of settling down in war-torn England. His advice referred to both me and my mother and we often harked back to it. The English felt we were foreign to them, sensing our lack of what they had experienced, the horrors of the Blitz, the bombs, the self-sacrifice and determination, the sharing that had bound them together more than ever as a homogeneous Island Race. Xenophobia was natural. Our points of view were cradled in different premisses from theirs. We had to tread with care, and if in doubt agree, or seem to, or at least not disagree with what was being said.

After he had gone my mother said: 'I can't get over how the scar changes him. Makes his face look more important.'

'What was he like before?'

'Before? He had a soft sensitive mouth. Now it's strong and narrower.'

Close friends like George and Mercia Relph were fond and welcoming, professional colleagues of Jill's less so, some were even hostile. Once she stopped our taxi, leapt out on the pavement and introduced herself to a fellow actress: 'Hello, it's me, Jill! We're back, how are you?' She held out her hands but the actress took a step back, obviously regarded her as a renegade returned only now that the war was over, to compete for the few parts available. Jill got back into the taxi. 'That was a mistake. Silly. Damn.'

At last we were able to go down to Apple Porch. A fully loaded Allied bomber had crashed into the woods half a mile away and the whole place had been declared out of bounds. All the windows had been smashed by the explosion and the garden was littered with debris. For weeks sappers had gone over the grounds with metal detectors and cleared everything away. The woods looked as if an enormous bite had been taken out of them, leaving behind a brilliant white crater of chalk.

Everything was strange: the flies buzzing everywhere, the coke-burning Aga in the kitchen, the fly paper drooling down from the larder ceiling spattered with black corpses, the lack of a fridge and the food kept under mesh covers, the butler's pantry with the glass, the scullery for everything else. Mrs Anderson noisily remembering me in the broad accent of Berkshire was the strangest of all. The only thing I remembered was the licence number of the little Ford: FLD 835. The car itself seemed as rickety as an old pram.

Uncle Jacky was demobbed and came to live with his wife Rosie in Apple Porch Corner, originally intended as a servants' wing. He was gruff, a Major, and at the age of only forty-five had decided that he had done his bit and was going to retire for the rest of his life. Poor Rosie!

My mother and I returned to Campden Hill Gardens. We went to see Larry as Sergius in Shaw's 'Arms and the Man'. The story has frequently been told but it is an axiomatic turning point in his acting, at the hands of Tony Guthrie as was the previous one with 'Henry V'. Larry could not find any reality in the part, and Guthrie asked him why on earth not, didn't he *love* Sergius? Larry's reply, as they walked down the Manchester pavement, was vituperative.

'Well,' said Tony, 'if you don't love him you'll never be any good as him, will you?'

This Larry described as the richest pearl of advice in his whole life, and he came to adore Sergius for his faults, his arrogance and absurdities. He invested him with all his imagination, invented a dreadful little jig for him to dance, each time tripping over his spurs.

His Hotspur, in 'Henry IV Part One', was beyond me. His next role was Justice Shallow in 'Henry IV Part Two'. Here he made himself the spitting image of his own father, having a lovely time using the gestures, the dirty little habits like wiping sticky fingers on the remaining wisps at the back of his bald head; then Ibo came to see it, and afterwards in his dressing room was inconsolable.

We went to see 'Richard III', from the front row of the Dress Circle. He came on stage with his hump-back and limp, his false nose, his left hand shrivelled: he had come to confide in us, then stopped, turned back, took out a key and locked the door. He sidled down to the very edge of the stage, chuckling and leant towards us as if to a mirror, to explain his fascination with all that was dark and terrible and what fun it was going to be, his laughter hissing, his consonants like whip-lashes. I felt close to him then, in that role, closer than before, because here was a character exposed in his every movement, every glance and pause. His speaking voice was modelled on Henry Irving's, his malevolent looks on Jed Harris, who was also the model for Big Bad Wolf.

We went round afterwards to his dressing room. He was still dressed as Richard, but had peeled off the rubber glove from his left hand and the false nose. He was furiously rubbing his own with spirit. 'So sorry, boysie, I simply had to. The itching, infernal interminable itching drives me bloody well mad.'

He held the false nose on to show how it fitted, altering his whole character. Jill was almost speechless with emotion at the greatness of his acting. Others crowded into the little room and he introduced me: 'My son, Tarquin, and his mother Jill.'

He relished their praise. It filled him with warmth which he exuded when he looked over at me, with pride, it seemed, and I bathed in the sense of assurance induced by reflected glory. He put his wig on the stand, stripped off down to his pants and donned a dressing gown, mouthing with a camp accent: 'You've all seen me bathing, 'aven't yuu.'

His adoring and whimsical dresser, Pat, passed round the whiskies as he plastered his face with cold cream and wiped off the make-up with a khaki towel. They all talked at once, trying to outdo each expression of congratulation.

I was too young to see 'Oedipus'. George Relph played a shepherd, so I sat in his dressing room during the performance and whenever he was back from the stage we chatted. He had played Buckingham to Larry's Richard. He told me how marvellous our food parcels from America had been. I asked what was so terrifying about 'Oedipus'. He said that soldiers just back from the war, still in uniform and awaiting demob suits, collapsed and fainted from the horror of it.

'Soldiers?'

'Yes. Last night there were several. One of them fainted during the interval, after it was over.'

'The Critic' was the very opposite. Larry as Mr Puff, in the cause of rumbustious laughter, took physical risks the like of which I have seen no other actor attempt, ever, culminating in a spectacular curtain fall, starting at the top left corner of the proscenium arch, clinging tightly, and swinging down like a pendulum to centre stage where he did a backward flip head-over-heels on to his feet. This brought the house down. The laughter must have saved many from the nightmares which Oedipus on its own would have produced.

Our crate arrived from America, too big to go through the door. The men jemmied it open on the pavement and we carried in the boxes one by one. The street was empty, the doors opposite locked shut and the windows sightless and sad. I went over to number 9 where there was a girl my age, and tugged the bell. It was her mother I addressed: 'Now that my toys are here I wondered whether you would let . . .'

'Go away.'

Yet on another day an old lady was crossing the road, tripped and collapsed. Within seconds half a dozen front doors opened and people brought pillows, blankets, glasses of water and affection for a fellow creature in distress. So there was a neighbourhood after all, caring but distrustful.

This kind of grit had contradictions. The most frequent complaint was a philosophic: 'It's always the same.' Ox-like persistence was the means to any end, the bowed heads of people standing in queues for buses, for groceries, with ration books in the butcher, outside MacFisheries, sunshine or rain, it was always the same.

The other complaint was an expostulation of outrage, a yelp: 'But it's not the *same*!'

Summer ended and I went to Cottesmore Preparatory School where Molly Williams was sending Alan and Brook. We three boys were now uncomfortable together, in school ties and caps, with grey flannel shorts and jackets, long grey woollen socks with garters and black shoes. We felt terrible standing on Paddington Station platform, lost, our mothers in hats. It was very early in the morning. Others eyed us. Some of the boys were tiny, others were huge. Everyone was white except for me, still brownish.

A dear old master pointed out the carriages reserved for us. The School had been evacuated to North Wales, not far from Snowdonia, an ancient building called Cors-y-Gedel Hall, allegedly with priest holes for the Catholics to hide from Cromwell's men. The journey took fourteen hours.

It was a well managed school, despite the fuddy-duddy wartime masters. We were taken for beautiful scenic walks up the surrounding hills. There were the usual football games, but also the exotic ones we invented when we slunk out of French dictation for gang warfare in the woods. These and the Welsh made for a happy term.

That Christmas I only saw Larry in his office. He gave me an envelope on which he had drawn some ivy and candles and a Father Christmas. Inside was a superb little Asprey's pen-knife in gold with my initials.

'Now,' he said. 'The tiny matter of your School Report. Not bad. In fact quite good. But just, I know it's difficult, I just think, I mean – just be *better*.'

I was crestfallen. He said that was supposed to be funny, but I knew nothing of William Wyler, Heathcliff or Wuthering anything. So he regaled me with a story of an old master at *his* school during the First World War, and an appalling oil of a boy. It was well-trodden ground.

'Smithkins,' he mimicked, 'and *where* is your essay?'

'Ooh sir, I left it upstairs.'

'Are you *sure* you've written it, Smithkins?'

'Ooh, yes, sir. When I finished yesterday evening I heard the Angelus and couldn't help feeling that God would be pleased with me.'

'Very well, m'boy, go and fetch it.'

And of course the toad was away for half an hour before he returned and handed in the essay.

'The ink,' said the master, 'is still wet.' He looked up benignly. 'But I believe you, m'boy.'

Daddy was now completely at ease with himself. He always was when acting. And how we laughed. The characterisation had been timeless.

My mother gave a cocktail party. I stood outside the front door, excited that there would be action, proud that they were coming to *our* house, a touch defiant at the wall-eyed houses opposite. Everyone came by tube or bus and the mere fact of having arrived gave them a sense of achievement. These theatre people came in strange shapes and sizes, and had astonishing vitality and bizarre reactions. Glen Byam Shaw was very distinguished, and his wife Angela Baddeley, by then more Mrs Bridges than Cordelia, could open her eyes even wider than Judy Garland. I gave her an orange.

'An ORANGE!' She clutched it. All conversation stopped. 'I haven't seen an orange for five years.'

Such odd people. The impossibly tall Tony Guthrie looked down at my upturned face: 'And what is the name of your school?'

'Cottesmore School, sir.'

'Yes, and what is it called?'

'Cottesmore School, sir.'

'You keep saying it's quite a small school, sir, but what is it?'

'Cottiz-more.'

'So grown up' Molly Williams said, damn her. Damn the long grey socks and prissy grey shorts, my turned-up pug nose that I could see profiled round my entire field of vision.

Leo Genn was in Service Dress, his Sam Browne on a peg outside. After acting as the Constable of France in 'Henry V' he had returned to his unit, and was among the first to enter the Nazi death camps. As he spoke in his rich dark voice the only movement in the room was a dachshund puppy tugging at his trouser turn-up unnoticed, so unimaginable were the revelations of mountains of corpses, bull-dozing them into lime pits, the horror of those still alive, just barely.

My mother got a part in a dull production of 'The Eagle has Two Heads' which made it to the West End. Her next opportunity was a film 'Escape' with Rex Harrison as a convict on the loose in Dartmoor.

Cottesmore withdrew from the wilds and reverted to its brick building in Hove. Luckily the headmaster Mr Rogerson moved the entire school again a couple of terms later to a mock Elizabethan mansion with the heaviest stone roof in Sussex in Buchan Hill Estate, complete with rhododendron tunnels half a mile long, a lake and a wonderful view.

Meanwhile at home, Alice had been to a National Health dentist and had false teeth. Teddy the carpenter never said anything, too personal, but John did: 'Doesn't stop her talking cockney', and winked. In his teens he became an oarsman and skier, and rather than change the way he spoke, or accept the straitjacket it imposed in England then, he went to Norway, married a local girl, established himself and held his head high simply as an Englishman.

11

Notley Abbey

In August 1946 I was taken to the theatre where Larry was directing Vivien in a revival of 'Skin of our Teeth'. She was playing Sabina, the scatter-brained tailspin of a maid in a silk slip. The auditorium was in darkness, the scene was lit and the actors on stage. A manager led me down the aisle and pointed to my father about six rows from the front. 'Hello, boysie,' he waved me towards him, gave me a soft kiss, put his arm round my shoulder and sat back to watch the rehearsal.

The actors were in workday clothes except for the elephant and the dinosaur who were complaining how cold the Ice Age was. Mr Antrobus, played by George Devine, was a confident and courageous American. There was a beautiful woman in a dull brown skirt and I asked who she was. Larry, focusing on the play, said: 'That's Bibs. You remember Bibs.' She was enchanting. When they finished she switched from an American accent to her English voice and said the armchair she had to carry was really far too heavy. She stood down-stage and looked pleadingly at Larry, called him 'Darling' and was reassured when he agreed to get a smaller one.

Vivien, translucently pale and beautiful, approached between the seats. Fourteen months had elasped since my arrival in England and this was our first meeting. She looked at me with love, called me 'Darling', and gave me a delicious kiss on each cheek, saying wasn't it thrilling I was going down to Notley with them that weekend. She asked me what things interested me.

'Music and playing the piano really, and shooting rabbits with my Uncle Jack.'

She made me feel that they were precisely the things which interested her too. I felt discovered, understood and cherished. She was master of that art, but in all the years that have passed since that first conversation I have never personally had any occasion to doubt her truthfulness. She, whose passion had deprived me of my father, did all she could to bring us together.

On Saturday morning my mother and I walked to Holland Park Avenue and waited for a taxi, my things packed in a soft suitcase. A bus went by. There were few cars. Trailing down the pavement outside the grocery shop was a long queue of people with their shopping bags and ration books, their sad faces, tatty clothes and old shoes.

A taxi stopped, my mother packed me into it and told the driver: 'Durham Cottage. 4 Christchurch Street, off Burton Court.' I was transported away, through the woebegone streets of London. Odd sights: a policeman in a helmet at a crossroads, a chimney sweep cycling in a top hat, piles of rubble and wooden stanchions supporting the houses still standing on each side.

In the narrow street gleamed the chrome grille and headlamps of a Rolls-Royce, outside a yellow gate. A maid answered the bell. We crossed a little garden. Durham Cottage was as dinky as Red Riding Hood.

I sat between Larry and Vivien in the front seat of the Rolls, George and Mercia in the back. The four of them had first driven to view Notley Abbey in the autumn of 1944, a fleeting visit after the completion of 'Henry V', with Vivien expecting a baby and about to start 'Caesar and Cleopatra', and Larry about to enter the lists of triumph he described in his letter to Jill a couple of months later. He had fallen in love with the place's gothic history. It had been founded during the reign of Henry II in the twelfth century:

> This Abby of Nutley, otherwise called Sancta Maria de Parcho Crendon, was founded and endowed by Walter Gifford, second Earl of Buckingham of Canon Regular of ye Order of St Austin, and dedicated to St Mary Anno 1162. Which endowments were confirmed by K.H.ll and by K. John . . .

according to an engraving I have dated 1730, a present from Vivien's daughter, my step-sister Suzanne.

Wolsey had stayed in the New Wing (fifteenth century) when he was having Christ Church built at Oxford. Then with the dissolution of the monasteries the Abbey itself, which was almost as long as Salisbury Cathedral, was razed to the ground. The wonderful refectory was gutted and the cloisters destroyed during the vast historical ruction which routed the pre-eminent power of the Catholic Church, whereby one third of all England belonged to Rome. Henry VIII's Armageddon released that land to his people.

All that was left out of the ruins were the domestic quarters, which remain with their cinquefoil lead casement windows and lichened roof.

Larry once said he loved the place 'more than people'. I wrote a description for Anne Edwards's biography of Vivien; it seems orchestrated but appropriate because everything that happened there was 'over the top' so much of the time.

Memory of it moves me deeply. In a great valley it lay – the heart of leafy Buckinghamshire, the River Thame meandering in weedy shallows through the elm woods, the willowed fields. This place where Henry V once stayed, breathed heraldry. In the attic were priceless frescoes of the emblem of Notley embracing the hazel nut and the lovers' knot. There was an exhausted sexuality about the place, regretful black rooks high out of reach, umbrella poplar trees silvering against the sky in unlabouring cascades, a cruelty unearthed in the corpses of monks once buried under the High Altar before the dissolution of the monasteries by Henry VIII.

It also had many friendly moments. On Sunday mornings you could lie in your bath and hear the village church bells pealing in Chearsley, Haddenham and Long Crendon.

On that first visit, once Larry had placed the medieval key into the gothic oak door, his mind was made up. Vivien realised how daunting a task it would be to bring the rooms back to life, starting with central heating. George and Mercia felt it was a divinely mad idea which needed people like Larry and Vivien to realise it. They dined with Del Giudice in a nearby restaurant. He who so adored Larry saw that he had to have it. He arranged for the capital to be advanced to him to buy the place at once, before the war ended and peace bumped property prices out of sight.

Next year they started decorating the servants's bedrooms, their own and George and Mercia's. Sybil Colefax, the interior designer, aided them, but even with her expertise the problem of actually finding materials and carpets was acute.

At the end of July, while Vivien was filming 'Caesar and Cleopatra', disaster struck her down with the loss of her baby. Within a few weeks of the end of filming she suffered an hysterical paroxysm and flew at Larry. The condition developed spasmodically over the years into manic depression, which came and went relentlessly, with normality between times and recovery of their love.

A year later, still underweight and with a cough she had had since before Christmas, and exhausted even more during the strain of the first season of 'Skin of our Teeth', tuberculosis was diagnosed. Larry was away entertaining the troops in Hamburg, with Ralph Richardson and the rest of the Old Vic Company, in 'Peer Gynt', 'Arms and the Man' and 'Richard III'. She managed to finish the run, and on the last night Larry took her to University College Hospital where she stayed for six weeks. She then went to Notley for nine months' recuperation. Larry visited her almost daily from London.

She stayed in their double bed and read voraciously, including the whole of Dickens. She called it the Pink Room because of its walls. The carpet was pale yellow, there was an immense fireplace and cinquefoil windows. With the coming of spring she could see the white blossom of two ancient pear trees, and began to develop a love for the place which was making her better.

George and Mercia's room, next to theirs, was the Blue Room. Later they were to decorate the Green Room, and years after that the suite they were themselves to take, up a further flight of stairs above the high ceilinged drawing room.

In May 1946, Vivien was well enough to accompany Larry on tour to New York. It was on their return that I first met her, at the rehearsals of 'Skin of our Teeth' for its autumn revival.

Their real life together at Notley then began. They invited the cast of 'Oklahoma!' down for the day. Howard Keel, a magnificent specimen of an American, epitomising everything that was big and healthy, thrilled war-torn London with his exuberant 'Oh what a beautiful morning!' and his sheer bounding energy. The showgirls were tanned and radiant. They were all just crazy about the historic old Abbey. Larry took them swimming in the River Thame. On the island between the river and the millstream was a fallen tree, a diving spot into a pool six feet deep. He showed them how. The girls followed, then started to come ashore. Their manicured feet sank into the river mud. It cloyed. Bubbles ran up their thighs and they hopped out in droves crying: 'But this is filthy. Honest to God it's really dirty!'

The house demanded that we wear evening dress to go down the staircase for drinks in the library, even when the only furniture at the far end was a couple of armchairs, a huge pouffe and a sofa Vivien had given Larry for Christmas. Sitting there were George and Mercia, Tony Bushell, associate producer of 'Henry V' and a friend from Hollywood days with Jill, and his lovely brown-eyed lady, Annie Serocold, with whom he lived in the cottage overlooking the river. Larry was shaking the cocktails.

Vivien sat on the pouffe, her long skirt spread round her, a wide belt made her waist tiny and she wore a tight black sweater. Jill had always said she was the most beautiful woman in the world – perhaps to justify Larry's desertion – but had been critical about her breasts. So I looked in their general direction and saw perfection. Those were the days for all who could to have bra-shaped breasts – to which no one, in Vivien's case, could have held a candle.

Everyone was very pleasant and wealthy.

There was something about Vivien's skirt: it moved up and down in a rhythm. Allen, the butler, announced dinner. Vivien thanked him and stood up. Her Siamese cat New Boy, now revealed, continued twitching his tail.

Tony Bushell's eyes were the sharp blue of Bunsen burners. He was tall, bald, a man with the vigour of a games-player and an unfulfilled desire to remain mysterious. He claimed that there was a large bear at Notley which rubbed itself against the front door of his cottage, making 'wuffley' noises.

After Puligny Montrachet with the fish, and well into the claret with the grouse, Larry told us of an apparition which only he and Vivien knew about: they suspected that she was a nun, a lost ghost who walked occasionally past the door of the Pink Room at about three in the morning. Vivien had heard her during her months of recuperation, the sound of her legs beneath a long habit. With such evidence it might equally have been a monk but that was never suggested.

They all knew of Vivien's health problems, but the air of too-good-to-be-true prevailed. George and Mercia went off to the Blue Room, I up the further half flight to the 'No Room', still uncurtained and incomplete, a table light with no shade, round which Vivien tied a ribbon to make it pretty. In one corner was a model theatre a yard square, with tiny wooden figures frozen in stillness for Larry's return to them.

Behind was an ogival door. 'The Tower,' Larry said. 'Want to come?' A single bulb lit a worn spiral staircase which made his voice resonant.

'Like ancient houses?'

'Love them. Cors-y-Gedel . . .'

'To hell with Wales. This is England.'

'Baba darling, can I come too?' crooned Vivien.

He led us into the attic, switched on a feeble light and we saw the arched oak beams under the tiled roof, faded cerise in the grooved edges, the surfaces grey. We followed him along duck boards. He pointed to the fresco of the triple sprig of hazel in pale brown, with green leaves and a lovers' knot beneath. 'Hence, I dare to dream, the change from Nutley to Notley, commemorating love?' Once within the Tower again, he said he wanted a double bath there. Vivien looked doubtful.

'Now', as his feet slapped the stone steps, 'to the oldest loo in England.' We went through my room and into a larger L-shaped one, fusty with emptiness. Within a tiny closet, beneath a recess large enough for a candle, was a hinged shelf which he lifted. 'A clear drop of thirty feet to an underground stream, piped into the river Thame.'

In the morning, dressing-gowned, I joined them in the Pink Room for breakfast. They were still in bed. Larry cut his toast into soldiers and dunked one of them into his egg. 'Come here, Tarkey.' He watchfully placed it into my mouth, something at the back of his mind. 'Get outside that and you won't be doing badly.'

They tried to make me feel part of the dreamland they were creating, as they did for all who went there. She arranged the flowers, selected the books to put beside guests' beds, kept lists of whatever they had been given to eat before, so as to avoid repetition. There is a bittersweet lyric in the South Pacific song 'Happy Talk': 'If you don't have a dream, how you goin' to have a dream come true?' They were trying to recover their love, after the loss of their baby, her first outburst of spluttering unreason, and her tuberculosis.

The first tree-planting was an avenue of limes straight from the River Thame between broad fields up to the brow of the hill, beyond the mead which was the grazing ground for old Blaunche Kyng. For more than a quarter of a mile the lime saplings, each staked and isolated from its neighbour, curved up each side of the drive and out of sight to the Aylesbury Road.

Larry's second 'Folly' was also successful. It was an S-shaped 'Where'er-you-walk' a hundred yards long down to the river to give some privacy to the cottage. The concave curve cradled the best of Vivien's herbaceous borders.

There was a medieval byre so they bought their first calf, and called her Sabina to tie in her birth date to the role Vivien had played in

'Skin of our Teeth'. Sabina begat Antigone, which begat Blanche, which begat Cleopatra. Notley butter was sent to me at school because of rationing and the cream was packaged for the White House restaurant in Percy Street.

Larry paid for his brother Dickie to qualify at agricultural school so that he could take over management of the farm. In the meantime the fields were leased out, and there were head gardeners, one of whom drove us crazy, with hooded eyes and an unmatched capacity for deflecting criticism. Larry mimicked the hesitancy the man used to concoct his counter-attack: 'Well, Mr Oliver, the, the, er, the thing is, I mean to say, is this. What yer uskin me, Mr Oliver, is to stop with the doing of the impertant things, and get on with doing of the inimpertant things.'

Before the tennis court was built Sunday afternoons were for walks. The three of us climbed up the hill past the dovecot. Vivien was not an 'outdoor' girl in the athletic sense of striding out, playing catch or scampering with the wind in her hair. She wore scarves or hats, moved demurely as we helped her over a stile, to be followed by Larry like a lord a-leaping.

There was a pasture and he explained that one of the best voice exercises was to bellow at the cows. If you shout or even raise your voice above normal speaking strength the tone too easily becomes metallic. His Macbeth had been criticised for that. It flays the vocal cords. Imitating the mooing of a cow caused the voice to gain resonance, so that great volume became rich and not rasping. He configured his throat and voice and bellowed. He loosened his collar and tie and brought his full diaphragm to bear. It was a glorious warm sound, not a snarl, more like the roar of a lion to let the pride know he was king. The cows were surprised.

A summer image is of Vivien in a cloud of butterflies, picking flowers, deep in the herbaceous borders with her basket and shears, watched by the Siamese New Boy. In the pantry she chose an elegant white vase, her varnished nails glinting as she darted the flowers into position.

'There,' she said, satisfied. 'Almost as much fun as picking them.'

We went into the library and she placed the vase lightly on a stem table. George and Mercia, Tony and Annie were there. Larry's face had an aura of joy as he watched her finger-tip the flowers with a touch of finality.

'So pretty,' she said, making her lips into a kiss as she did so: 'Pooritty, aren't they, Baba darling.'

I had never before seen a man and a woman in love. Theirs had a depth of experiences shared for eight years, remembered passion, loss and fearful illness, and now rebirth of all they had ever had.

I had watched Vivien pick the flowers for Larry and wanted to be a part of the two of them. It was a powerful longing that could only live through the denial of the one really deep love I had in life, my mother. So different was Notley it seemed that this moral truth did not have to be faced. It was another world.

This separation was essential to stability. It was breached when Vivien telephoned me at Apple Porch to ask whether I had received her birthday present. I had, and had written a thank-you so all was well.

Eva was sitting in a deck chair under a tree with Jill, gazing over the View.

'And how is your father's new wife?' demanded Eva.

'Mummy,' said Jill gently, 'she's his wife, and Tarquin is fond of her.'

Eva heaved a turbulent sigh. That evening we sat in her Chamber of Horrors, listened to the six o'clock news and learned of the further communisation of Eastern Europe. 'The world,' said Eva, 'is in a terrible state.' Poor Warsaw.

Once when Vivien dropped me back at Queen's Grove I could not resist showing her my new kitten. My mother was upstairs and I realised it was not a good idea. I grabbed Mishu and took him out, leaving the front door open. 'Lovely, darling,' Vivien said from the bottom of the steps, blew a kiss and left. She never did come in.

For his part, Larry confined his enquiries to Jill's health and whether she was successful in obtaining work. He resented the divorce settlement which bound him to give her a meal ticket for the rest of her life. This had been at the insistence of Eva. The magnitude of the recognition he owed her for his sense of direction as an actor and as a director, when he was still floundering, had soured. Cosmic loathing displaced the love that used to prompt the words 'Hello my darling Mum'.

At Notley, the summer of 1946 was the first to be filled with flowers, with happiness sharpened by their sad memories. Weekends were established as sacred. After the Saturday night show, friends would forgather at Durham, have a quick sandwich and then drive the ninety minutes to Buckinghamshire. At 1.00 a.m. the butler helped with the luggage, and dinner followed informally.

Weekends were hard work for him, his wife and the cook, but the rest of the time was free.

There would often be twelve of us, so some had to stay in Thame. While the drawing room beams were being treated against death-watch beetle we crowded into the library, and after dinner on Sunday the games were fairly restrained, mainly cards.

Larry took the Old Vic Company for six weeks to the Century Theatre, New York. Vivien insisted she was recovered enough to accompany him on what became a triumphal tour, with Hotspur, Justice Shallow, Oedipus, Mr Puff, and Astrov in 'Uncle Vanya'. She, as always, needed only four hours' sleep. He with his workload needed twice as much, and was often denied it at her insistence that they go night-clubbing, partying, merry-making of any kind. The nervous energy of New York coupled with the drinking she was supposed to turn aside put her on a 'high', which though uncontrollable was very appealing.

They returned to London exhausted.

Larry added King Lear to his repertory. I saw it from my crows-nest in the Dress Circle. His hypnotism was overwhelming, his roaring strength during the storm, the pulsating energy. In the second interval my mother and I stayed fixed to our seats.

The third Act opened with him in tatters, a mad old man, vines clinging to him, daisies in his hair. My reaction was an outburst of childish laughter: that man in tats and bare feet was my Daddy. My mother shut me up.

'Yes, I heard,' he said afterwards in his dressing room, eyes loving. 'My son's laughter. Only a son could so laugh at a father.'

The embrace of Notley was upon them. The huge drawing room was now carpeted, decorated and welcoming. In the library the curtains had been replaced with white ones carrying the hazelnut emblem with the lovers' knot. Roger Furse had had these printed when he was working on the sets for 'Hamlet'. The design appears on the walls of one of Ophelia's scenes.

After New Year 1947, Larry greeted me with the words: 'Your father's not a knight.' Ralph Richardson had been knighted in the New Year Honours and *he* hadn't. 'The king doesn't like me.'

His antidote to tiredness and disappointment was, as so often, a further cartload of energy poured among all those around him, this time in the form of The Game, from a man who had the night before ended a week of 'King Lear'.

I was in John Mills's team and was given 'Suck it and see.' He said it was just up my street, which I couldn't understand, but it was easy enough to do. I gave Vivien 'Steady the Buffs' which no one guessed, making her mock furious with me. Someone, perhaps good friend Roger, gave Larry 'Spivs and Drones'. He stuffed evening handbags under his shoulder pads, articulated his pelvis like Sammy Davis Jnr and of course we guessed 'Spivs'. He stuck out his tongue, blew between bulging cheeks like a flight of bumble bees and leapt over chairs, on to the piano, did heads over heels, jumped as high as he could, grabbed his knees mid-air and landed with a bounce into the sofa.

'Halcyon days,' he yelled, jumped up, leapt again and crashed down onto the sofa, again and again as if to ram into his mind that this was real, real, real, that he was having a good time, wasn't he, and therefore so was everyone else. Then, even when playing the fool, he seemed tapped into some force that drove him on and on, as if the only way he could relax from monstrous overwork was to aspire to exactly the same extreme in over-play; as if unhappiness, however deep, was something you could excrete if you pushed hard enough.

The first to be downstairs next morning was the critic, Alan Dent. He was helping Larry prepare the script for 'Hamlet'. He had the face of a purple emperor and the gentlest Scottish accent. While we waited for the others he taught me cribbage: 'Fifteen tu, fifteen foor.'

Larry believed that the only way he could be convincing as young Hamlet was to have a very young Ophelia. He chose Jean Simmons, aged sixteen. The part of his mother Gertrude was played by Eileen Herlie, who was also his junior, by twelve years. His choice was for a cast in no way associated with him in the public mind. This made Vivien feel she was on the shelf.

In springtime I saw him at Denham Studio in a hairdresser's chair. His head was covered all over with a steaming towel. 'Hello, old cock, hang on a bit. In a minute I can come out of this.'

The hairdresser checked his watch, leaned over Larry and, solemn as a mortician, revealed him. The head which had been covered with dark hair, occasionally cut into tortured shapes for the likes of Henry V, often hidden beneath wigs, now shone like a banana in a smoke-house. He was ash blond, even his eyebrows and lashes. He studied himself closely in the mirror, his face aglow and pink.

'Your forehead has changed too,' I said.

'Damn right. I plucked it up half an inch, to give myself an arched Hamlet brow, to cease having anything to do with myself at all.' That must have reminded him of Jill.

We careered off like madmen in a station-wagon with fat wheels, the sections of an aluminium canoe rattling in the back. At Notley we assembled it and launched ourselves downstream. We paddled and sang, he baritone, me treble. We came to some thick reeds, pushed as far into them as we could, then turned back.

Next day Terence Morgan, a youthful Laertes, arrived with his pretty wife. I accompanied him and Larry outside to a fine old ash tree overhanging uncut grass. They wore tennis shoes, cotton trousers and T-shirts; they carried swords and rapiers, unbaited, with sharp points. No gloves, body guards or masks.

They faced each other, presented their sword-tips up, lowered them, and swished them in a series of arcs. They crouched and circled in the sequence they had rehearsed many times. After warming up they sped up their lunges and parries, snatching away each attack with fewer and fewer nano-seconds to spare, their expressions were of fear. They poured with sweat. Larry shouted out for more rage, more rage. He stood back against the tree and Terry lunged at him again and again, the pointed sword getting closer and closer before being deflected.

They rested, wandered around and recovered their breath. Larry looked up into the branches and affectionately patted the bark. Once he had failed to parry in time. Terry's point stuck into the bridge of his nose. Half an inch either side and he would have lost an eye.

Before lunch we all sat in the drawing room with the sun streaming in. There was an air of expectancy, the chat merely a veil over anticipation. Allen came in and bowed a trifle stiffly.

'Good morning, Sir Laurence. Lunch is served, m'Lady.'

'Thank you, Allen,' Vivien purred. There was a pleased silence while Allen withdrew, which of course Larry broke; 'Don't you *love* it? "Sir Laurence" comes so trippingly off the tongue.'

It was that evening that he stood in front of the library fireplace, a champagne glass in his hand and delivered his peroration on how happy he was. He had always dreamed of the kind of love he now had with Vivien, had always wanted the splendid career he now had, and Notley fulfilled his deepest historical hopes of living in such a place. And not only that, there was a Rolls Bentley in the garage and he had a knighthood, things he had never really sought.

The effect was to make the rest of us feel excluded, in some kind of vacuum. This was filled by clinking glasses and Mercia wondering whether his knighthood would make me an 'Honourable'.

'No,' he said. 'For that his father would have to become a lord. A *theahtah* lord. The noble Lord, Lord Long Crendon?'

The following morning as I watched him and Terry fencing again we were approached by the gentleman farmer who was our neighbour. He was the previous owner of Notley, a gaunt man whose ancestors' names had for centuries been hewn into the gravestones around Long Crendon church. He excused his intrusion and they paused from their fight. 'Merely wanted to congratulate you on your knighthood. And,' a mysterious pause, 'to say quite simply how glad I am, that Notley has *got* you.'

After a few attempted pleasantries he swung his stick into the ground and stalked up the hill towards the dovecot. Notley Abbey had been occupied by his family for several centuries and he resented the Oliviers.

That afternoon Larry and I had to go to Eton together, a year ahead of time, to meet my future House Master and have the proverbial afternoon tea. It was a dreadful introduction. 'Deadly' Hedley took an immediate dislike to us. He was humourless and Larry thought he was a dried up old haddock, but he does deserve more sympathy than the story allows.

We parked on the gravel outside the front door – a bad start. Hedley came out to meet us, saw the Rolls and was miffed. He had pointed features, deep-set eyes far behind strong horn-rimmed spectacles and, horror of horrors, hair as blond as Hamlet's.

'Wow!' cried Larry, forcing the pace, 'well, well, *well*!' He bowed towards the schoolmaster to show the top of his head. 'But mine is growing out at the roots, unlike yours!'

Anyone would have blanched at Larry's unexpectedness, but Hedley made it into a confrontation with his tone of reprimand: 'How do you do, Sir Laurence?' He turned and led stiffly through the hallway, and out into the sunny garden. Mrs Hedley was easy on the eye, charming and relaxed.

My mother arrived from London. We all stood and my father introduced her as 'Tarquin's mother, Miss Esmond' which made me feel illegitimate. Hedley was a bit surprised but she affected not to notice.

Over tea my mother said how much she had enjoyed acting at the Windsor Theatre and wondered what was showing. An easy enough opening.

'Oh,' said Hedley, 'something terrible by Chekov.'

'Don't you like *Chekov*?'

'His characters, so many of them, such failures.'

'Aren't we all?' my mother asked.

'I should hate to consider myself a failure,' he replied. He had been a classics scholar at Eton, gone straight to King's College, Cambridge, with other Old Etonians, and returned to the school as a master. Boys' maids had more experience of life than he . . .

In the summer heatwave the Rolls collected me from Queen's Grove. Vivien was at Shepperton filming Anna Karenina. The girdles and sheer weight of nineteenth century Russian clothes made her unbearably hot. She was unhappy with the director, and even more with Ralph Richardson playing her odious husband. He played it for sympathy, hamstrung the drama, and removed any justification for Anna entering into the disastrous love-affair with Vronsky which drove her to suicide.

She came off the set and kissed me. She gathered up her skirts, turned and said: 'This dress makes me look like the lady with the big bottom.' I followed her down to see the rushes of her and Ralph.

'What do you think of him?' she asked.

'Very nice,' I said, happy to be positive.

'Exactly, and that's quite wrong. He should be a brute.'

Back in her dressing room she nervously lit a cigarette. This seemed incongruous. 'Looks so funny, in those clothes.'

'You like them?'

'The most beautiful I have ever seen.'

She was taken aback. 'Well, I must say. How sweet of you.'

She leant towards the mirror and tweaked away her long false eye-lashes and laid them in a little dish. She started loosening her wig. 'I just wish,' she said as the dresser helped ease the netting from her temples, 'I just wish I had a straight nose. I'm thirty-five and don't look too bad, but a turned up nose is so boring. Only sort of nose to have is a straight one. Like Garbo.' That, from the woman with one of the loveliest noses ever.

A few weeks earlier she had accompanied Larry to Buckingham Palace for him to be dubbed knight bachelor. The pictures of him, a blond Hamlet smiling shyly in morning clothes, with her beside him in a black suit, make him look slim and youthful. The conductor Malcolm Sargent was knighted the same day so they asked him down for the weekend.

The opportunity to impress the master of the Promenade Concerts was heartily prepared for. Larry had shelves built in the little room beyond the drawing room, and his records marshalled into order. Malcolm arrived. The gramophone was playing something 'with body'. For a while they chatted, Malcolm bent on singing for his cocktails as well as his supper. Then he creased his smile into its most charming. 'Would you mind if I asked you to turn that off?'

Larry was flabbergasted. 'The *gramophone*?'

'If you wouldn't mind.'

Larry obliged, then mincingly asked: 'Don't you like myoosic?'

'It's just, well, how would you like it if I played you recordings of John Gielgud's "To be or not to be"?'

12

Down Under

For almost the whole of 1948 Larry led the Old Vic tour of Australia and New Zealand. Vivien was to shine as Sabina in 'Skin of our Teeth' with him playing Mr Antrobus (George Devine's part), was Lady Anne to his Richard III, and Lady Teazle to his Sir Peter in 'School for Scandal'. Like Jill before her, Vivien adored being on stage with him. This was the first time for eight years, since they had lost all their money on 'Romeo and Juliet' in New York.

Now it was to be different. Everyone knew that his Richard personified greatness. There was magnetism and fearful danger, the Spanish 'Duende', where to be near carries a sense of trauma, of being enveloped by his 'dark' power. What this meant for Vivien during the scene of his seducing Lady Anne must have varied, depending on whether she were spell-bound or spell-rejecting.

It was a triumphant tour; dramatically, politically and financially, and a disaster in other ways. The only close friends they had with them were George and Mercia.

The first letter he wrote to me was four days out to sea:

RMS Corinthic

Feb 18th (1948)

Please . . . write to me c/o British Council, 489 Bourne Street, Melbourne, Victoria – will find me for the next five months or so. We get to Cape Town about Feb 20th and I will send more stamps from there. I do hope you are up and about by then.

(Cottesmore school had been smitten with chicken-pox.)

Bibs is getting gradually less tired and so am I. We took a terrible beating all last year with all that work, but with three more weeks of this sea we should be strong as horses by the time we get there. The weather is getting lovely and warm and we should be crossing the Equator in a week or so, where we shall be roasting I expect.

We shall be opening 'The School for Scandal' in Perth on March 20th and then go all over the place . . . we shall be home some time in November so we shall try to see you at Christmas. My dearest love and Bibs' too to you.

That made me feel a part of them. Aged eleven, after three years of knowing them, we now had special links, separate from those between me and my mother. At night I would pray for her, then Eva, Jacky and Rosie, maybe the cat Mishu, and finally 'Daddy and Vivien'.

His postscript cut across this separation:

My love to Mummy please.

Apparently he thought it did too, because there is a further PS:

Hope the Rugger goes well.

This re-established the direct line from father to son.

It is difficult to imagine what the now wonderful cosmopolitan Australia was like in 1948. The people were welcoming then as now, but their provincialism, their feelings of being literally 'Down Under' and at the end of the line, made them especially susceptible to taking offence: a curious mixture of brassiness and umbrage.

Consequently the impositions on Larry and Vivien were not the merest of morsels, but huge demands upon their time and energy, as England's, maybe even the world's, most 'glamorous and romantic couple'. As ambassadors of goodwill, from the Old Country, they were stuck with having to pretend this role in front of crowds, politicians, and gatherings where he had to behave in much the same way as he had in the Albert Hall in 1942. And this was in addition to being tour leader, director and leading actor, plus the persistent concerns over poor Viv's mental health.

For my birthday he sent a parcel, contents now forgotten, with every single Australian stamp stuck round the label, nineteen of them ranging from 1/2d, to the £1 engraved with the King and Queen in Coronation Robes.

Australia Hotel, Sydney

July 21st 1948

This letter may arrive early I fear, and the parcel which follows
it by ordinary mail is liable to come late, but . . . I will try and hit
the right spot with a cable on the day. Here are some stamps.
There is also a complete set on your parcel so that, unless some
thief gets at them, you will have an unused and a used set – they
were each stamped with meticulous care by the postmaster here
who sent you his best wishes. Bibs and I are having a really
amazing but quite . . .

The rest of the letter is lost, as are the others he wrote from the
Antipodes, and my memory can only recall them partially.

They had, of course, to see many local offerings of theatre, most of
it gutsy, made more unseemly by the Australian accent which in those
far-off days grated excruciatingly on the English ear. There was one
surprise: the young Peter Finch. He impressed them so much that
Larry invited him to England.

Their accumulating exhaustion (at least it was the cool Australian
winter) led to rows, back-biting, recrimination and Viv's own pitiful
outbursts. These were an illness and had nothing to do with her
personality or love of him, but they could not be hidden from their
colleagues whose loyalty was such that there was never a word
breathed outside.

Into this maelstrom the Old Vic Board lobbed a grenade equivalent to nerve gas. By way of acknowledging the triumphant tour
which was to yield a profit of £40,000, Larry was sent a telegram
saying that he, Ralph Richardson and John Burrell, the third member
of the artistic triumvirate, would not be leading the company for a
further season. No reason was stated.

The tour struggled on to New Zealand.

On board ship, after their final departure, he sent me a letter. His
knee cartilage had finally given out during the fight in Richard III. He
drew a sketch of himself on a dockside baggage platten, being hoisted
over the ship's rail by an enormous crane, with an arrow pointing to
'me!'.

In their absence, Durham Cottage had had its front door moved to
one side, so that the dining-table no longer had to be moved to let
people in. Upstairs the tiny bedrooms were enlarged.

Notley had been threatened by an attempted invasion redolent of Toad Hall and the occupation of weasels and stoats while Toad was in gaol. Luckily Tony Bushell and Annie were there to repel the attack.

Before dawn one autumn morning Tony was woken up. This was no wuffling sound, no mere bear. He peeked between the curtains and saw nose-to-tail headlights all the way up the drive. He clambered into wellington boots, duffle coat, deerstalker and seized his stick. The entire hunt were gathering and printing their proud hooves into the lawn he had nurtured like a cricket pitch.

This was a man who had served in the Guards Armoured Division and fought his way with a pistol out of a tank surrounded by Germans. He strode squarely and angrily towards the Master of Foxhounds, shook his stick and yelled; 'GET OUT!!!!' Somewhat surprised the Master looked down, touched his top hat and was about to say 'Morning' when Tony shouted again, hustled through the pack of hounds and shouted again: 'You heard me, GET OUT!' He whacked the Master's horse on the rump, shook his stick again and the entire hunt realised, even the hounds, that they had better leave before they got hurt. So they withdrew, over the bridges, up the drive, followed by at least fifty cars.

The Master of Foxhounds sent a reprimand and signed off with the style: Captain, Coldstream Guards.

Tony replied –

Sir –

We are not troubled by foxes at Notley.
If we were, they would be shot, by

Yours sincerely

Anthony Bushell
Major, Welsh Guards.

After their landfall Larry and Vivien stayed at Durham Cottage, his future plans for the Old Vic now castrated by its power-grabbing board. There she told him what he had already feared for some months in Australia, and increasingly and more undeniably during the weeks of the homeward journey. She did not love him any more.

He was thunderstruck. His passion for her still made everything that had preceded it seem a shadow. With her love now denied he had to come face to face with what he had destroyed in order to cling to her. What his mind had sought to warn him, his heart had to reject. He could not accept it.

Notley beckoned to them both. They drove down at the end of the autumn when the place was glorious and mysterious. The L-shaped No Room had been fully decorated, ready for them, bathroom en suite. From the bed there was a clear view of the millstream and the river, and the island in between where Larry had put a white marble statue of Venus.

Outside, the cloister wall had been realigned to accord with the original form. The drive now encircled the house, enabling more convenient use of the front door by the staircase, and leading away to the garages. This revealed two huge stone piers, as large as those in Salisbury Cathedral. In the ambulatory was a cache of ancient tiles, mostly broken.

Vivien decided that the cloisters should be shaped with arcades of clipped yews, a white garden and a catalpa tree in the middle. The gardener told them that when digging out for an asparagus bed several jaw-bones and craniums had been unearthed. This located where the high altar had been and they arranged to have it delineated by a semicircle of trees.

Notley had indeed 'got them'.

Also while they were away, his film 'Hamlet' had been given a Royal première, and its growing popularity with audiences, not only in England but world-wide, more than justified his act of faith in underwriting so much capital expenditure on the house. It was as if his career was no longer an end in itself. He was exhausted with acting. The only reality for both of them, the only love that remained unquestioned, was where they stood. They must both have wondered whether it would hold them together.

That spring, at lunch, I asked what he would have said in his speech to Her Royal Highness Princess Elizabeth and Prince Philip had he been present at the 'Hamlet' première. 'A fuw well chowsen wirds', he started in Australian. 'Probably' in county English, 'ending with something like: wouldn't you prefer an experienced man of the world, like me, to that fumbling young blond?'

We all laughed, Vivien with hysterics. With tears pouring down her cheeks, she looked out of the window at the daffodils and the rose garden beyond and pulled herself together. When she turned back she seemed content, looked softly at Larry and we were relieved.

Vivien's parents, Ernest and Gertrude, were there, so after dinner

Viv and I played Newmarket with them while Larry read a script. Then we all sat back in the sofas, they with brandies, and listened to records: an often repeated orgy was Sibelius's Violin Concerto, first played by Ginette Neveu with earthy passion, to be followed by Heifetz, playing it as if it were the purest distillation of the soul.

Energy was restored. Larry had brought cricket nets and coconut matting from Australia which we unrolled and pegged out on the lower lawn. Every visiting male was co-opted into batting and bowling, even Vivien's old father Ernest. His lofty expression at the crease was redolent of Empire. Larry overdid his bowling and strained his right shoulder. Very much in character he then bowled left-handedly.

The English public were to see Larry and Vivien together on stage for the very first time in 'School for Scandal'. It opened on a freezing 20 January 1949, after hundreds of people had camped out all night on the pavement in an orderly queue for tickets, despite both Larry and Viv going to them to explain that every seat had been sold. Vivien at last evoked the critics' approval as Lady Teazle: for the new depth to her voice, the mellifluousness tweaked with irony to deliver unexpected comedy in many shades. For the first time her talent, long acknowledged on screen, was recognised in the theatre as on a par with her beauty.

Larry re-opened in 'Richard III' to renewed and grateful praise. The old rhythm of life was re-established: weekends starting after the Saturday night show, to end on Monday afternoon. Malcolm Sargent came down to Notley again. So did the gargantuan Orson Welles, with his new and tiny bride: Vivien took me naughtily to one side to wonder how *they* managed. I said there's always another way and she told me not to be disgusting.

Next day we played bowls on the newly mown lawn. Orson was not built for bending. After much grunting he just managed to wedge belly between knees. Cantilevering his great bulk was fit to make his eyes burst. After a few rounds his composure burst: 'This makes cricket look like a *game*!'

At dinner Malcolm's exertions fell far short of wit. His conductor's manner was arrogant and condescending. We weren't buying it. He persisted on his morality model, about a man who did not wish to go to bed with Vivien not being more moral than the man who was really tempted but resisted – heavy stuff which she managed to detain at her end of the table.

Undaunted he turned towards Orson and Larry, at the far end, and announced that he was going to explain about nine/eight time. It is a tragedy that Orson never played comedy, with *his* look of fathomless disbelief. 'Nine/eight time,' proceeded Malcolm, 'quite rare, no triplets or quavers, just nine semi-quavers, as in: "Lon-don-is-a-beau-ti-ful-ci-ty", up to nine like that with no note accented, "Lon-don-is-a-beau-ti-ful-ci-ty".'

Orson's sense of the ridiculous took over: 'Glad he likes London. Wouldn't last a minute in New York.'

After dinner Vivien asked me to play the piano. I did my not very good best, and it kept Malcolm quiet. Then Larry hurriedly put on a new recording of the 'Pathétique': another improvement. Even so, the soaring tragedy of the great final movement was too much. Orson rose in his magnificence, leant back against the piano and wailed in his deepest bass: 'Poor old Tchaikovsky. Wadda madda boy, come to your friendly Orson, you poor old guy . . .'

In the morning Larry showed me their new bedroom, the Georgian furniture Vivien had chosen, the painting of roses by Winston Churchill which the great man had given to her. Larry wondered whether they would get to know the ghost better.

'What ghost?'

Angrily he said: 'You know perfectly well we have a ghost.' I had forgotten.

'It's a nun: legs hissing under a long garment, hence nun. We thought she was returning to this room.'

'So you've kicked a nun out of bed.'

This made him laugh. He opened his wardrobe door, showed all his ties hanging in line, the MCC and Garrick ties bright as sweet-wrappers, and an equally vivid tie with stripes of red, purple and pink. 'The Tallulah Club,' and he told me the story.

Vivien started to complain openly that it was wrong for Income Tax to be charged on their joint incomes instead of separately. At nineteen shillings and sixpence tax in the pound she had a point: 'It punishes us for staying married. We ought to be rewarded for that. It's difficult enough as it is.'

Larry disguised his misery in his weekend role of country squire. He had an eccentric tweed jacket built, with four buttons, cuffs with turn-ups, a yellow waistcoat, a birds-eye cape and a deerstalker. It was not quite Sherlock Holmes, no pipe, violin or cocaine, but exaggerated for the work he did: trimming adventitious shoots off the lime trees, adjusting the rubber supports round new saplings, checking the hazels' bud-grafts along the where'er-you-walk. His unhappiness showed when he re-wound the cable of the electric hedge cutter, watching the carefulness of his own hands. He missed his horse, Blaunche Kyng, who had died.

He wrote to Jill.

Durham Cottage, Friday April 8 (1949)

From a father's point of view in dreaming of his son's career I have always found myself greening up with envy of Bronnie [Bronston Albery, owner and manager of theatres] as he watches young Donald stalking about the New and slowly taking over responsibilities. To me there have always seemed few occupations more delightful than administering a theatre with imagination and dignity.

I love acting of course terribly in my heart, but it's terribly exhausting, and if one just lacked that particular nervous energy necessary for success in the job, or one just didn't come off, for no apparent reason, I think I'd rather be Bronnie than anyone. Anyhow I have determined to own a theatre before I die, with the vague idea that Tarkie might like to inherit it – a little *shop* – a *nice* little shop – all one's own with polished handrails and professional stuff going on behind the footlights. Tireless in interest and experiment.

I wonder if your idea was the same?

P.S. One somehow thinks the grandchildren might have a taste for the other side too. All jolly vague, of course – just dreams. I haven't got a bloody theatre yet & probably never will have but first L. O. Productions is building gently but slowly (I think – hope?) in organisation – pity if it all fluffs out when your little friend hits a bus.

P.P.S. The Old Vic was a fine dream you see for old Ralphie and me, as our work could go on, or we could think so. But we've been shaken up from that dream now. I don't know what old Ralphie will do – start his own shop perhaps, he thinks, he's just marking time and getting his breath now, like me.

This seems a distilation of his genius: 'Dreams', that 'particular nervous energy' and the 'other side': reaching beyond the horizons of self towards transfiguration.

He had told Jill that the two things he most wanted were to be a good husband and a good father. How hard he tried to be both, and how far he succeeded, given the constraints of his priorities.

To build on Vivien's success, without outshining her himself, he decided to play chorus in Anouilh's 'Antigone' with her as the outlawed princess flung into poverty by the tyrannical Creon, played by George Relph. I heard him his lines, page upon page of exposition translated by Christopher Fry. It was so naturalistic that I found myself looking up from the script, thinking he was talking to me personally.

'Come on, Tarkie, follow the fucking thing.'

'Sorry.'

'"Wives they're afraid of, kids that are afraid of them . . . I will tell you about Creon."'

'Yes!' I asked eagerly.

'Follow!' he commanded.

When he had finished, checked the crosses I had pencilled in, he rushed up to his room. In half an hour he was back, eyes blazing, word-perfect.

His choice of 'Antigone' for Vivien provided depths of pathos no one suspected she was capable of. Her beauty defeated, smudged with dirt, clothes ragged and walk reduced to that of one trodden down, were extraordinarily emotive, and her voice softer and lower, revealing tragedy with a horrifying caress.

Next day was the start of the week I would go to Eton. We were alone in the drawing-room. He had finished his lines and sat on the arm of the chair I was in. There was a long silence. Quiveringly he lit a cigarette.

'Why are you shaking, Daddy?'

'Well, I,' he inhaled deeply. 'Well, old cock, I mean, of course you, you know all about sex, don't you.'

'Yes, my headmaster told me, and my Uncle Jack.'

'He was a wonderful lover, your Uncle Jack.'

Anything to change the subject.

'Really?'

'Quite wonderful. Ye-es, very good lover indeed: but that's for later. You've been warned about bigger boys and taking advantage. Seldom happens but it might. You're small for your age and the youngest in the school and you'll be wearing bum freezers. Unfair somehow.'

He stubbed out the cigarette and delivered himself of the message I dimly remembered when, as strangers, we were wandering back from our first dinner together in Hill Gate Village, and which I was now able to understand. Retrospective knowledge, that Vivien had told him she no longer loved him, makes his words of love for me more poignant. He was tense, filled with anxiety and my instinct should have been to fling my arms around him; but in the deep armchair, with him perched so high, I couldn't.

The first morning at school there were letters from my Mama, Eva, and Vivien wishing me all the very best, and one from Larry written during a performance of 'Richard III'.

> Darling Boy – Whenever I've not been actually talking on the stage today, I have been thinking of you – & sometimes in the middle of some great dramatic moment (so-called) my thoughts have wandered to you, to the terror of the prompter and the bewilderment of the other actors on the stage. And now, while Clarence is roaring away in his cell, I hasten to write just one line to welcome you and bring you my love, the first morning you wake up at Eton.

'Being an Etonian', even in monkey jacket and high starched collar, seemed stride after stride to be an entirely new experience. I thought seriously, but fatuously, that I had arrived, that whatever happened in the rest of my life everything would be fine, somehow, and I would be able to go anywhere and be welcome.

It is strange to recall from a letter to me from Eva that rationing was still in force four years after the war.

> Apple Porch, May 3/49
>
> . . . I've had some lovely butter sent to me, real Jersey cow, so I thought you might like some so here it is. Am awful cold & I'm going to bed with my hot water bottle . . . two of the puppies are sold . . .
>
> Your Gran.

Larry's hope that I might go into theatre management was not shared by Jill, who saw it as more of a wish-fulfilment for him than for me. As for acting, she entirely shared his opposition to my taking it up, even at school. 'Be your own man, not someone's son', they both insisted, and trotted out statistics of the odds against success, of having to wait at table for months when out of work, and with my name being resented for any job landed as supposed preferment. I have since seen some of my baby-star films and am sure no talent was denied.

However, my need for emotional outlets and desire to perform were strong, so I was fortunate in being taken for the piano by the School Precentor, Dr Sydney Watson. Thanks to him, Hedley allowed me to cling to music, a subject of which he was ignorant.

Apart from the usual school mysteries, new friendships, and a lot of hard work, that summer term ('"Half", Mummy, don't say "term"') was a series of afternoons practising in the Music Schools, on my way to the Thames under Windsor Castle. I had a narrow straked boat called a 'Whiff', with fixed seat, and sculled far away and all alone round Lower Hope, Upper Hope, past Athens and Easy Bridge, up to Locks and back, happy that William Gladstone had done the same.

During the summer holidays I flew with Larry and Vivien to the South of France to stay at a grand old villa called 'L'Oulivette', on a hill overlooking Cannes. It belonged to her ex-husband Leigh Holman's sister Joyce and her French husband. They were all there, together with my step-sister Suzanne. I took to her as immediately then as I had when we were being evacuated on the *Scythia*, even though she did say she had never really needed a young step-brother!

This extended family was a curious pot-pourri of past betrayals, divided loyalties and present laughter. We rented a fishing boat and picnicked around the islands. Vivien in a two-piece swimming suit was something of a disappointment, not very trim or sporty, but she did dive, even if belly-flops, and she did swim but not much.

I liked Leigh's dry sense of humour. 'Just how,' I asked him, 'are we related, you and I?'

'Strictly speaking we're not,' he said legalistically.

'But loosely speaking.'

'That's quite different. I am your step-mother's first ex-husband.'

'First?'

'Whatever happens I shall always be that.'

Larry might have said 'IAGO!!' but I wouldn't swear to it.

Leigh being there showed the extraordinary loyalty that Vivien inspired. She also gave loyalty that withstood every trauma, except deception of herself by others. Larry realised that Leigh's forgiving presence, which was to become more frequent, was of solace to her.

After a week with them, Leigh and Larry took me to the airport to meet Jill, and they drove us both along the Corniche to Le Lavandou.

Vivien had read Tennessee Williams's new play 'Streetcar named Desire' and felt she could identify with the tortured Blanche Dubois, while not wishing to foresee the effect upon herself of realising night after night the searing descent into madness. With her new status as a tragedienne, Larry also thought that she would be marvellous. Here at last was a modern play of immense power and greatness. Our old friend Jessica Tandy had played it on Broadway opposite a young and thuggish Marlon Brando – a moth to a gorilla.

Vivien's gifts made her the only choice for the West End and this caused them to override objections from John Gielgud and other close friends, on the psychological dangers. Perhaps Larry thought that this devastating role about instability would somehow help. Whatever happened with the part later, when it opened that October in the West End it established her as a top stage actress, in addition to her Oscar-winning screen supremacy as Scarlett O'Hara, but at unfathomable personal cost.

Larry meanwhile realised the dream he had described to Jill the previous April, by taking a lease on the St James's Theatre. With about one thousand seats it was his preferred size, and he loved the burgundy-coloured seats, gilt lamps and mahogany. He strengthened Laurence Olivier Productions (LOP), set up a year earlier by his agent Cecil Tennant, by bringing Alexander Korda to the board to join Roger Furse the designer, Tony Bushell the producer, and himself. Now that he had his own theatre to run he appointed Lovat Fraser as General Manager.

He opened his first season with a stylish production of 'Venus Observed', a verse play he had commissioned from Christopher Fry, who had written two previous ones: 'The Lady's Not For Burning' and 'A Phoenix Too Frequent'. During rehearsals he and other actors, including George Relph and the young Denholm Elliot, walked up St James's to Savile Row for their tailor-made clothes to be fitted, and down towards the Palace to Lobbs for their buttoned shoes. The sets were expensive, using an authentic telescope complete with the mechanism for keeping star time, and a newly installed revolve stage.

At the end of the play, as the Duke of Altair in the garden pondering fate after his house had burnt to the ground, he felt that the final curtain was *never* coming down and rose to his feet as it did so. As he stood on *his* stage and took measure of the applause between bows to the audience, he thought it was not a huge success but decent enough; his guess of thirty weeks was accurate. A few weeks later he directed the Australian Peter Finch in a light play 'Captain Carvalho' which did very well.

The moguls insisted that Vivien play opposite Brando in the screen adaptation of 'Streetcar' to be filmed in Hollywood. Larry, mainly in order to be there with her, accepted the lead in 'Carrie' opposite Jennifer Jones. He *said* the piece that attracted him was his suicide sequence, but that ended up on the cutting-room floor. It was generally a down period for play-writing and he was bored with reading bad plays, dated plays, plays that didn't work. At least 'Venus' had given him wonderful poetry, even if it failed dramatically: how can you expect an audience to bathe in be-yoo-tiful words when the house is on fire? In his disenchanted state and needing the money he went, looking forward to being directed by his mentor William Wyler.

Vivien's performance on screen, released in September 1951, won her second Oscar. Larry's performance in 'Carrie', on the other hand, made you wonder not how he did it, but why. The reason was to be with Vivien and give her his constant support.

For the Festival of Britain he decided that, with Vivien at the height of her powers, he and she together should attempt two related peaks: Bernard Shaw's 'Caesar and Cleopatra' and the infinitely more demanding Shakespeare Cleopatra to his Mark Antony. In the film opposite Claude Rains she had been a bright and bewitching kitten of deviousness and youth, beauty matched by intelligence. To play again the role that had exhausted her into miscarriage shows her determination to rise above past loss, in order to act opposite Larry. Her attempt to trump this role with that of the older Queen Empress, to whom Mark Antony had given Asia Minor's south coast as a wedding present, shows her courage.

They opened at the St James's with Caesar on 10 May 1951, and with Antony the following day.

When they were settled in to a monumental success with the two plays more or less alternating, I went to his dressing room and watched him in vest and pants, making up as Caesar. He sat before the mirror, naked bulbs blazing all round it, a bust of Caesar to one side. In front of him were trays of powder, puffs, nail scissors, clippers, pots of various creams, rows of pencils and sticks of grease-paint on either side, and a couple of stands with wigs. He placed his cigarette in the ash-tray, leaned towards the mirror and examined his face: the moment between one entire personality and the creation of another.

He picked up a tiny concave of rubber, rubbed adhesive in with his little finger and placed it on the end of his nose, and then again with another in the middle. He added false eyelashes. As they dried he wiped his hands on a khaki towel. He squashed a sponge into a bowl of olive green suspension and daubed it all over his face. He stood and applied it to his forearms, and his dresser Pat sponged his legs.

Comparing him to the bust of Caesar's head I could see the shape of the nose was perfect, but the rest was still Larry, the colour of the Incredible Hulk.

The pencil markings around his eyes took him about ten minutes each, sitting back with a hand-held magnifying mirror, smoothing lighter shades with a little finger after applying them with a brush as fine as an eyelash. He moved his eyes round, and checked with the Caesar. He drew the wider lines on the forehead, deep ones curving harshly into his cheeks, then the highlights necessary to give them three-dimensional substance. After the detailed work he put on the wig and set about concealing the join half-way up his brow and around his temples. Finally he fluffed power all over his face and dabbed it with the towel.

We had chatted, he had puffed a cigarette between long periods of concentration. He studied himself archly in the mirror, now Julius Caesar entirely.

'What day is it?'

Pat's reply horrified him.

'But that's Antony!'

She corrected herself: 'No, it's Thursday.'

'Thank Christ. Otherwise someone would have to go out front and announce' – he put on a sergeant-major's voice and a toff's accent – '"Laydees and gentlemen, either wait and hour and a hoff, or else hev the other pley".'

The eyes were Larry's smiling through Caesar's features. He had cast a spell on his face, knew it was good, and could open up his own again as if under an umbrella.

I once watched his Caesar from the wings. At the end of his first scene with Cleopatra as he declaimed 'Incorrigible, incorrigible, away!' and the revolving stage sped him in my direction, he saw me from centre stage and the eyes reverted to his own, as easily as turning a page.

That night, as Pat helped him climb into his armour and buckled him, and as he placed the laurel wreath around his head, he said: 'Now is the time, the very moment in time.' He sat magnificently in his full regalia, sword clinking down from his belt. 'The time that every actor has the strongest craving for a num-num.'

He took a sip of water, gargled and swallowed with distaste.

'Water. At my age.'

There then entered a tiny, sunlit girl in bare feet and white robe, with masses of hair tumbling over her shoulders. 'Tarkey,' Vivien said, reaching up to kiss my cheek. 'You're huge!'

For the young Cleopatra she looked the essence of simplicity; but for the older raddled beauty, she etched cruel lines of sensuality, dissatisfied lust for power, and adopted an unforgiving cast of mind. She too was master of the art of make-up, still acknowledged forty years later by the Theatre Museum which used her magnificent Cleopatra as the model for their exhibition called 'Slap'.

As one of the most beautiful women in the world she was perfectly cast as both Cleopatras. Her suicide after that of Antony was more moving than any I have seen since, though other actresses, even ugly ones, often received better reviews. Her looks, and her winning of two Oscars in films when none of the others had even been nominated, blinded critics to her talent on stage. They would not accept that beauty itself is a talent, and a sine qua non for Cleopatra.

The Oliviers' French background always excited Larry and was one of many reasons France was his favourite country abroad. He felt a special kinship for the French, their actors, literature, civilisation and countryside. This was personified by his admiration for Jean-Louis Barrault and his Académie Française. He was delighted when Jean-Louis agreed to open in the St James's with his wife, Madeleine Renaud, and Edwige Feuillère.

They came down to Notley, sat on the floor and joked with us after lunch for the entire afternoon. Suddenly the room was filled with a red light. We rushed outside and stood in awe of a sunset which daubed every cloud into flames. Jean-Louis' lined and extremely mobile face was stilled as we watched the end of that day.

He gave me some advice which went something like: 'In France the ladies know who they want.'

'*Who*?' I asked.

'Précisement. They say to man: "Voulez-vous coucher avec moi ce soir". If the man says no, fashion insists the lady slaps his face.' His eyes disappeared into a magnificent toothy grin.

After they had left we missed them. 'They really are just as nice as us,' said Vivien.

Laurence Olivier Productions took the two Cleopatras to New York where they opened at the Ziegfeld Theatre on 19 December 1951. In addition, Larry then directed Rex Harrison in his own previous role in 'Venus Observed', to bring to America a piece of contemporary English drama.

His first letter:

17 West 54th Street, NYC

Thurs 21 Feb. 1952

. . . You must have been seriously worried about me lately –
because it must have seemed that nothing other than my sad
demise could possibly have been responsible for *such* silence!
Such deep and lengthy silence.

This actually is, I believe, the very first handwritten letter I
have sent home certainly for many weeks, if not since I have
been here. There have been many business epistles, stern and
close-typed, scores of cables and even some phone calls, but *no*
quiet, civilised, handwritten *letters*.

However, as it should be, the first comes to you herewith. We
are reasonably well, reasonably successful, & reasonably happy, *all* within reason however; the governing reason being that
we are under quite a bit of strain. The job is extra tough, chiefly
because of the size of the theatre, which is vast and acoustically
most imperfect. We are having to fairly *bash* the things over full
strength all the time; this is neither the best, subtlest, most
artistic or winning way of showing off one's acting, and the
consciousness of this is depressing.

Bibs has been poorly. I have been working just a bit too hard,
rehearsing 'Venus Observed' (In Philadelphia with Rex) while
playing (Caesar and Antony to V's Cleopatras) travelling to and
fro getting the train on down there and working *v* long hours to
get the thing on here.

It is on now, and though I feel comfortably satisfied with the
result it is not an absolute *sensation*. I have had some quite rude
notices on my direction too, which *stopped* me with surprise and
mortification! I've gotten quite used to being criticised for me
acting, well now it seems I've got to get used to me direction
being thrown things at. Oh dear, Oh dear *what* a gloomy letter.
Vivien is in the bedroom with her throat doctor at the moment.
Oh Gawd there I go again.

For his next project he had decided to surprise everyone by *singing*
the baritone Macheath in John Gay's 'Beggar's Opera'. As ever, his
preparation was scrupulous:

I am working madly on my singing voice every day now. I have done so on and off now for more than 20 years, as Jilli could also tell you. Well now I'm giving myself one last chance in order to try and ring a little change in my rather sombre career from time to time. Wish me luck, Thank you.

Next week I'm starting on a bout of physical training to get myself into better shape. It has been worrying me dreadfully to think that you would be beating me at tennis any day now! Worse, I might not even be giving you a game and you might politely be saying you were tired whenever I suggested one, and I should sneak up on you having a quick bash with Tony Bushell!

Oh I do so hope you're alright and happy and doing finely, that the music is good and the writing – please send me any little snippets you would care to.

At the age of fifteen I discovered girls. My mother and I had spent the summer with Danish friends we had met in California, and their platinum blond daughter, Inge, had set my heart a-beating, especially when, out late canoeing on the sea towards the Northern Lights, we capsized. Then there had been a chance meeting with an aristocratic French girl on the beach at Deauville – where Sir Richard Burton had first seen Isabel. Finally Virginia, from nearly next door to Apple Porch, to whom I managed to give my very first hurried kiss under the mistletoe, just before her parents drove her away after Christmas dinner. At last, a deed to prompt a report to my father.

Same letter, later date: the following Wed 27 Feb 1952 –

Just as a spur to my already smarting conscience arrives today your second angelic letter. You are a *dear* chap to write to me so sweetly. I am enjoying so much your good description of all . . .

My *dear* boy! The international spirit you show in your choice of girlfriends is very laudable, though I fear it may be a severe tax on your diplomacy as time goes on – such hazardous procedure may well endanger world peace, or are you in training for the diplomatic corps? Otherwise I'm afraid such a very ubiquitous love-life may well consign you to a Naval career! French, English and Danish. I'll try and pick on one for you from New York shall I? and one from Jamaica – a nice black job if we go there to visit Noëlie on our way home. Anyway dear boy my kindest regards if you would like, to Virginia next time you see her. Yes, I did meet her Mum I am sure.

We close here April 12th and my plan has always been to get home before you go back to Eton. But if we stay with Noëlie, which I think we rather should, to get a bit of sun to revive us a bit, we may be running it a bit close.

Rex did & is doing brilliantly on 'Venus' – it had a huge advance and they are living on that at the moment, but they may pick up with the daily box office booking as time goes on. I do hope so. It was all a great effort . . .

I really must write to Christopher Fry now. I have as yet given him no report on his play here – it's getting a bit embarrassing.

To Jill he wrote from the theatre on 6 March 1952.

. . . This town is the most dreadfully unpeaceful place just as it always was. Our season here has been very decently successful, by which I mean we have played to huge houses and enormous money, but somehow it doesn't seem to feel awfully happy. Of course the theatre is vast & we have to yell our guts out and bash things over which is all a great strain . . .

The smaller theatres are all disappearing now because they can't make them pay. Do you remember when we first came here there were 73 theatres alight? Only 30 now. I think London has a little more. Very sad.

. . . When anything goes wrong in these conditions – the extra effort required to play in this huge theatre – it is very hard to get it right more than very slowly. Lynn [Fontanne] was saying that she usually stays off, but the theatre drains of people whenever we announce Vivien is off, so we are hoping that she'll get better all right and not have to be off again.

The previous letter I have of his to Jill was the one written in 1944, of the appalling overwork which led up to Vivien's miscarriage. That no letters survive in the interim between them perhaps indicates his need for Jill's support during periods of prolonged 'especial frenzy'.

There is an undated draft of a letter from Jill to him. It indicates that, despite the unusually close father-son communications by letter, there were shortcomings. After all, whenever I stayed with him I was travelling light, with a suitcase, no space really mine, nothing left behind, no real sharing, and only for odd weekends, one or two each school holiday.

T. has been thinking a lot about you lately. When Mercia and I had him out ten days ago he said he very much wants to get closer to you. He says he doesn't know you and can't talk to you freely because he never sees you except with other people. If he needed a man's confidence he would go to his uncle Jackie rather than you because he wouldn't be nervous and he feels closer to him.

He said that if in the next two years you and he still remained strangers, after that it would be too late, because his mind would be fully formed and you would have had no part in the formation of it. He has reached an age when Mum ought, for the time being at least, to take a back seat.

His problems are male and should be discussed with a male . . . He is missing not having a father and has been for some time . . . I feel sure his thoughts and feelings are very like what yours were around his age only in many ways he is more mature. He certainly thinks deeply and has more sensitivity than I had at 16 . . .

At that time he described his relationship to me as less paternal than wicked avuncular. I was determined to be more to him than a nephew, but could not escape the fact that I felt I belonged to him infinitely more than he felt he belonged to me. When I was asked whether I was Laurence Olivier's son this put me in a false position. Rather than say simply 'Yes, I am', knowing the way he felt, I would reply 'Yes, he's my father.'

The two Cleopatras closed in early April, Larry and Vivien went to Jamaica for a much needed holiday with Noël Coward in his lovely house 'Firefly', overlooking the tropical beaches and palm trees between Oracabessa and Puerta Maria. It was close to Ian Fleming's house 'Golden Eye', which Noël, quickening the lives and wits of all, called 'Golden Ears, Nose and Throat'.

Their state of mental, physical and nervous exhaustion was appalling. In 'real' life Vivien was better at acting 'All things bright and beautiful' than Larry was. He had a heart to heart with Noël which failed utterly. He was told by the Master that if anyone was close to a nervous breakdown it was *he*: poor judgement again.

Resting did them both good. Larry continued his singing, which must have prompted many a pinch from Noël.

On a Sunday Vivien suggested that they (Noël and his manservant-cum-constant-companion Coley, Larry and herself) go to Mass in the local church. To her delight she saw the service sheets were in Latin. The Jamaican parents in the pews around them were huge, the little girls had ribbons in their pig-tails, the little boys were bright as buttons. The singing was hearty and the flat accents gave 'Jamehkan flehvor to Currubeen Luttin'. Noël tittered that the prayers seemed constantly to repeat 'Oracabessa, Puerta Maria'. They then hastened up the hill for some good stiff Bullshots.

My fourth summer term started before their return and it seemed an age since I had seen them. Larry had never been to see me at school, neither at Cottesmore nor as yet at Eton. This was commented on by Hedley, and the sorts of boys who in every school pick on any peculiarity in others. My mother and I implored him to make a special effort to come down for the Glorious Fourth of June.

There is the undated draft of a letter she wrote to him:

About Vivien coming, have you asked her? I feel sure she will realise that there are lots of people who are old fashioned and narrow-minded and might make dirty cracks about the three of us going together.

Personally I don't give a damn, but it would be hurtful to Tark . . . as he is very fond of V. It is not as if we're an unknown family. You and V are world famous and you can't make yourselves inconspicuous. I don't think V will be offended. She was so very charming and understanding when she spoke to me.

Like all the other boys I was in top hat, tails, with carnation in buttonhole and a rolled umbrella. Larry was dreadfully late. I left my best friend and our mothers and sought him in the crowds, the car parks, among the picnics. I felt alone and strung between a swagger and bursting into tears. Then I was told he had been seen in the crowd round the cricket match, softly cruising in the Bentley. I saw him at the wheel, forehead furrowed, lost as lost. Vivien's profile through the open window was the prettiest I had ever seen. In the back seat, the bags under them even bigger than the eyes, was Robert Helpmann, like a goldfish. After pretended pleasantries Larry and I waved them goodbye. He and I then sought an angry Jill.

He prevented me from hurrying. We ambled. He was indeed recognised. Approving glances came my way. It was good; I tried to look as if I wasn't absolutely thrilled. Then I saw Jill's taut and livid face. She turned and saw us, what had happened between us. It was the first time we were father-proud-of-son-proud-of-father. She clapped her hands with delight.

Something took him away to prevent the continuation of this wonderful day. Whatever it was, I wrote him a scorching letter, followed rapidly by an appeasing one, which elicited a wonderful reply.

Durham Cottage

17 June 1952

Dear child of heaven,

You really sound crusty in your letter. I am terribly sorry about the 4th. Please don't be cross with me about that sort of thing, it just couldn't be helped and in my sort of job it just never can be. You will understand, as soon as you start such a thing, that a job that depends on ideas is uncontrollable in the ordinary 'office hours' sense.

When *you* are writing your books, plays or whatever, you might decide to take a day off, but you wouldn't be able to if your publisher was waiting for the work, or your producer was anxiously trying to get a new scene out of you. Well it is like that with me in most of my work.

At the moment Fry, Peter Brook and I are all writing a film of the 'Beggar's Opera' as you know, and all the studio departments, all the casting, all the designing wait for the finished result. Even your darling Mummy is impatient with me sometimes and she is an actress and really knows well enough the position and would be sympathetic with my side of the question if well *prodded*.

It is now the 20th and I've just got your second letter. Oh dear Oh dear.

I'm dreadfully sorry, my dear boy, but I had better not come to Henley [Royal Regatta] as I should only be an infernal nuisance, and interrupt the routine of everyone else's day. I have appointments in Town until 11.30 and again they start at 4.15.

It is such a shame. I should really have loved my day with you all.

He then addresses the problems I had been trying to put over to him,
about the stresses, strains and aches of my being 'in the clouds' with
Virginia.

> I have been giving a great deal of thought to the situation and I
> have come to the conclusion that we ought to try to be a little
> more sensible about it.

The situation was actually quite commendable. She and I wrote fairly
crusty letters daily, and when we were alone together in the holidays
I stroked her breasts. No more: a perfect liaison for sixteen-year-
olds. She was a nice intelligent girl and very pretty.

> Just consider what the present situation is doing for you. Delight-
> ful thoughts and dreams, beautiful as they may feel, are lux-
> urious; over-indulgence of such luxuries, which I think you are
> prone to, is not good for a person; over-indulgence of anything
> has been shown from the beginning of time to be the enemy of a
> person's manhood and his proper fulfilment of life. (Except, I
> regret to say, over-indulgence of work which has never been
> shown to hurt anybody.)
>   You see, these wild horses that natural instincts are, are
> things that you must be sure to have control over. See that
> the reins are *firmly* in *your* hands. *Don't* let them take you
> where they will, because they don't know what's good for you,
> or care.
>   Don't forget. Nature herself has only *one* interest, *one*
> concern throughout the entire gigantic realm of her animal and
> vegetable kingdom – *procreation*. Nothing, *nothing* else. She
> doesn't care how she gets it or who gets hurt in the process.
>   Just recognise that all the romantic ecstasies, all the rosie
> reveries, the stoppings of the heart when the phone rings, all the
> exciting and bewitching variations of Love's sweet dreams that
> mankind is subject to, are basically, simply and solely Wicked
> Old Nature's cold-blooded calculated *Bribe*, to bring children
> into the world. Simply that.
>   Acknowledge Nature, of course, and admire we must, but we
> *must* be *firm* with her, or she'll pitch us into all sorts of trouble.
> She doesn't care about *us*.
>   Take those reins into your hands. Say . . . 'No, no, no, come
> on now, work, business, life . . . I'm not going to dream it away

in idle provocative speculation. I'll write that sonnet when I have proper time.'

And don't forget when adjudging your 'Times and Places' dear boy that a *bed* was *primarily* designed for *sleep*!

It was a letter which completely took me over and became a part of my life, that he had taken all the time and trouble to compose such a philosophy made his love shine through from every sentence.

At the time I did not know how wrong was that trite old cliché about overwork never hurting anyone. In Vivien's case it caused the miscarriage that preceded her mental problems, and in his, years later, it caused such an uproar in every cell of his skin and muscle, dermatomyocitis, that I was advised he had six weeks left to live. In the event it led to a sharply disabled old age.

In the 'Beggar's Opera' film one of the locations Macheath galloped through was alongside Frensham Pond in the gorse of Surrey. We arrived the night before at the hotel to dine with the director, Peter Brook, and his beautiful bride, the actress Natasha Parry. They were waiting outside in the dark and she, in a full white cotton skirt blazing in our headlights, threw her leg into the air vertically above her head, captivating us all.

That was about the only happy moment: the film was shaping up badly and between scenes Larry wore a face of thunder. Vivien told him at least to smile when the press came to photograph his Macheath on location, but he wouldn't. His loathing of 'spikes', as he called all to do with that kind of reportage, did him no good. The film was 'Bad-mouthed' long before its release.

Vivien was preparing to act in a big-budget film 'Elephant Walk', produced for Paramount by Irving Asher. It needed sub-continental vegetation and elephants and the location selected was Sri Lanka.

Opposite her was cast Peter Finch.

The inevitability of what happened tempts a belief in fatalism, or a disbelief in human judgement. The fact is that Larry liked Finch from the start, gave him his first West End role, which succeeded, then had him act in 'Daphne Laureola' with Dame Edith Evans, which was very successful, helping to prevent LOP from becoming FLOP. And the man was newly married. Loyalty and safety seemed written in.

The hothouse climate of Sri Lanka incubated Vivien's exhaustion. The dynamo in her mind that always burned away any natural desire for sleep, was a further impetus to self-destruction. The locations were lush, the climate tropical, and her appetites burst night after night outside on the hillsides in the arms of Finch, who was, after all, a gypsy with Aussie urbanity but no conscience whatsoever, extremely attractive, fun, flirtatious and sexually charged.

In England, Larry was immersed in post-production of the 'Beggar's Opera'. I wrote to tell him how much I liked my Modern Tutor, Oliver van Oss, such a civilised man after Hedley who despised him as a dilettante.

Durham Cottage

2 Feb 1953

Van Oss sounds a delightful chap, and indeed I have always heard so from other quarters.

Vivien seems to be alright in Ceylon. I cabled her after her reported accident, and also the Paramount people, from whom I received 'Miss Leigh's accident purely publicity'!

I cabled her again saying 'The Daily Telegraph informs me you had cancelled evening at Night Club. I am going to buy a horse.'

To which she replied 'Cancel horse. Went to a night club after all.' So apparently all is well.

. . . I've not written to V yet and must do so now.

From Sri Lanka Larry received a call from the producer to go out and help. On his way to Heathrow airport he picked me up from school, and we went to the departure terminal to have lunch together before his flight. It was strange to sit in Eton tails in the airport café.

'Nonsense,' he said. 'You're the only properly dressed person here.' I still felt like a waiter.

He wanted to warn me of what I had known subconsciously for years: there was something wrong. He said it had started after they had lost their baby, nearly eight years before.

This shook me. It had simply not occurred to me that they could ever have wanted a baby, let alone conceived one, the way they lived; they weren't parental people. Appalled overtones welled up within me. He told me what a beautiful little foetus it had been, quite perfect; it had a penis, and would have been a little boy. I was horrified.

Ever since, he said, there had been the rhythm of disorders. At the top of the cycle she would drive herself harder and harder, accelerating all the time and then changing her gears *down* from top to third, and accelerate harder and crash change down again, seizing up the engine into a spiral that burst into depression. He had been advised that the condition was incurable.

' "Whom the Gods love," ' he quoted, ' "They first send mad." You know, in Jamaica, Noël told me I should have taken her in hand years ago. He knows nothing. When she is herself she is herself. I try to come to terms with her illness. The doctors can't cure it. The most terrible effect it has is to make her hate, really hate, the one she most loves. Well, to judge from her hatred I can tell the one she really loves most is me. Take comfort from that, I suppose.'

I asked how he had been able to be so loving despite these terrible problems.

'You know, I actually find aspects of it attractive; the sheer gutsiness of her trying literally to challenge the world, her defiance. And the love-making has never been better.'

The details of her breakdown are the stuff of the tabloids. It occurred finally in Hollywood. It was absolutely total. So was the press exposure.

He replied to a sympathetic letter from Jill:

25 March 1953

Darling Jill

I am most deeply grateful to you for your most generous thoughtfulness in writing such a lovely letter to me. You were right in guessing that I do most desperately feel the need of friends just now. It has been a very bad time.

Getting her home was an incredible nightmare. As you may have gathered, she set up the strongest resistance, and of course as naturally follows when things go this wrong, I was to her her worst enemy. She has suffered terribly and will be very ill for some time.

But none of the horrors of the last ten days compare to the feeling of relief that somehow the mission was accomplished and that now she is safe in, I believe, the best hands in England. No one can see her for a bit and so I am taking the time to recharge the batteries against whatever the future may hold – just in fact what you prescribe.

I had the loveliest time with Tark. He was terribly sweet and dear to me and for the first time neither of us minded the silences in conversation. It made me so happy. I think he sensed all was not quite well with me.

Even his own life, although not plagued with such mental health problems, did have the extreme highs and lows of a storm-tossed sea. Perhaps he was therefore more adequately equipped to come to terms with one who could be storm-crazed.

With the constant and painful blare of the tabloids, and the obviously acute need of sympathy, these problems were not the sort that could be discussed at school, even with a man as understanding as van Oss. Music became a tremendous relief, at an age when emotion can assume the status of the sacred. (Special it may be, but not the Holy Grail.) At least the piano was a disciplined outlet.

Vivien returned to Notley to recuperate. She stayed in the Blue Room to be closer to the servants' wing and still have a view of the garden. I went to see her. She was thin and worn, her breasts almost flat under her nightdress, but she was shiningly happy, as if nothing had happened. I brought her a little radio in case she wanted the news. Night had lifted once again.

13

Recovery

A couple of dozen relations and close friends gathered in LOP's offices in St James's to watch the Coronation on television and the Procession pass outside. Each received a Coronation Mug labelled: 'With our love and welcoming thoughts, wishing so much we were with you.' Larry was keeping Vivien company at Notley.

Noël Coward was politely condescending to the American actors. Jill and Vivien's mother Gertrude knelt outside and watched the Procession from the balcony. Several ladies and gentlemen dozed off in front of the television after the Queen was crowned.

We watched seemingly the entire British Empire march by, and finally the fantastic gilded Coronation Coach. This was followed too closely by a jeep, as if a fairytale prince had become a toad. The champagne flowed and Noël Coward was furious the Americans talked only of the Queen of Tonga, instead of entirely about *our* Queen.

'How wonderful Queen Salote was,' they were saying, 'in an open coach, the torrents of rain in her face, how she won our hearts, her lace handkerchief soaked.'

Noël's patriotism was about to burst.

'And who were those two funny little men behind her?' they wondered.

Unable to bear it any longer but not out of disrespect to the Queen of Tonga, he said: 'Her lunch.' My godfather's judgements, like his wit, came down like a guillotine, never a miss, no reprieve; sometimes the wrong head was summarily chopped.

The original passion between Larry and Vivien, their uneven

though adored performing talents, and their aura that relations and friends would not believe could ever become stale, kept alive in the two of them a belief that would otherwise have evaporated. For the selection of plays there was not much around in terms of new product that Coronation Year, yet the occasion pleaded for 'the both of them' to be together on stage: normally a concept Larry deplored; it was so limiting to be typecast as a couple. 'Romeo and Juliet' and the two Cleopatras were exceptions.

Vivien's health was improving. They read plays and plays, even though she was still in bed. They were looking for a light comedy. Isolated from the world, they relished the near secrecy of the valley they were in, as if the sun shone from the sky only for them. One morning I accompanied him for a walk along the Thame. The river-bank was alive with birdsong, thick with reeds, bullrushes and wild summer flowers. We cut armfuls of kingcups and carried them home, stuffed them into champagne buckets to take up to her bedroom like trophies.

His wish to remain a good husband, and the depth of his commit-ment, added to his gravitas. Emlyn Williams came for a weekend with Molly, and was strolling with us. He asked how it was that Larry could stand it all. Larry gave a deep sigh, looked up at the lichened roof beneath a warm sky and said: 'I just look at the place, and think everything will be alright. I love it all so.'

'I'm much taken with Vivien's mother Gertrude,' said Emlyn.

Larry smiled, scenting a bejewelled worm of Emlyn wit. 'How so?'

'She seems so respectful towards actors. Asked me what we did with ourselves in the daytime.'

'And did you say . . .'

'That we played with ourselves? No dear boy, she's terribly grand for that.'

The play Larry chose was perfect for Vivien's rehabilitation: 'The Sleeping Prince', a light comedy by Terence Rattigan. That there was so little choice is indicated by this soufflé being made into a film 'The Prince and the Showgirl' (a title that tells the entire story) with Marilyn Monroe, and even after that into a musical by Noël Coward.

I heard him and Vivien their lines together, as they smoked in the drawing room. For the role of the Archduke of Carpathia Larry got his old producer friend Alexander Korda to read out all his lines in a thick Hungarian accent –

Vivien as Jennifer Dubedate in 'The Doctor's Dilemma' (*Angus McBean*)

'Then, venom, to thy work.' He stabs the King (*Rank Organisation plc, from 'Hamlet'*)

Directing (*Rank Organisation plc, from 'Hamlet'*)

'And with a look so piteous in purport
As if he had been loosed out of hell
To speak of horrors, he comes before me.'

Jean Simmons as Ophelia, her chamber decorated with hazel sprigs and lovers' knots from frescoes in Notley Abbey (*Rank Organisation plc, from 'Hamlet'*)

The Max Factor Salon
London: Eve Gardiner

Eyebrows &
Socket Line
Black Pencil

Eyeshadow
Blue/Green No7

Eyelines
Black Pencil

False Eyelashes

Rouge
Clear Red No1

Face Powder
Ochre

Foundation
Panstick N2
Very Pale

Ageline
Brown Pencil

Lip
FR2 pinky/red
outline to darken

Body Make-Up
Pancake: Special 135

Vivien's make-up from Antony and Cleopatra (*Tim Fowler, courtesy The Theatre Museum, Angus McBean*)

Notley Abbey

Father, still as Duke of Altair, and son after the first night of Fry's 'Venus Observed' (*Felix Barker's collection*)

Caesar and Cleopatra (*Angus McBean*)

Antony and Cleopatra (*Angus McBean*)

Larry and Viv (*Topham*)

Vivien and Larry in 'The Sleeping Prince' (*Angus McBean*)

Vivien as Lady Macbeth
(*Angus McBean*)

Macbeth: sketch for the
portrait by Ruskin Spear (*by
kind permission of Mary
Spear*)

Salvador Dali's portrait of Laurence Olivier as Richard III, commissioned in 1955 by Sir Alexander Korda. Dali said: 'I see the rhinocerous in Sir Laurence, so that is probably what I shall paint. He is two-faced, a split personality (*Courtesy of David Metcalfe. The portrait now belongs to Captain Peter J. Moore and is part of his collection in the Salvador Dali Museum, Barcelona*)

Richard III, on location in Spain with Anthony Bushell

Vivien, Kay Kendall, Noël Coward and Lauren Bacall (*Charles Castle's collection*)

Marilyn Monroe's arrival, with Arthur Miller, to film with Larry in 'The Prince and the Showgirl' (*Topham*)

After the first night of 'Titus Andronicus', Larry in his dressing-room with Jean-Pierre Aumont, Ginette Spanier Seidmann, Maurice Chevalier, Vivien as Lavinia, and Douglas Fairbanks Jnr (*The Illustrated London News*)

Vivien with her end-of-life companion Jack Merivale and Robert Helpmann (*Dinah Sheridan's collection*)

Larry's old age in the Malthouse, Steyning, with me

Larry, from the portrait by Emma Sargent, after serious illness; despite the loss of his fingernails and the strength of his legs, his shoulders shrunken, the glory still shines from him, 'like a nimbus'. (*National Portrait Gallery*)

Eightieth birthday at the National
Theatre, with (right to left) Richard
and his wife Shelley, Tamsin, Julie-
Kate, Joan, Larry, and me (*Alan
Davidson*)

Larry admitted to hospital in October
1988 (*Topham*)

Jill attending Larry's memorial service
at Westminster Abbey (*The Times*)

My Darlink Boy [He starts a letter from Durham Cottage,
1 November 1953.]

We've had a decent enough tour. V. is bewitching in the piece &
I enjoy my part very much. The play is a very cunning piece of
mechanism and a good evening seems to be had by most people.
I think you'll enjoy it alright. It's light, of course, but has en-
chantment, absolutely no 'message' and it's a great relief to me
not to be appearing in something that the poor audience has
come to more than half out of a vague sense of duty.

We took the Bentley all round the country with us and
motored from date to date, the sun obligingly shining for us
every Sunday. We got caught napping in our ignorance one
time. I had always imagined Manchester was right in the North
and that Glasgow would be just a little run across the border;
well, by way of the great lakes it turned out to be 270 miles!
I thought I'd never stop driving. England is so surprisingly
beautiful in unexpected places.

I must stop now, the sounds from the bathroom next door tell
me Baba is ready for bed.

The 'Sleeping Prince' was howled down by the critics. They wanted
the great actor to do great acting all the time; they blamed him for
hanging back for Vivien's sake, with some justification, but they
forgot his own occasional need for respite. A horse cannot run the
Grand National every day.

At the end of my summer holidays Jill was cast in a strong supporting
role in the film 'Night People', starring her old friend Gregory Peck,
and the gruff and argumentative Broderick Crawford before he was
typecast as a reformed alcoholic cop. Interiors were filmed in the
studios of Munich. The director, Nunnally Johnson, was an old boy-
friend of Jill's. She rose to the stretched medium of Cinemascope. The
German technicians were efficient and friendly and with the Oktober-
fest in full swing in the beer halls we all became well acquainted. One
long weekend Jill and I drove over to Salzburg, the next we flew to
Venice, our first adult times together.

In London Danny Kaye was enjoying a huge success in his one-man
show at the Palladium. Larry and Vivien put on a threesome frolic
with him in a midnight matinée as part of 1953's 'Night of a Hundred
Stars', for theatrical charity. Danny then came down to Notley for the
weekend. His mimicry was often camp and his films have since dated

badly, but at the time he was the funniest man alive. For Larry this represented a challenge. As has been written elsewhere, Danny made me laugh so much at dinner that I literally fell off my seat.

The story continues. Danny had with him his wife Sylvia, and a boring business manager who, seeking to please, had brought a most awkward present: a huge cheese-cake that we had to eat as dessert. When we had helped ourselves Larry imposed an air of dreadful formality. The cheese-cake was awful. By means fair or foul he wanted to get the bigger laugh. He and Danny excruciated themselves with revulsion, with frowns at each agonising swallow and fastidious use of napkins, their deadly serious etiquette made the tears roll down our cheeks.

'Vivien,' Larry said eventually, 'there is only one thing to do with this cheese-cake.' He took it in the palm of his hand and squashed it into his face. Whereupon Danny rushed over to lick it off. Larry went out to wash in the pantry.

In that particular contest the set-up was funnier than the pay-off. I can well imagine that whenever they were together Larry felt compelled, no matter what, to rise to the challenge of being funnier than Danny, no holds barred for the sake of a joke.

He popped in to see me at Eton.

Friday 4th December, 1953.

I did enjoy seeing you on Monday. I do hope you don't mind my being untalkative. I am rather prone to silences by nature which makes me dull company at times, but it is a joy to me to feel I don't have to make an effort with you. So much of my life seems to be taken up with being something I'm not feeling like. And my knee does depress me too and was hurting and still is, damn it.

I've been to 6 of the world's most expensive doctors who have a fine time practising their serious expressions and then tell me that I must have hurt my knee somehow.

It's v. painful during the show.

With that inside information I saw him in the play. After the Archduke had been fondling the showgirl for a while on the sofa, he straightened his leg to its fullest length in a kind of relief. I mentioned this afterwards and sympathised about the obvious pain he was in.

'No, old cock,' he said. 'That was merely your father being filthy.'

National Service loomed for the following autumn. I wanted to join the Coldstream Guards and asked his advice about the interview with Regimental Lieutenant Colonel W.A.G. Burns DSO, OBE, MC, in Birdcage Walk. He replied –

For the question you were worried about –

Q. 'Why do you choose the Coldstream Guards?'

A. 'Because it's the best Regiment, Sir.'

Q. 'What makes you think that?'

A. 'Everybody knows that, Sir.' (Not too cheekily, you understand.)

He was curiously obsequious with the English Establishment, unsure of his ground.

During his visit to Eton that afternoon he said he would like to meet Dr Sydney Watson, my piano teacher. We went under College Arch, along the inside of the Tumbrils, the sound of football in the far distance. Sydney stammered his delight at seeing us and hm-hm-hm-beckoned us in.

Sitting alone with Dr Watson while you played your prize-winning piece was a memory I shall treasure for many a long year.

Despite the critics' contumely – and they did have a point – his play made good money from delighted audiences even though Vivien looked less a showgirl, more an archduchess. Their dread of having to sell Notley subsided. Things were looking up. Money was found for his third Shakespearian film: 'Richard III'. In his excitement he wrote in pencil –

Friday May 18 [1954]

Just a line while I am eating a sandwich to bring you my love. Richard III is ON. So you can imagine there is no spare moment for me now. It's OK. I intend enjoying it. I am sick of suffering under things and letting them make me unhappy. If one isn't careful one gets into the habit of every job and every so-called pleasure becoming a burden – something that has to be just got through, it's bound to seem like that when one gets overstrained or tired, and one looks forward to nothing. Now with V. so much better and you always so angelic and making me proud of you – Life is taking on a different aspect.

The previous week he had come down to watch me in the final of the Junior Sculls, a race in shells with sliding seats for those awarded colours, called 'Lower Boats'. It was a long race, all the way up to Athens, round a flag and back, two and a half miles perhaps, far longer than Henley. My mother ran part of the way. He ran all of it. The winner, easily, was a giant of a man called John Mead, I was second, and an equally long way behind was another giant.

So his pencilled letter went on –

Last Monday night the Harrisons [Rex and Lilli Palmer] came to supper. We talked a lot about you & while I was undressing slowly I had another drink and indulged in that fatal musing instead of penning a few words to thank you for making me so proud of you that day. So here it is now, then I *ought* to be *musing* on the Battle of Bosworth etc. etc. It is nice to think about what Marsden [John Mead's housemaster coach] said: as you get on, weight will matter less and technique more and more . . . we shall muse about Henley in 3 or 4 years' time . . .

In October 1954, after the start of National Service I received a postcard from Bosworth Field with a Spanish stamp: Torrelodores, a bull farm close to Madrid, addressed to 23066250, Recruit Olivier, Brigade Squad, Coldstream Guards, Caterham.

This place is rich in so many beautiful ways and our location is a dream place. I wanted a tapestry-like background. I certainly got it.

The location had been discovered by Tony Bushell, once again Associate Producer, far from the pylons and vapour trails of England. Unfortunately the early autumn rains had failed and the grass was silver. For the first shot, therefore, they had to disguise it technically. They set an overlay on glass in front of the lens, so that it filmed painted green meadowlands spread between the actual trees. After this modest counterfeit the audience would accept that they were ever after in England.

A second postcard, of the Escorial's Hall of Battles, with the plumed and helmeted chequerboard of infantry and cavalry regiments, continues –

> I have attempted to copy the picture overleaf in one or two battle shots though I don't suppose anyone will know it. The work has been really gruelling and not as unlike yours at present as you might think, but satisfactory and I am happy with it.
> Baba has been with me almost all the time.

For the shattering climax of Richard's death Larry drew on a long past memory, from when he was in Roland Gardens with Jill just after they were married. He had bought her a kitten. It enchanted them with its play and its purring, but when on its own wrought such havoc with their sparse furniture that they called it 'The Enemy'.

One day, when Jill was rehearsing, Larry lay in his bath and watched the kitten chasing a ping-pong ball. It bounced towards the landing. He stretched over to push the door shut and keep the kitten inside. It darted out just too late and the door broke its neck. Larry leapt out of the bath and grabbed it to his chest to bring it back to life. In its death throes the claws tore his flesh with each spasm. Pouring with blood, the kitten now soft and limp, he telephoned Jill in floods of tears: 'I've killed The Enemy.'

The catharsis of the film: after Richard's throat is cut, it is these spasms he thinks of during his own horrifying convulsions, 'Fighting off death', as in a vile enraged reptilian orgasm.

While on leave I went to Denham Studios, looking a complete nincompoop in battledress, boots like mirrors and shaven back of the neck. Larry, in full make-up as Richard III, *sans* wig, was behind the camera checking on angles, while on the ground, seated side by side with legs stretched out in tights of differing pastel shades, were three theatrical knights: Ralph Richardson, Cedric Hardwicke, and John Gielgud.

As we drove away for the weekend he confided that he was deeply dissatisfied with Ralph. 'The old bugger won't accept direction. I take him with extreme delicacy out of earshot, when nobody suspects, and try to coax him. "I'll think about it," he says, and bloody well goes on playing for sympathy. Buckingham should be detestable, how else can people be expected to fall in love with a villain like Richard, if they like his sycophant?'

For Christmas I gave him and Vivien a Worcester thimble I had found in Chester, while at Officer Cadet School.

> . . . it looks lovely on V's chest of drawers, with the other bibelots in her room . . . Getting v *v* exhausted now, but only a few more weeks.

'Her' room? This was the first I knew of it. My weekend there had been 'Family' – Tony Bushell and Annie, George and Mercia Relph, Ernest and Gertrude Hartley, Glen Byam Shaw and Angela. Glen told us he had lectured at a boys' school, and heard one of them saying: 'And isn't Bernard Shaw remarkable for 92?'

Mercia was on form. That week she and George had had to go out for dinner in London. They set off too late, which was George's fault. It was raining and he hadn't brought an umbrella. They couldn't get a taxi and so that was his fault too. They stood in the rain at a bus stop. She asked to borrow his hat. Eventually the bus arrived and they sat down in front. He hadn't any change.

'I've loathed going out with you,' he roared, 'for the last twenty years!'

'Speak up!' she retorted. 'The people at the back of the bus can't hear!'

With Larry committed so many hours of the day, leaving Notley before dawn and frequently returning well after dinner-time, Vivien was feeling very down. I went for a walk with her in the dewy morning, preceded by her new Siamese, Boy-Boy. 'Look how pretty he is,' she said, 'shaking his little feet.'

That afternoon while she wandered alone up the lime walk with her cat, Larry and I strode bracingly up the other side, past the dovecot. Now that I was in the Army he gave me an affectionate and encyclopaedic dissertation on the joys, problems and intimate details of love-making. He was far more of a sensualist than anyone, least of all he, has ever suggested, a marvellous blend of deference, affection and relish.

When we turned back we could see across the valley of winter trees. Vivien was nearing the top of the far side, the cat still with her, the leafless saplings etched to her left and right.

'Look at her,' he murmured. 'Shaking her little hips.'

'How you must love her.'

'Frankly, in her present state I do not love her mind. But her body, yes. Actually we're trying to have a baby.'

The difficulty of our relationship thundered in my blood again.

'Yes,' he went on. 'Thought it might help her. I was worried I was sterile. Tests showed I'm as fertile as Hercules.'

I felt, immaturely, that my whole world with them was under threat. I had yet to start a world of my own.

In the spring I cabled from Officer Cadet School that I had been commissioned in the Coldstream Guards, with the First Battalion, to be stationed in Chelsea Barracks. (This meant I would be an Ensign, with bearskin and scarlet tunic, carrying the colour in Changing the Guard at Buckingham Palace, sojourning in St James's Palace when on Guard Duty, and giving lunches there with brother officers, enjoying the fruits of the debutante season.)

The telegram reached Larry after dinner at Notley. The post-production of 'Richard III' was pleasing him more and more. He knew he had a masterpiece to edit. In high spirits he penned a verse or two on the back of an envelope and dictated it long distance over the phone to the operator. It was past midnight when the sergeant on guard came into our company lines and woke me: 'A fookin' long telegram for you, Sir!'

He had printed it out on buff Army Forms, line running into line in neat handwriting –

Bravo! Resplendent Ensign, you young blade, But why dost 'tempt to put thy father in the shade With plumes, mirrored leather, gold braid? Could'st not remain a Private economical? Must Dad now find thee Wardrobes astronomical, For whom the way must now be Tragical not comical?

   Must Dad now curb his splendid voyage into wrong, To keep his son in wine in women and in song? While St James's to the Palace from the Theatre throng Fashion insists true feelings be denied And this sonnet must my doting pride.

The greatest change was my no longer having to wear his old clothes, cut down to size and fitting me like a scarecrow. My suits were now made at Anderson and Shepherd – apart from the tails he gave me which he had worn at Vivien's Oscar ceremony for Scarlett. Father-hood was blooming:

The shirts are alright at Coles. You'll want at least a dozen . . .

That same spring of 1955, old Eva died aged eighty-five, after a vigorous life and an old age full of laughter. Jacky and Rosie had moved before to a cottage beyond Henley, where they lived out the rest of their days. With no thought given to the alternatives, and accepting the bad advice of Donald Krolik, Jill sold Apple Porch at once, and almost everything it contained, at the bottom of the market. The place had had the opposite effect on her from that of Notley on Larry and Vivien. It had enabled her to become a hermit, sucked in by peace and plenty, continuing to accept Larry's alimony until he himself died. She had virtually retired from the theatre, and had acted in only a couple of films in the previous few years. Many of her friends thought she should do more.

On the other hand she devoted immense effort to charity work. She was a most effective chairman of the Actors' Orphanage Welfare Committee. With money raised largely by the annual midnight matinées, they assisted in finding accommodation for war orphans, maximised payments from local councils and helped pay for private education. As the orphans grew up, the Actors' Charitable Trust developed Denville Hall in North London, where old actors and actresses could live out the rest of their lives, each with their own room with their own books, paintings and furniture. In addition she was chairman of the Theatrical Ladies' Guild from 1948 to 1982. Apart from the satisfaction she derived, this brought her into contact with the theatre people she loved.

After an early lunch at Notley, Larry, Vivien and I hurtled over to a cinema near Denham to see the first showing of the final cut of 'Richard III'. William Walton, composer for Larry's three Shakespeare films, was there, Roger Furse the set designer, Tony Bushell and other creative and technical behind-the-camera people. I felt then, as now, that this film would outlive all his other work in generations to come.

Afterwards I navigated William Walton, and his strong-faced ebullient Argentinian wife, Suzanna, cross-country to Notley. He was aware from my overwhelmed and inarticulate burbles that I worshipped his music, all of it. I showed them into the Pink Room and laid their suitcases on the bed. He saw the irregular configuration of paintings hung up and down the wall, just like written music.

'What a splendid tune for Larry,' he said, and sang –

Definitely Waltonesque.

His ashen complexion and pale eyes made him look like a Lord of Appeal without a wig: unbelievably different from the passion of his music. I loved his sense of humour. When discussing conductors, he said of Sir Thomas Beecham: 'A musical version of Malcolm Sargent.'

He took so strongly to Notley that Larry asked if he would like to have the cottage now that Tony Bushell and Annie lived elsewhere. So it happened that, with Suzanna looking after him, my favourite living composer wrote the score of his opera 'Troilus and Cressida' in our valley. I am unable to think of the place or of his music and separate the one from the other: baroque sensuality rooted in almost legendary history. 'The pain that is ecstasy,' Troilus sings, ending on the basest bass note of absolute lust.

The Brigade of Guards' shouts of command vary between officers and sergeant-majors, the seeming effeteness of the former releasing the unsurpassable strength of the latter. Even so I thought that my voice had muscled up enough to have a shouting match at Notley with Malcolm Sargent and Larry. 'Escort to the Colour,' I yelled, 'present ARMS!' Malcolm did his modest best. Larry undid his shirt button, his neck swelled, his chest heaved in air like a whale and the sheer volume of his voice reminded me of the full organ in the Albert Hall. Vivien clapped her hands with pride and said that the only person she had ever known with greater lung power was the Wagnerian primadonna Kirsten Flagstadt.

The first time I had guests in St James's Palace I invited my mother, George and Mercia, and Malcolm Sargent. The Captain of Queen's Guard and the other two officers were relaxed and welcoming, slightly surprised at the schoolboy level of Malcolm's jokes. This encouraged me to invite godfather Noël on his own for dinner. He was delighted to accept and telephoned Jill to ask what I was like.

My mother thought quickly and no doubt objectively as she drew breath. 'He's pompous, patronising, and slightly ridiculous.'

'Oh,' said Noël.

At least she had not waved goodbye to her directness. *She* was still inside herself, somewhere.

In his diary he wrote 'It was a perfectly sweet evening. Three very young officers and one slightly older one. Lovely manners and good old shabby, traditional glamour.'

The confidences Noël shared with me about Vivien and Larry were couched in censorious, finger-wagging terms. He was didactic, clear cut and unforgiving. Although sympathetic about how awful their problems must have been for me, with that dreadful publicity, clearly he had no idea what they themselves had suffered.

His brilliant wit and energetic one-liners kept him in everyone's mind as the funniest man alive, but there was no way Larry would ever want to act in one of his plays again. Their friendship became mainly for old times' sake. He it was who had first made Larry famous, but he had become dated.

On the other hand, John Gielgud remained very much a star in Larry's firmament. His choice had established Larry as the most exciting Romeo, twenty years earlier. And then, after seeing Larry's Richard III on stage, he had presented him with the sword of Edmund Kean which now hung diagonally on the library wall at Notley. His Clarence in the film of Richard, his professional acceptance of direction, made Larry feel he ought to be repaid. So he was invited to direct Larry and Vivien at the next Stratford season's production of 'Twelfth Night' or (appropriately) 'What you will'.

We drove down in the Bentley that spring, with John Gielgud and Vivien in the back doing the *Times* crossword at speed.

'Me or Mummy, five,' read Vivien.

'Maori.'

'Redhead who proposes easily, six and three.'

'Probably,' said Larry at the wheel, 'something "top" or "cup".'

'Ginger Pop,' said John.

'Pop the question,' Vivien laughed. 'What a lovely clue!'

On the farm Larry's brother Dickie had taken over the management. Investments were in hand – four deep-litter sheds each for five hundred hens to lay eggs, and the piggery changed from breeding sows to fattening piglets in ten times the number of sties. The lunchtime conversation changed accordingly.

'Yes,' said Larry as gentleman farmer, 'the sows got a disease of the uterus, so we went over to fattening.'

'Don't be disgusting,' said Vivien.

'And we've opened up a bridge from the Mead to Willow Island.'

'A pretty bridge?' someone asked.

'A sort of, well, *rolling* bridge.'

'A rolling bridge?' asked John. 'A rolling bridge gathers no foss.'

So everything got off to a cracking start; much better than a previous visit when John G. announced in a panic to shake us all: 'Do you realise – I'm *fifty*!' We were horrified.

At Stratford, Larry and Vivien took a house near the theatre. He arrived with a dozen fledgling ideas for Malvolio: different walks, accents, gestures and characterisations he wanted to try out with the rest of the team. Immediately from the dress circle came John G's minatory ebullition: 'Oh Larry, for God's sake. Don't. So vulgar.'

Everything went from bad to worse as John's start-stop interruptions and complete lack of preparation ('I wanted first to see what the actors could give me') drove them into a frenzy. At one of the rehearsals I attended he admonished a character actor William Devlin, who was just trying out a little emotion: 'Oh! For God's sake don't bleat, Billy-yeyeyeye' causing the old actor to withdraw in tears. 'Oh for God's sake stand byeeeee.'

With opening night drawing ever nearer, the moves were still being changed, even where minor accidents occurred: 'Oh keep it in, keep it in, so *pretty*!' when Vivien, as Viola in boy's clothes, pinged her sword against a bell. To Johnny's chagrin, Larry had to forget the generous thought that had prompted the exercise and take over the direction himself, at the very last minute: too late to prevent the production being a bit of a mess.

Then Glen Byam Shaw directed 'Macbeth'. Under his all-seeing and all-forgiving eyes Larry and Vivien were able to develop their roles in extraordinary ways. I remember her sultriness, the deep notes in her voice, the sudden flame of ambition making her drive him into murder; her conscience dragging her down into madness; his majestic and tortured presence, supreme guilt at what he had done despite foreseeing the result; their most terrible hours; his craving of her – 'There's pleasure yet' – as he yearns with the utmost soul of his being for her belly. Only a woman as mature and beautiful an actress as she could have been believable. Both he and Noël Coward considered her the finest Lady Macbeth of our century. Everyone knew that he was the finest Macbeth, ever.

Many have said that the resemblance of the play to their own life, and the tragedies they had faced together, made their interpretations great. It may well have been so. I believe that the 'Vivien experience' did as much for him in 'Macbeth' as she had done ten years earlier when she filled the hollow man that he had been on film, with the passionate Heathcliff, Nelson, even Henry V.

As before, some critics said that Vivien did not measure up to Larry. No actor of either sex has. No actress that I have seen has come close to her Cleopatras. He may have had to rein in his Mark Antony but there is nothing unusual about an actor doing that for the sake of a production. It's called teamwork. In 'Macbeth' they matched one another to perfection.

I bought a car, a 1937 Morris Eight with spoked wheels and an engine the size of a sewing machine. Weekends at Notley became almost regular.

Noël Coward visited and he and Larry settled in for what promised to be a very long night with whisky, having driven back from 'Macbeth' at Stratford. Noël could not get over how moved he had been and needed time to unwind. As I left them and went upstairs I heard Noël's insistence: 'But Larry, *dear* Larry, I've told you time and *time* again, my diction is puffickt!'

In the morning Noël and I went for a quick-paced walk up the drive. At great speed and in one breath he said; 'Now tell me, Tarquin, as your godfather I feel it incumbent upon me to enquire after your religious life.'

'Well,' I paused. 'I was confirmed, I think baptised. God is in heaven.'

'I see. What do you do about sex?'

'I write passionate letters to a French girl I met skiing and fell seriously in love with. Her name is Jenny.'

'Wet dreams, that sort of thing. I've tried it myself. It doesn't work.'

We hustled past a few lime trees. He glanced at me. 'Are you at all queer?'

'No.'

A few more lime trees. 'Not even a little bit?'

'No.'

Another tree or two. 'Oh . . . Pity.'

At lunch I said how wonderful it was to have my father and godfather in the same dining room. Noël barely drew breath before riposting: 'That is one of those excruciatingly boring remarks which ought to be profoundly moving!' How we laughed!

Some time later he wrote to Jill, undated –

We've discussed everything under the sun – even religion! The way he speaks of you is proof positive. You are so obviously, apart from being his mother, his greatest friend in the world. This I think is probably the highest of all compliments.

Godfather Ralph had referred to 'Laurence's splendid fury'. Many years later Franco Zeffirelli described it as terrifying, that dreadful skill some actors have of choosing the most upsetting and telling word to crush. I once provoked this, stupidly and unthinkingly, being at that age –

Notley Abbey

No. Tarquin dear. Last weekend's behaviour simply will not do.
And you must please never do such a thing again. To phone up
at eleven at night & say you were not coming on account of too
many 'late nights' is altogether too thoughtless. 'Late nights' is
no excuse whatever either for breaking appointments or for any
other sort of poor behaviour any more than is any other form of
self-indulgence and you mustn't plead it.

I really must advise you to pull your socks up in the matter of
good manners, otherwise the regiment of which you are the
smallest & smartest officer will be the only place where you are
welcome shortly.

Cripes!

He did not indulge me quite as much as my lapse suggests. I
received a letter from Stratford Memorial Theatre asking me to pay
for my seat for 'Macbeth'; 'You haven't, your Dad won't, who will?'
So I sent a cheque with a ditty about my having earnings from a
book on the sex life of ghosts. They replied that they were pleased the
pen was proving more profitable than the sword – a little exchange
pasted into the battalion's scrap-book under the heading 'Trouble in
Paradise or who pays for the seats chez Olivier'.

With 'Twelfth Night' providing an uncomfortable canter and the
soaring heights of 'Macbeth', the company went into rehearsal for
'Titus Andronicus' – a Grand Guignol play so difficult that it is
seldom performed. Larry's lines were among the most complex he
had ever faced. With these colossal professional demands gobbling
every ounce of his energy, a further manic spasm turned Vivien
to Peter Finch, who was also staying at Stratford. Larry became
resigned to not being able to do anything about it. The show had
to go on because at that stage there seemed no sense in entreaty,
or indeed any kind of appeal to someone who was so very far from
being herself.

The genius of the director, Peter Brook, produced of Titus a
theatrical experience so overwhelming that even the most articulate
critics' paeons read a bit like heavy breathing; especially when they
came, inescapably, to reveal the plot's eruption into so many corpses.

Peter Brook had worked on the music himself. It was spine-
chilling, created by taping the strings of a piano being plucked, then
laboriously editing out the initial 'Ping' of each note, retaining only

the eerie and dwindling resonance. The sound, once heard, is never forgotten, unearthly and cruel. It gave credence to the horror, made it believable that Titus, the war-bitten general trying to ransom his son, had struck off his own hand. The sound of the wrist bone being crunched through, the final convulsive slice, the actual parcelling away of the hand into a shroud for his black enemy Aaron to seize and lope away with, all this was so shatteringly real that in terms of audience statistics, more people collapsed and fainted than at 'Oedipus'.

The cast was magnificent, except for Vivien as Lavinia; from her own personal point of view, this was as well. She normally gave so much of herself to a part that it would enter too deeply into her psyche for her own good. Bad dreams visited her when she was not suffering her usual insomnia. When she was herself she regarded sleeplessness as a blessed means of being awake for more of life, in thought or more likely in reading. But during her bad times it must have come close to what Macbeth had to say about murdering sleep. She never quite shook off Scarlett, nor Blanche in 'Streetcar' which she said had sometimes made her feel she was herself going mad. So it was a mercy that she stood well outside the character of Lavinia, and did not try to put herself through recreating what it must feel like to be raped on your husband's dead body, then have your tongue torn out and hands cut off.

Larry let his guard slip. Finch took advantage of this when Vivien invited him down for weekends at Notley and he sometimes behaved as if he were the host, at mealtimes or in the drawing room telling his anecdotes, acting out his stories, with just a touch more energy and enthusiasm than anyone else. In fact, but for the truth of the situation, it could have looked as if we were having a good time. He was amusing and intelligent and every now and then would ignite Larry's spark of glorious regaling and impersonation. Kindness and good manners prevailed. One night when Larry took Peter for a late night heart to heart, set to get down to an ultimatum from one man to another, Peter made a comment about something irrelevant and Larry sat down and laughed, in his exhaustion and being forced to live with unreality.

'Macbeth' bound him and Vivien together. Little deeds of hers still appealed to him, like her selection of presents for members of the cast. She was stumped when it came to the girls who had played the secret, black, and midnight hags. She eventually chose gold champagne swizzle-sticks: witches' brooms.

My battalion was transferred that winter from Chelsea to Krefeld, near Dusseldorf, to join 2 Div., British Army on the Rhine. We marched behind the Band through the streets of London in pack order, the only gleam being our forage hats and boots. My mother, Larry, and Vivien were all at Victoria Station to wave good-bye.

As soon as the Stratford season was concluded Larry arranged for Vivien to have a rest cure in secret in Germany, away from the tabloids which dwelt on what her illness made her do. Since this was no true reflection of herself, it was and is irrelevant, mere pandering to base curiosity. The only human truth these eclipses revealed was the seemingly infinite and forgiving devotion of Larry.

On his way back he dropped in to see me in barracks, and was much taken by my brother officers. My Commanding Officer and his wife invited us to dine at their house. Larry returned to London on the same train as one of the company commanders, Major Le Fanu.

The two of us spoke little of his reasons for coming to Germany. Our sadness and hopes for Vivien did not call for discussion. The fey language in his letter was for his own cheer.

St. James's Theatre SW1

Monday Jan 9th [1956]

Dearest Boy, For Vivien (In secrecy to keep away from the tabloids) don't put her name on the envelope but simply put –

Freifrau von Roeder
Hoohenfried
Bayerisch Gmain, Bayern

. . . I adored seeing you, the journey back was not bad and your Major Le Fanu very nice to talk to. I got the bridal suite on the boat & didn't ask anyone to share it with me. Peter H [Hiley, his general factotum] met me at L. Strasse [Liverpool Street] and we took the Major to his Club.

. . . I had a lot of business with Cecil [Tennant, his agent] on Saddy and also today & saw Miss Marilyn Monroe at the cinema in Staines (!) in 'Seven Year Itch'. She's certainly easy to look at.

Things (Tabloid reporters scraping for more on V's health

etc.) start buzzing as soon as I get back so I'm cutting and running again on Wed. to the Seidmanns in Cap Ferrat & so on to the WWs [Waltons] 2nd night [of his opera 'Troilus and Cressida'] in Milan on the 14th and down to Ischia [their home] with them from whence I shall write.

Marilyn Monroe's business partner and manager, once her stills photographer Milton Greene, had bought the rights to Terence Rattigan's 'Sleeping Prince', wanted Larry to play opposite her, and also to direct the picture, to be called 'The Prince and the Showgirl'.

Then came a postcard from Ischia, Jan. 23:

WW's opera was received poorly enough in Milan to place W. alongside Verdi and Puccini whose first efforts were likewise fated.

V. has left Germany now and is home for a few days & will I hope join me here about 28th or 29th as her rehearsals are postponed a week.

Noël Coward cast Vivien in his diaphanous light comedy 'South Sea Bubble', with Peter Finch. My Mama wrote:

Daddy seems to have hit the headlines in a big way – first Daddy and Viv with their new house [which had been the Waltons'] and return to England. Then Peter Finch crying into his brandy in the Evening and Sunday papers, having given up playing opposite Vivien in the Coward play, and saying how much he loved Larry. Then Larry in New York with Marilyn Monroe; that went on for days, in all the papers.

My brother officers were discreetly sympathetic about the Finch hullabaloo. They did not have to say much; everyone knew all families have problems. The other ranks, mainly Geordies from around Newcastle, with a strong moral code, were more outspoken, angry at the press for making so much of an illness. My father's patience they took for granted, but Finch – that cynical lecher – left them nearly speechless apart from the 'F' word.

The move from Durham Cottage, long overdue because it was the size of a doll's house, followed Vivien having a nasty fall down the tiny staircase and hurting herself. Hate mail arrived with the horrifying wish that she had broken her bloody neck.

Lowndes Cottage,
Lowndes Place

Sat 25 Feb 1956

. . . One of two tiny paragraphs in the papers may have told
you that the Monroe thing is on, and I had the full treatment
from the press in a fearsome week in N.Y. from the 6th to
the 10th with Cecil Tennant . . . People ring me up for interviews now and I decline, saying I've had all the publicity I want
for years to come. Anyway all that is satisfactorily concluded
and I think you'll like and be amused by Miss M. alright – it
looks like being quite a lively summer.

I have a maddening Midnight Matinée to organise & appear
in next week, after that I shall be able to get on with the
script with Terry [Rattigan]. This should take us probably till
end April, leaving May to make the Shooting Script in, and
June for welcoming the little lady and her entourage and
testing etc, & we should shoot July, August, Sept, sort of
thing.

. . . V. has finished her first week of rehearsal with Noël and
all seems to be going well. She's being wonderfully well (though
rather scared) and her most sweetest self, I know you will be
glad to hear and your heart to feel.

Of course my Hol. was fairly buggered up by having to come
home when poor dear old Alex [Korda] died. I had to make
his funeral oration which was a difficult job rather, and V.
and I had to do a thing each on the T.V. last week for the
dear chap.

. . . On Thursday Baba is giving away the prizes for British
Film Academy, and as old Richard got Best British Film, Best
from any source, and Best Performance she'll be giving 3 of
them to me so it might be fun, & rather amuoooooooosing.
Richard continues to run at the Leicester Square and the beginnings of its provincial career are promising.

Noël has become 'foreign resident abroad' now which means
I have to take the presidency of the Actors' Orphanage which is
a bloody bore frankly.

* * *

LAURENCE OLIVIER, Lowndes Cottage

Mar 7 1956

. . . Our Midnight Matinée on Monday at the Coliseum was not a
fiasco as we had feared thank God. V., Johnnie G., John Justin
and I did the Screen Scene from 'School for Scandal'. Then later
. . . I did a recitation which started seriously and then got interrupted by Nigel Patrick in one box and Frankie Howerd from
another and ended in comical disaster which went alright & at the
end I made a thank-you speech & we got out about 3 a.m.

I'm off to N.Y. again on Saturday but back next Thursday
15th. It's a groaning bore & I hoped I had got out of it until it was
explained to me that the Ambassador in Washington had invited
President and Mrs. Eisenhower & Lord knows not who, to
'meet *me*' & I ask you – how do you get out of that?

Wed 18 April 1956

N.Y. & Washington fine and exciting but as usual absolutely
killing. You see you arrive at 7 in the morning *their* time – which
is noon *your* time. Everything is later there and if you get to bed
at 3 a.m. the first night it is *8 your* time and so you start off with
a 24 hour day.

All went well, but by the time I got to Washington I was
teetering a bit & a bit burning hot behind the eyes. I know of no
torture quite so exquisite as that when staggering with exhaustion, you have to be pleasant to strangers, or trying to make
intelligent replies when they are being pleasant to you.

I had lunch at the White House in a sort of commissary with a
lot of State Governors and people, & then Mrs Eisenhower took
me all over the White House, showing me all the bedrooms,
closets, bathrooms etc – it really was very charming, but she said
she didn't think the President could possibly come to Richard
that night, as he hadn't been out since he was ill, & anyway it
would be a bad precedent as how would he ever refuse others
etc., also he had seen a bit on the T.V. the day before, so in my
mind I gave up hope, & said '*please* tell the President that should
he come it would be the most wonderful honour, but I would
forswear any such, rather than tire him for an instant etc.'

I then had to go to the new National Picture Gallery & have my photo taken against what seemed like every picture in the place. I finally got to the Embassy where I was staying & Lady Makins saw my condition & suggested I go to bed for an hour. I couldn't sleep, of course, as I had two different sorts of speeches to make out – one if the President *did* come and one if he didn't.

At dinner there were a few people and everyone was very pleasant – the Ambassador had to keep popping out to the phone because of the Jordan situation.

When we got to the theatre Mrs Eisenhower's sister told me that the President *was* coming. I don't mind telling you a great lump of pride came into my throat – it was the first time he had ever done such a thing, & it was for a British picture & all that, & I was moved beyond anything to think that our little picture had got the Queen in London, & the President in Washington & I desperately tried to get my speech straight in my mind.

Not easy when people keep putting a microphone in front of your face for a few words on the air, or shoving you in front of a camera for the same thing on the T.V. and for newsreel cameras.

Finally the President came beaming up to the portico & I felt a lot of things had been worth a lot of trouble. Inside the theatre somebody made a speech & I was given the Key to the City of Washington & left to gulp out my own effort.

. . . After it was over I went to a big do where I solemnly shook hands with 600 people in a queue! The planes were grounded next morning & I just got a train to N.Y. where I just got the plane back to London. That was the Thursday.

Baba, Alan Webb and I drove to Notley on the Saturday & decided to stay the night there on our way to Manchester for her opening which went splendidly beyond expectations.

She has come up beautifully in these last four weeks, getting better in her part and better & better in herself from the very depressed state in which she started the work. She is immensely charming in it and as funny as the part will allow. It is Noël at his lightest but it is I believe what the larger section of the public enjoys – 'Witty lines' and all that – piquantly relaxing without the *slightest* danger of any exercise for the imagination or intellect.

Puss is better and sweeter than for many years – pray God it can keep like that & life can be heavenly again. *When do you get back?* Goodeeeeeee! Tout va bien chez nous . . .

Then ten days later, about developing the script with Terence Rattigan:

> The work goes well and our first full treatment should be through about the middle of the week. We shall have to give it a terrible combing over as it looks like getting on for 3 hours!
>
> Tony and Annie Bushell (happily married couple now) are with us this weekend and Alan Webb.
>
> V. will add a bit to this –
>
> Tarkie darling. I was so really touched by your angelic wire for the first night. I wish you were here today for Notley is looking simply ravishing – the avenue of daffodils up the orchard is a wonder. Larry has been an *angel* of help with the play & we are both well & looking forward to seeing *you*. Fond love darling, Vivien.

For the first time in so very long they really were enjoying the happiness they deserved together, with Vivien in her 'smasheroo' and Larry beavering away with Terry at their script, and the prospect of glamour and money with Marilyn. Notley was galloping into spring.

I was confronted by a curious arrival in the Olivier family: a cork-tipped cigarette. Larry assured me that they were delicious, personally blended by himself, which was nonsense, and a source of income at tuppence a thousand. This eventually aggregated to £40,000 a year. Meanwhile I wondered about the contumely from my brother officers, and how to minimise it.

Rather than hide I stood up at lunch in the officers' mess to tell them. None of them noticed me, because of a stange regimental custom that has us wearing hats at the lunch table. The peaks conceal everything but the food. I declaimed my little piece and they looked up, munching, their eyes mild. 'And on the back of every packet of these it reads,' and I camped it up, a bit like Penelope Keith; "Benson and Hedges are renowned for their high quality products. Olivier, with the special tip, maintains this tradition."'

Part Four

14

Final Loss

Under Dickie's fraternal management the farm made Notley self-financing, with piglets fattening, flurries of hens laying, greenhouse vegetables, and a skilfully managed hundred acres of arable land and pasture. For the first time in his life Dickie was doing the right thing for himself, and for his wife who had conceived his first-born child.

Larry's attitude to his elder brother, whom he described as fat and dull, was on the whole dismissive. He would impersonate his voice, mannerisms, walk, until just before Dickie came into the house when he would flee to avoid him, leaving the rest to keep straight faces.

While I was in Germany, Larry and Vivien were uplifted by an occurrence which made it seem as if God was smiling on them: the one thing they both thought would save them. She conceived, at the age of forty-four, twenty-two years after her daughter Suzanne had been born.

They decided to keep it a secret from all except closest friends. Any leak would have damaged the bookings for Noël's play. There was still some time before the baby could be considered safe. Besides, secrecy had helped to make their very first love together especially romantic. This, added to a sense of legitimacy, gave them a kind of rebirth.

At the far end of the orchard Larry planted an oak sapling. Some considerable distance beyond he planted a right angled line of Lombardy poplars, with the tallest on the extreme left and right, and the shortest in the middle to give forced perspective. Round about he added a few decorative trees, had a fence made with a gate, and a little sign which read: 'St Molin's Wood'.

They were enraptured by the unlikelihood of having a baby, together, at last. Their friends may have been sceptical but they were more than willing to share in the joy, except for Noël who was fractious then and later. He saw with objective professionalism that it was, whatever the outcome, no good for his play. This may even have added to their delight at feeling like naughty children.

One Saturday night, after they and a few friends had driven down after the theatre, had dinner, and were winding down in the drawing room, the phone rang, unconscionably late. Larry guessed that it was a reporter. He adopted the entirety of a Mrs Bridges, twiddled imaginary hair curlers, and with the plummy voice of a dignified yet outraged woman in respectable service who had just been woken up, spoke into the receiver: 'Hellew.' Pause. 'Hew?' Another pause. 'The Diley Mile? A wot? A BABY!!! Ew, it *will* be a surprise for us beelow stairs!'

He knew exactly what he was doing. The reporter knew exactly who had taken the call and could do nothing about it. It won a respite of twelve hours for the home team.

In Germany I read the headlines in the tabloids and felt pole-axed. I regret that I took the news itself very badly, as well as the manner in which I received it. For this Vivien never forgave me, until the day of her death.

Lowndes Cottage, Friday 13th:

Dearest Boy,

I have just put in a telephone call to you and I can only hope I get through alright. I am dreadfully sorry you should read our news in the papers and I imagine you must have done by now, I mean about Vivien and me having a baby.

You once said to me that you would not like it at all if this should happen, and so I have been rather funking telling you about it. It was silly . . .

Noël too thought Larry a dreadful coward for not telling him earlier than he had. Four months into pregnancy would not allow Vivien much longer on stage, so finding a replacement in time was far harder.

Larry's letter to me continues:

We have just had our phone conversation. You sounded very unhappy. I am awfully sorry.

You would be terribly wrong if you thought that anything could ever diminish my love for you, or interfere with my thoughts of you. In fact some instinct tells me that this could easily and kindly bring us closer together once we are used to the idea. I wanted to say something of this on the phone, but those wires are the least satisfactory method of human contact.

We had been keeping so quiet about it because of Vivien's play and the embarrassment of it getting out before she was replaced, then in the extraordinary way that things get in the air, it happened. The night before last at 2.30 in the morning the *Daily Mail* rang up and said they were printing the story unless it was positively denied. I had to get a general announcement made. It all came so suddenly I couldn't let you know in time.

. . . I beg of you to try and feel happy about it, it is a thing that pleads for joyful feelings.

Fri 20 July

Your letter was a bit Hamlet-like . . . Believe me I am not making light of what you feel, and I am most dearly touched by the way you describe what our relationship means to you, but for my part I tell you that our relationship is only in its early stages.

Some years ago I arranged my life so that I could never be a father to you in the accepted sense of the word – I could hardly 'abandon' you again as I did then. I have always hoped to redeem that circumstance by one day providing something broader for us than a normal Father-Son relationship, which I myself found to be a somewhat restricted one. My heart rises to greet this more and more every day. You may have kids of your own in a few years time. Should *that* make any difference do you think?

Mon Aug 6

It was a great comfort to hear from you, though I will not attempt to answer, as the answers will come out of life and experience, in which humour and human realities should be allowed a freer hand than perhaps they have been lately . . .

I start the real shooting tomorrow morning on the film. Vivien stops playing this Saturday. If you could possibly find time to send her some affectionate wishes it would be cheering for her.

We shall be at Notley all through the film which will take 3 to 4 months. I am *so* looking forward to seeing you but please let me know when, the place is apt to be flooded with guests with the film and all – so give me the nearest date we can expect you soon.

Sat 18 Aug

I can't tell you how grateful and relieved I am to receive your angelic letter and to feel from it that that old bubble of humour of yours, which, though so light, is yet the strongest armour that people like us can be born with, has reasserted itself.

I must have posted my letter just before the headlines screamed that Vivien had lost her baby boy, the same day Dickie's wife delivered her daughter. It really did seem, like some character in literature, Jude Fawley in *Jude the Obscure* perhaps, that her life now was eternally hamstrung by the furies' mocking: 'You shan't! You never shall again . . .'

Some minutes ago too, a very sweet telegram came over the phone from you. Thank you for this sweet thought which is a very great blessing to both of us and more especially comforting and helpful to Vivien in her most unhappy time. She is making a gentle and brave recovery from her ordeal & I pray will emerge complication free, in a while.

Please let me know what you would like for your 20th birthday present so that I can join the labour exchange and draw some overtime . . . What date shall you enter the gates of learning?

The film is tough going, but reasonably alright.

A couple of weeks later I was home with my mother in Queen's Grove in the rainiest of English summers. I telephoned Larry during his lunch break at the Studio.

'Daddy! How *are* you?'

'Well,' a resigned voice, 'you know. Very tired.'

'How's Marilyn?'

'Doesn't even believe me when I say it *shouldn't* be raining this time of year.'

In Pinewood studios there was a wall of security to keep the press out, provided in the form of guardsmen. I longed to talk to them and ask what they thought, but they were not my men, I was no longer a serving officer, and they were there to keep outsiders at a distance.

On set, beyond the lights, the cables, the camera crew, roamed a tetchy Marilyn Monroe in a long white evening dress with short shoulder sleeves. To me, the only feature that was any good was her tiny waist. Her face a marshmallow, her curves too bulbous.

Larry introduced us. Her eyes were a soft and pretty blue. Her lips formed into her lower-than-born-with smile, as taught. Her skin was damp from the hot lights; she did have a bit of a niff about her. The greatest sex goddess in history, which she was then, and ultimately the object of the sympathy of millions for her unhappiness and suicide, was a phenomenon that rapidly bored and gained the dislike of almost everyone in the studio.

The beginning had made her sound such fun. In New York Arthur Miller had told Larry of her first visit to his parents when they were engaged. His mother had insisted on the acme of Jewish food, Matzoh Ball Soup. Marilyn had a healthy appetite, and gobbled it up including the meat balls. Father Miller had her served some more.

'Such a charming girl, Arthur, loves our Matzoh Ball Soup.'

She finished her helping again and was about to be given even more, when she sweetly declined. Father Miller looked worried.

'You mean you don't *like* our Matzoh Ball Soup?'

'Oh,' she replied, 'I just love it. But gee, isn't there any other part of a Matzoh you can eat?'

Her star entry into England on the arm of her new husband was a stunning show. Her manager Milton Greene had coached her superbly for the opening Press Conference, attended by a multitude of reporters and photographers. By the time she arrived, extremely late, these busy gentlemen were out for her blood.

First question: 'Miss Monroe, how would you define the American way of life?'

In a kinder tone, Larry repeated the question to her.

She shrugged prettily. 'Oh I dunno. How would *you* define the *British* way of life?' and flashed her teeth in a coy smile they liked.

Second question: 'Miss Monroe, we have read, er, several times, that all you have on in bed is Chanel Number 5. Is this true, Miss Monroe? Are you sure you have nothing else – *on*?'

She giggled deliciously: 'Maybe the radio.'

They adored it. She enchanted them.

At work, she proved impossible to direct for comedy. In the flirtatious scenes the Prince had to coax, invite simperingly, while the Showgirl had trippingly to shy away. M. was as subtle as a schoolgirl throwing up.

'Darling,' explained Larry after exasperated days of her 'Method' anathema to comedy, 'imagine you're a little stream, a lovely dancing little brook scintillating and pivoting round little stones, laughing over your shoulder at each one of the prince's predictable approaches.'

The situation became desperate.

There was a scene in the showgirl's dressing room of her sitting in a strapless gown opposite a mirror. She had to pat her hair, elbows high over her head, yielding to camera-left a soft image of under-arm and cleavage. She fluffed her lines a few times. While taking a breather she leant towards the mirror and nudged one breast to swell above the bodice, then the other, and looked teasingly up at the lighting boys on the scaffolding.

'Shall we,' said Larry. 'Please? Darling? Once again? Yes?'

She sat back, arms in the 'up' position and looked under each in turn, then at the reflection in the mirror, pulling a face. She said, 'I'm kinda worried about my armpits.'

Nonplussed, Larry coaxed, 'Are we ready to go?'

'I said, I am worried about my arm-pits.'

He looked helplessly around. He leant close to her ear and whispered: 'Darling they look marvellous.'

'Okay.'

'Action.'

She forgot her lines again and repeated her concern. The boys in the scaffolding who had enjoyed her cleavage now grimaced at each other, pulled their noses, stifled their titters. She scrutinised the areas of her attention. 'Could you darken 'em down a little?'

Out of context that was a reasonable request. Unfortunately her un-professionalism, lateness of three or more hours, the tantrums, had exasperated even Sybil Thorndike, who was playing the Dowager Queen Mother.

'Couldn't you darken 'em?'

So they did, resignedly. When that failed to please, one of the make-up girls blurted out: 'I suggest you stick some crêpe hair there, dear, they used to grow it in those days.'

She was aghast: no sense of humour at all. On the other hand she was the producer, employing everyone, including Larry.

One Monday morning I left Notley with him at crack of dawn. His routine was to have a mini Britvic bottle of grapefruit juice in the library, and then in tweedy clothes drive the Bentley along country lanes. At the studio, after being made up as a Carpàthian Grand Duke, he had a British breakfast. Bumble Dawson, the costume designer, came into his room in a tizzy. I stood to peck her cheek and to her surprise so did Larry.

'Well,' he smiled. 'Not usual to stand for old Bumble.'

We sat. She sank her stern in a big chair.

'Marilyn,' she gasped, 'had six eggs for breakfast and then screamed for six more. She insists her bottom looks lovely in a too tight dress, shows off that she isn't wearing panties, and that men don't like girls with panties on . . .'

'What sort of men?' wondered Larry, mock devious.

Bumble snorted a laugh, leant back and her bosoms heaved her tumult away. She turned to me.

'We have had to make half a dozen different-sized dresses to cope with her weight gains and losses.'

Marilyn's great gift was how the camera, still or screen, loved her, best illustrated by the sequence in Westminster Abbey for the Coronation of King Edward VII. She had to sit in the Nave among lesser foreign and Colonial dignitaries, while her Prince was with the Peers and Peeresses, further East beyond the organ screen. As director, Larry's head was just beside the camera lens, and I was standing a couple of feet behind. A soupy tune, selected by Marilyn Darling to induce appropriate emotion, was playing loud.

'Action . . . Now Darling, quite ready?' he asked. 'For sure now? So we both are . . . Right. Fine. Just you and me. We're in the Abbey for the Coronation . . . I want you to feel surprised to find yourself among these foreign ladies and gentlemen. A little amused by the moustache next to you perhaps? . . . Fine. A little more? Lovely. Now, look down to the organ screen and see if your Prince is looking back at you. Be a trifle disappointed that he isn't. Look up now, sigh at the beauty of the music. Roll your lovely eyes slowly up, slowly down. Allow a tear to form, build a little, look up again. Let the tear drop. Feel wonderfully happy, uplifted in a way you have never been . . .'

Or some such. At the time of filming it looked okay. On screen it was much much more.

Back in his room I asked what was the awful music. 'The Londonderry Aire,' he said.

'Not "derrière"?'

There are other stories about the making of that film, most of them mean without mimicry to soften them. Even Larry, who preached the importance in acting of loving the character you play yourself or you'll never be any good, and also having appropriate feelings about how delicious was the girl he had to seduce, described her as having the shape and mind of an amoeba.

He and the then pregnant Vivien had given a reception for M. and Arthur Miller at Notley Abbey. It was a maelstrom of a day, invaded by photographers uninvited, while Larry and Milton Greene had to keep from view a Marilyn who had fallen asleep tipsy. Apart from that, she and Arthur stayed in a mansion in Surrey called Parkside House.

We were intrigued by Milton Greene, the developer of M., and invited him down. He was a disappointment, as when he said belittlingly to his young wife, with baby: 'Of course you're right, dear. Girls are always right.'

Yet, was this resignation to be wondered at in such a man? He had discovered a critical mass of putty, made her world famous, and like a care-worn Aladdin, trying to keep himself neat and composed, wondered what on earth to do with the genie he had released. Her next film was 'The Misfits', written by her husband.

As for any woman, Vivien's miscarriage represented the denial of the greatest achievement in nature. But for her, four months into pregnancy, only a couple of months away from the foetus having a chance of survival, and after the public ballyhoo at the conception, then again at the loss, there was the extra hangman's noose of knowing that the last chance had gone. The fact that she, once again, had not enjoyed the feeling of sharing her body with her own baby, was no comfort.

As soon as he could, Larry took her away for a holiday.

Torremolinos, 13 Jan 1957

. . . All has been well apart from the usual complaints attendant upon an overdue hol. – gout, tummy troubles etc. I have actually swum 3 times. Diamond cold but delicious & quite a lot of warm sun. We hired a car and toured this place, Córdoba, Sevila, feeling much refreshed.

He was pleased that I was at Christ Church, Oxford, the 'House of Christ', 'Aedes Christi', names that appealed to him for the college that Cardinal Wolsey had started having built while staying at Notley four and a half centuries earlier. My life was being smiled upon in the form of Philosophy, Politics and Economics, with the most wonderful tutors: Oscar Wood, Robert (now Lord) Blake and Roy Harrod. My tall room-mate and I both rowed on the Isis.

I stroked the House's first Torpid in bumping races, in which a queue of accurately spaced rowing eights tear off at the sound of a gun and try to catch the boat ahead of them. Larry came down to watch us row a practice course. Halfway through, along the overhanging willows of the Green Bank, I used to give a spurt, goaded on by imagining the first subject of Brahms's First Piano Concerto.

The fourth and final night of the actual bumping races was the following Saturday.

Laurence Olivier	LOP Ltd	Marilyn Monroe
	presents	
	The Sleeping Prince	

Feb. sometime, 1957

I've written to Jill and asked her for dinner on Saturday evening and Jackie and Rosie too. It's about the best plan I think.

It was a lovely afternoon last Saturday and I did so enjoy seeing you. I shall be bringing Dickie on Wednesday and look forward to possibly a dewy moment of breathless returning peace afterwards. All my love and strongest wishes for an exciting and splendid week.

Rowing was more effective in bringing him closer to me than school concerts and piano recitals, which he never attended. Ecclesiastical music was even more taboo. Before my voice had broken I had been in the choir, as he had, eventually becoming the 'Keeper', a ribbon round my neck with a medallion, and carrying the Cross. He did not wish me to describe to him the solos and descants. They had meant so much to him as a boy, too much perhaps for him to face now. He had turned his back on all that, yet it still had power to move him. Once he had had to go to a service in Christ Church Cathedral. To his delight the anthem was by William Walton. In the Order of Service was a footnote which pointed out that Walton had been an organ scholar at 'the House', and gave the dates. This, Larry said, made him wonder about becoming religious again.

The roof of Christ Church Boathouse carried a further family contingent, of Vivien, Alan Webb, Graham Paine (Noël's constant friend, wearing a pink tie with no idea that it represented the mecca of rowing: the Leander Club), and a maelstrom of undergraduates and other parents. On the towpath Larry and Jill waited opposite the top of the Green Bank. Downstream were all the Eights, one behind the other for the start.

Surrounded by all and indeed sundry, Larry began to tell Jill of his amazing experience a few days earlier in a taxi. He said he suddenly, absolutely unexpectedly, had the change of life. All over, just like that.

The start gun fired, and the crews belted off at forty to the minute. The crowds started to run and cheer, carrying Larry and Jill ahead of them. They both plodded over Long Bridges and along the straight towards the boathouses, Larry continuing to shout calmly about how there was this pressure at the base of his spine, a sort of dull orgasm.

'A dull what?' Jill yelled.

'Orgasm!' he roared over the shouting. 'And I felt my head blow off and I knew it was over. Have you had it? Change of life I mean?' By which time she was breathless.

The Christ Church crew was rowing behind me with excitement and precision. We were closing on Magdalen College as we straightened up for the Green Bank. There is always something special about the House bumping Magdalen. It seemed to me a pity to hasten the pleasure: it was good to know that Larry and Jill were gallumphing down the towpath and punting for us. I was happy that Vivien and the others were on the roof of the boathouse. I waited until we bounded out into open view at the end of the Green Bank, right opposite them and the huge crowds all over the University Boathouse opposite, to spurt and strike Magdalen like lightning.

Larry cupped his hands and gave an Olivier bellow from the far riverbank. 'And what wonderful timing for the bump! Ahaaaa!'

He wrote in his autobiography that we ended up as Head of the River. It may have felt that way to him, that we were the best, but there were still a few crews ahead of us at the end of that season.

Mon Feb 25

. . . and what a gorgeous week. All, all, all love, delight, and pride for which I am so grateful is yours.

He was so very happy, as were my mother, Vivien, everyone. We made our way back to my rooms in Peckwater, the whole crew and their parents. There were congratulations and praise on all sides, nothing like it for the parental givers nor for the filial receivers. The crush was considerable but wherever Vivien stood there was space around her, as if she were royalty . . . Her beauty and happiness radiated, making some of the mothers and girlfriends anxious, until she spoke to them and put them at their ease. Whenever she moved people made way for her and returned her smile.

The year before my mother and I had been to see John Osborne's 'Look Back in Anger'. We did not believe that his barrowboy, with such zestful and articulate preoccupations, could have sold many sweets, but we came away shocked and uplifted. It was the most *dramatic* play we had seen in a long time, although not well structured, nor as controversial as Noël's 'Vortex' had been in its day. It was slated in the dailies, and rescued in the Sundays by both Kenneth Tynan and Harold Hobson.

This new voice got through to Larry the second time he saw the play, and he said that on reading it the words leapt from the page. He felt he might have found an answer to his need. The thought of Old Father Christmas having to trot out Lear again, for want of anything else, had been depressing him.

At the First Night of Osborne's 'The Entertainer' in the Royal Court Theatre I had no idea what to expect. The previous week I had collected Larry at the end of a rehearsal. He was wearing the character Archie Rice's trousers, which were like sponge bags, too short, and they flapped as we crossed Sloane Square. He looked terrible.

'Where *did* you get that haircut?' I asked.

'One of those joints where the barber's little finger sticks out from the electric clippers: for a thorough job. Then at the end you can be sure he'll whisper, confidentially: "And will there be anything else, sir?".'

The little Court looked shabbier than ever. Clusters of lights bunched down from the proscenium, and there were boards lit each side with announcing numbers, like a music hall. The orchestra sounded abysmal, and we were at a loss. My mother and I looked at each other uncomprehending. The lights went down, the curtain shot up and there was Archie Rice, a down-at-heel comedian, approaching us half-way between a strut and a waddle, doffing his terrible grey bowler with a pantomime wink and booming: 'Gooood evening, ladies and gentlemen, Rice is the name, Archie . . ' to be interrupted by a vicious screech from the violins, and Archie bantering to the conductor: 'Oh Charleeey! . . . It's going marvellously well Charleeey, audience is loving it . . .'

Never have I blushed more. He had previously been Titus Andronicus.

There were wonderful actors, his son and daughter played by Richard Pascoe and Dorothy Tutin, his father by his favourite George Relph, and Brenda de Banzie as his wife. It was a tumultuous, moving theatrical experience. Afterwards in his dressing room there was adoring yelling and speechlessness. A fellow actor was muttering: 'And Brenda de B., wondering whether she had stolen his thunder. As if anyone could . . .'

After another night's show, having read the reviews which had tried to explain the play, people were just as excited and perplexed: Archie's seedy tap dancing; the loss in Egypt of his son Sergeant Rice, where 'The Playing Fields of Eton have surely got us beaten'; war against the establishment; the tragedy of a failure refusing to give up entirely; his self-disgust for what he had become, and the laying bare of his soul, physically, visually as he crumpled like a tight ball of paper at the news of his son's death, to rise at his recollection of a negress singing a spiritual.

In the corner of his dressing room, as still as sculpted marble, was the aquiline face of Yehudi Menuhin. When almost everyone else had left, Larry was wiping away the remains of his arched charcoal eyebrows. He cried out: 'Yehudi, my dear fellow, I had no idea you were here. Come . . .' Yehudi approached and looked at him in the mirror. He said: 'If only they could write that for the violin.'

For some reason between places to live in London, Larry and Vivien were staying at the Connaught Hotel. It was less than a year since her miscarriage. She was not welcomed by John Osborne and the so-called Angries, nor had she been a part of what was happening: too old for the daughter, too beautiful for the wife. Life for her was frustrating and claustrophobic.

At Notley the predictable effect on her did have its lighter moments. Ernest and Gertrude were there, plus Ginette Spanier, a directress of Balmain and her husband Paule-Emile Seidmann, Stephen Mitchell the impresario and others lamely playing tennis. After dinner on the Sunday we realised that Vivien was no longer with us. Gertrude was afraid and insisted that we all ought to search along the river in case she had tried to drown herself. She was shocked by Dickie saying that usually V's night wanderings were in the mead beyond the garden. The word 'usually' from a man so unimaginative convinced her at last that Vivien's problems were more than tabloid exaggeration.

We wandered out into the night in twos or threes, fairly light-hearted because we knew Vivien would be fine by morning. We wondered about finding the 'Thin Lady' in a Charles Addams cartoon, or perhaps Lady Macbeth feeling her way downstairs. It was a long search. When we got back we found her tucked up in bed sound asleep. Next morning she was up by nine, in the garden with a hat, clippers and a basket of flowers.

Marlene Dietrich came for a weekend. Vivien set her to work on dead heads in the rose garden. We were working along the surrounding walls with jam-jars filled with syrup for the wasps to drown in. These we hung amid the espalier apricots and peaches. Some of the fruit was far too high so we stood on each other's shoulders. Marlene wanted to help and gave Larry a leg-up. With his heels either side of her soft platinum hair, she straightened up and stood under him, like a plinth.

'To the left, Marlene, further to the left.'

She tottered, obedient and gasping.

'More yet, *that's* it.' He stretched as high as he could and hung the jar. 'Down now.'

She was fun at the time, but she never described this in her book. All she wrote about Larry was that she had once seen him act in the London theatre, but he had then appeared in a television commercial and forfeited her respect.

In the evenings Larry retired soon after dinner and Vivien kept everyone else up far too late. She drank too much but slurred not a word. Her enthusiasm carried us all. Then, just before we poured ourselves upstairs to bed, she struggled to write down what everyone wanted for breakfast, her chin pressed against her chest, writing pad held at arms length to help focus her eyes. She looked up and smiled for our approval. Next day her hieroglyphics were deciphered by Dickie's wife Hester who went above and beyond the call of duty to help.

The Stratford Memorial Company reassembled for a tour of 'Titus Andronicus' to Paris, Venice and Eastern Europe. Larry sent me a postcard of Venice which he posted from Zagreb.

June 7th, 1957

. . . Yes this is definitely the most beautiful place in the world (Venice). We are having a rather fabulous success but in other ways, apart from all the social engagements, life is not being easy. Our curtain calls took over 20 minutes earlier this week in Belgrade. We called them the 3rd Act! We had to postpone here in Zagreb owing to the scenery being 8 hours late.

Then a card of Zagreb;

This is not the most beautiful p. in the w. but not bad and better than Belgrade. The Marshal [Tito] came himself on Tuesday and was very agreeable.

Larry said that Tito had the beaming, broad-faced self-confidence of a spiv, with diamond cuff-links and shirt buttons, determined to show how spankingly go-go everything was in Yugoslavia. The Marshal fluttered a commandeering hand in the air and a drinks trolley rattled up.

'Drinks!' His eyes glinted. 'Cocktails? We have everything here: *White Ladies*?' So they had their first White Ladies in twenty years.

This tour is very gruelling. We give 3 perfs within 24 hours. Sat 3 & 8 & Sun 12 noon! & then off to Vienna.

In Warsaw there was an imposing statue outside the Theatre and Larry asked who it was.

'That,' said the Polish dramaturg in deference, 'that is the great, great Polish actor Solski.'

'Really. What sort of roles did he play?'

'Everything. All his life he played everything. When he was eighty he again played Hamlet.'

'Hamlet – at eighty! Must've been quite a hole left behind when *he* died.'

'Yes,' was the fatalistic reply. 'And what relief.'

On their return to London, the entire company shredded with exhaustion and Vivien out of control, they staged the production of 'Titus' in the Stoll, a stately theatre with ornate brass balustrades, scheduled to be demolished. A similar fate was being debated in the House of Commons for the St James's Theatre. Vivien seized the cause as a relay sprinter grabs the baton for the final lap. She called a protest meeting in the St James's.

Larry, exhausted as he was, felt it was a lost cause because the theatre had been condemned as a hazard: fire engines could not get through the arch which led to the stage door. Vivien's efforts accelerated into a march on Trafalgar Square. Then as the guest of Black Rod in the Distinguished Visitors' Gallery of the House of Lords she gave voice: 'My Lords I wish to protest at the demolition of the St James's Theatre.' She had to be hustled out, but her efforts although unsuccessful won much sympathy, including an offer of £500 from Winston Churchill who nonetheless wrote to her that as a parliamentarian he could not approve her methods.

In this condition she agreed to taking a holiday separate from Larry. She was keen on his going north, to Scotland, with me because we were going to seek locations for the film of 'Macbeth'. She of course would be Lady Macbeth, for the first time in one of his Shakespearian movies. This would at last fulfil an ambition she had cherished ever since 'Henry V', where she was forbidden by her contract with Selznick to play Catherine, and 'Hamlet' where Larry wanted women completely dissociated from his public persona. 'Richard III' had had no part suitable.

Ever since she had first set eyes on him, at the outset of their love, she had wanted to be a bridge to his greatness and had achieved this in significant instances: now for Lady Macbeth, in which she knew he believed her to have been the best in his lifetime, was a further progression to this goal: it clasped her to him in a way which her illness might eclipse but could not destroy.

For me our holiday, father and son together, was also the answer to possessive prayers. Larry's idea was that we should appreciate better the Scottish landscape by painting it, the two of us, side by side with our easels.

Before we set off there was a joyous lunch party in the garden for which Vivien rose sparklingly: 'Make sure you find some excellent Blasted Heath,' she told us. A number of Americans were there, including Eddie Albert who had acted in 'Roman Holiday' with Gregory Peck and Audrey Hepburn, and from the continent Jean-Pierre Aumont and his new bride Marisa Pavane, who was even more beautiful than her twin sister Pier Angeli.

'Yes,' Larry explained, 'Tarkey and I are going painting with gouache.'

In my ignorance of acrylic, my blood froze: 'With whom?' I demanded. I knew the sort of man Gouache would be: one of those unshaven, talented people with dirty fingernails.

Vivien was all set to have her holiday with Leigh in Europe. We fondly kissed everyone good-bye, Larry let me drive the Bentley and Eddie Albert scattered white rose petals over the bonnet as we left.

We put the car on the train, had a sleeping compartment and awoke in Perth. Routinely after breakfast we would drive with picnic hamper and map-read to the day's objective. The first was King's Peak, Dunsinane. We set up our easels, daubed paint to palette and looked towards Birnam, across a verdant and tame valley: hardly a blasted heath. The only liquid we had to mix with the gouache was White Burgundy. This dried too fast, giving a pointilliste effect.

Next day we scoured the hills opposite, sure that Birnam would be of gnarled oaks with twisted leaves. But it was a tufted spread of baby conifers, undeserving of: 'I looked toward Birnam, and anon methought the wood began to move!'

We drove into and climbed up the Cairngorms. We added stones to their little topknots and took photographs: across the glowering grandeur of the Grampians and wondered how on earth all the paraphernalia associated with 35 mm filming – the fleets of trucks, canteens, portable loos and make-up wagons and wardrobes, the lights and reflectors, the generators and all the people – could possibly cope with some of the tracks which led to the best locations.

No matter which hotel had packed our picnics, the basket contained a circular cheese box with a picture of a bright country girl. The ingredients we learned by heart: margarine, colouring, non-fat milk solids and emulsifying salts.

We stone-stepped across violent mountain streams: gingerly at first, until we had both fallen in, become braver and leapt from rock to rock like mountain goats. We found that Scottish law allowed genuine travellers to buy drinks at any hour of the day, so we did. We numbered the film rolls and indeed each photograph of each angle and referenced it to large scale maps. We measured the ground of possible battlefields, and paced up hills to see whether skilled photography could make a small battlement seem huge from below and serve the purposes of two or more castles from various sides. At dinner we discussed plays, films, biographies and novels and music, interspersed with much beguiling regaling.

I asked why he had never played Othello. He said that Ralph Richardson and Tony Quayle had played the role convincingly, and filled it by their sheer size. As yet he did not feel he had built up his physique enough, maybe one day he would. I wondered whether he would go to Africa to get the feel of the character.

'Christ no. Place scares me shitless. Besides there's no real need, if you have the talent, to find the person you want to act, nor to go to a place you want to write about. You can place yourself there in your mind. The only artist who could really justify travel is the landscape painter, if he wanted to get the precise shade of colour for a particular effect.'

We discussed 'Hamlet' and tried to get at what precisely it was that set it apart from all others as the greatest play ever written. His own intuitions had come mainly from the season at the Old Vic, directed by Tony Guthrie. One of the frustrations of discussing role interpretation is that it is actually impossible to refine more than a hint. An entire human being is involved, each one of his myriad nerve ends or a combination of thousands of them may be called upon for a particular nuance, so any labelling with mere words is bound to be rough. His performances affected him and his audiences mentally and emotionally and we cannot now imagine how. He said that in that play he let the audience into him. Physically his neck measurement increased by an inch and a half.

'The thing about young Hamlet is that you have really to level with the audience, admit to them that you aren't actually role-playing, becoming someone else, lying to them in that way. It is actually yourself that you have to reveal. The lines make you do this. It's not smart in the sense that acting is smart to be different, Romeo as a lover, Sergius as a braggart. This one you have to get the audience to trust and accept *you*, as you are.'

I pondered. 'You mean it's the difference between being a lover and a husband.'

'Yes!'

After Kyle of Lochalsh and the Western Isles we turned South, through the sweeping bleak rock faces of Glencoe and across Rannoch Moor. In our three weeks we had found locations which promised well.

Once over the border, back in England, Larry's mood changed into bleak despair. There was Vivien to return to, and Notley . . . ? It was only a matter of time.

We stopped at a traffic light in an industrial northern town. A kindly grey-faced woman ambled across in front of us. 'What am I to do?' he murmured. 'See *her*? That woman? She's my age to the very day. Fifty: and who wants her? What has she got to look forward to? Where's the sex in her, and who the fuck wants to be touched by her?'

As we drove on the silences ached more and more.

'Since Vivien turned her back on me, you must understand, I have had recourse to a few sweet obliging creatures.'

Rather than get dreadfully serious I composed some comment that made him smile, and after we drove on things seemed easier. Then: 'Thing is, whatever the hell nature's real interest is, the human heart demands that it be wrapped up in ribbons called "love". I don't really believe that I will ever be able to love again, certainly never as much. They sense this. One friendly woman pleaded with me while we were actually in bed. "Please," she said, "I know it can't ever be true, but it would help so very much, if you could just manage to say you loved me, just used the words – I love you." You see?'

And to think there are those who say, as if by definition, that actors are incapable of deep feelings.

With Vivien still in Italy we had my twenty-first at Notley, with my mother there and many older generation friends whom I had known so well and for what seemed so long.

My mother and I then drove through France in her Jaguar, to Italy where we had what was for five years to be our last holiday together. We went to Maggiore, Como, and stayed at La Locanda, San Vigilio, on Lake Garda, for her to find again that history was repeating itself. For these were precisely the places which Vivien had visited a few weeks earlier.

When Vivien returned to England she was excited by Larry's news of our Macbeth peregrination. Absence had made her heart grow infinitely fonder but this time round Larry was on the hunt elsewhere. This was made nearly impossible for him by press gentlemen. That 'silly season' it seemed there was little else to write about. Even when he and I were in Scotland as father and son, barely a day passed without a photographer accosting us, or a keen wee interviewer writing some cock and bull story about his going to the local theatre. So wide were the ripples from the running story of Larry and Viv that when I was in Italy with my poor old mother there were photographs of the two of us in the local Garda newspapers.

Larry at one stage fell for a young actress and they became quite serious about getting married. She on her side had a devoted admirer, say 'Frank', who had been round her for months, felt that at last he was making headway, and was beside himself with jealousy. This time-worn set-up gave rise to a scene of touching human awkwardness.

'Frank' learned that Larry had arranged to spend the night at the actress's house. He was determined to prevent this, to confront the older man and warn him off. His will-power was compromised by Larry being a hero of his, for he was among the greatest of the stage-struck. He waited outside her house and realised eventually that Larry was already there. The actress must have been cooking for him.

A bedroom light was switched on. He became frantic. Passers-by looked strangely at him, a loiterer. He could not bring himself to ring the doorbell. There was nowhere to sit. He lifted the lid off the dustbin and saw a bottle at the bottom. He picked it up, broke off the neck into a jagged edge and determined to scar Larry for life. He stepped into the dustbin, squatted down and lowered the lid, leaving a crack to peer through.

At about two in the morning he could see a Rolls slide to a halt the other side of the dark street. This struck him as strange. As the cramps ate further into his bones the car door opened and a beautiful woman walked up and down in the shadows. He wondered how on earth she expected to do business in that part of London. She looked in his direction. He crouched lower to let the dustbin lid shut completely and huddled in complete darkness.

He heard footsteps inside the house, gripped the bottle-neck and braced himself. The front door opened quietly. Larry clicked it shut behind him, put his hat on, calm and sad and harmless. 'Frank' held up the dustbin lid and stood ready. He saw how his hero looked, dropped the bottle-neck and said:

'Hello Larry!'

He was hardly noticed. The car across the road was Larry's and the woman beside it, Vivien. After her intrusion Vivien finally scotched the affair by making an unexpected call with her mother Gertrude on the actress's mother, and put the fear of God into her.

She was determined to fight for Larry's love. Two-thirds of their fifteen years together had been punctuated by the rhythm of her mental illness. She had lost his baby, twice. She still had Lady Macbeth. She still had Notley.

15

Midnight

That autumn Larry opened again in 'The Entertainer', with Joan Plowright playing his daughter. Usually one dislikes whoever takes over a role that has previously been wonderfully played. Joan was the exception. I had seldom seen such range and intensity kept so well in hand.

Then he took his set designer friends Roger Furse and Carmen Dillon with him to Scotland.

> We went up to Lochalsh . . . It's hard to believe but some of our Ref Nos aren't marked or noted. We want the ventricle of your young memory. Lots of photos missing of course.

This was followed by another card from an aeroplane:

> Dear Boy I meant to write a little good-bye or phone. I'm on my way to New York, for two or three days, be back soon after the weekend. Just to send you my love is all this is for.

Finance for 'Macbeth' was forthcoming from Mike Todd, Elizabeth Taylor's husband at the time, whose new process 'TODD-AO' had been used to film 'Around the World in Eighty Days'. The gentlemen's understanding was that Larry's film would be shot in this medium. Nothing had been written into a contract.

'The Entertainer' opened in America in January 1958. Vivien stayed in London for rehearsals in 'Duel of Angels' by Jean Giradoux, translated by Christopher Fry. It opened at the Apollo in April.

Larry sent a card from Boston on 7 February with a picture of a Mademoiselle Yvonne: 'Demure despite her nudity, she gazes quite sans crudity, upon the skulls both thatched and bald of patrons who are often called: Great Gourmets'.

'The Entertainer' is wonderfully successful here, so now it is only next Wed and that will be my last 1st Night of this piece . . . Georgie Relph is off ill again.

Hotel Algonquin N.Y. Sunday March 2 1958

All goes well here. The audiences sit in respectful attention – not laughing much – I don't mind that except I lament the 'draught Bass' and the 'Nun's Story'. They applaud vociferously at the end which is very nice.

Hotel Algonquin, N.Y. Sat Mar 22 1958

I can't tell you how pleased I was and still am . . . over the New College Sculls . . . How *ever* many lengths is 17 seconds? Can we have the cup at Notley?

Geo and Mercia send much love. Geo much improved in health.

Poor Mike Todd.

Mike Todd had been killed in an aircrash. No agreement on 'Macbeth' had been made in writing. Alex Korda was dead, Del was no longer around, so Larry had to try on his own to raise the money. He had adapted the play for the screen, written the shooting script, completed the budget and schedule and in fact much of the development.

I am slightly on tenterhooks about Macbeth – the money seems a bit obstinate about coming forth and I hate the idea of all that work for nothing, & feel a bit foolish that I can't get enough confidence in me – still the industry is in a shocking state and I suppose it's not really to be wondered at.

Vivien doesn't sound too happy in the play and I worry for her a good deal.

She hated 'Duel of Angels' which had lines in it about the denial of love. The news about 'Macbeth' upset her even more. All she had left uniquely to offer him was Lady Macbeth, where she was the best in the world, and it looked as if the Scottish play too was waving a flag that said: 'You shan't!'

I used to drive over from Oxford to see her at Notley. There were friends there, but without him it was not the same. She wrote:

> I am so thrilled with that lovely little book. It has the best pictures I've seen of cats of all sorts and I do think it was sweet of you to send it to me . . . There's a clue in my X-word today – 'A party for Eights Week'? Five letters. I wish you were here to give me a hand.

'Bumps' perhaps?

I failed to get into the First Eight for the second summer running, and rather than stroke the Second Eight again I decided to concentrate on sculling.

Algonquin, New York, Sunday May 4 1958

I was terribly hurt for you about the VIII.

Apparently I had taken it fairly well and he continued –

> You will have a much happier life than I have, whose great weakness has been the most bloody awful baby-ish sort of black-dog sullens, and it has wasted God knows how much time and scorched up in bitterness what could have been wonderfully pleasant hours.
>
> I have had a teasing time lately money-chasing for Macbeth. It's not really my job & it's a bit humiliating and I'm not sure I've done myself much good by it. Anyway I begin to see the writing on the wall about myself as a film producer. Richard III simply did not do as well as the others even in England, and the 'Prince and the Showgirl' was disappointing in the box office. So the proper sort of confidence among the industry has gone & it's a bad time to be peddling things outside it.
>
> Don't worry I'm not too discouraged. I have had a lovely whack at it over 15 years & I was lucky to get the chances, and it *is* a troubling task which seems to take just a bit too much out of one.
>
> There is still a hope but *v* faint & even if it does come off the

recent peddling has tired my spirits & dulled my enthusiasm a bit, and made me a little more sharply aware that my own confidence in the project is not honestly 100%.

. . . I'm giving a big party on Thursday sailing round Manhattan which should be fun – I do wish you could be here.

Vivien seems gay & bonny and her success must have been good for her. Have you seen it yet?

At Oxford, as adjuncts to lectures, research, essays and tutorials, my sculling and piano playing were curious two-handers, with demands which were almost incompatible. After losing the final of Marlow Regatta's Junior Sculls by six feet, I drove to Hugh Trevor-Roper's house (now Lord Dacre) to give a recital. With callouses to do justice to the feet of an ostrich I played the delicately tortured 'Sarnia Suite' by John Ireland, and two Chopin nocturnes, after which the keys were awash with sweat.

It happened over and over again: win through to the final, and then be beaten at the very end by a bigger or even just a taller man, with more leverage.

Then there were the Oxford Royal Regatta Challenge Sculls, the centenary of that event. In the first round I drew John Mead. My mother was there. The short course started at the top of the Green Bank, the two of us sculling abreast. At the boathouses I was half a length down, thinking hard and wondering whether so much training and love of the Isis would ever make me look anything but ridiculous. It was very lonely but for the shouts of 'House! House! House!' from my Christ Church tribe. Rage and humiliation became a surge of energy and in a splendid spurt I took two lengths off him when he least expected it, and I was able to hang on, diminishingly but grimly, to beat him by half a length – thirteen feet. The final I won easily.

I telephoned Larry, now back at Notley. He remembered the name Mead.

The following week for the University Sculls, over the full course, no one beat him. He broke the record which had stood for almost forty years, by a full six seconds.

Larry was pleased with my trophies, the cup was just large enough to ice a bottle of champagne, and the slim silver box engraved with a hundred names had two silver sculls etched in arabesques, nestling in royal blue velvet.

Larry's brother Dickie was diagnosed as having leukaemia, with less than six months to live. After discussing things with Dickie's wife

Hester, Larry agreed that he should tell him. His need for comfort and counsel during Vivien's bad times had brought the two brothers much closer, although Larry still found it difficult to resist impersonating him when he wasn't there – so well that you couldn't help thinking that he was.

Once Dickie had recovered from the news and his loving concern for his about-to-be widow and two little girls, his mind took him back to a moment of glory at Dunkirk: he had commanded a Motor Torpedo Boat in the war and rescued many troops from those beaches. He expressed the wish to be buried at sea.

Then he, thrice married, now at last happily so, unburdened himself of a philosophy that is trite, bittersweet, and identifiable to almost everyone. He spoke in an Edwardian accent: 'Women are all the same, you know, really. I mean everything starts pleasant, desiring to please. Nature looks after you as the children are born. That's all. Time goes by. The baby screams down the house. Then they get cold on you. You . . . you find a little something on the side. To keep the peace at home you wonder about more confounded babies, each one gains a year's respite. Then they turn their backs on you. There's rather a lot of talk about privacy. So you go to the pub, take up bridge, wander about a bit. Then they get suspicious. Become sorry. Want to come back. But it's too late.'

I like 'Rather a lot of talk about privacy'.

Sat, 17 December 1958

The funeral (secret believers us all) was a splendid thing. It was a fine ship – a mine-sweeper they had laid on for us, and not a little boat. His coffin was draped in the Union Jack, and the White Ensign flew at half-mast astern of him. It was very moving, as we drew out from the dock, that all officers on watch and any hands on the decks of all the ships which we passed, stood at the salute while his coffin on the port rail sailed by. I couldn't help feeling how pleased the darling old boy would feel.

Everyone was kindness itself and we were treated with the greatest courtesy, never for a moment being made to think it was the great privilege which it undoubtedly was.

The poor darling had an oddly hard and disappointing life, but it is wonderful that it took such a blissful crescendo in its last 5 years, the great happiness that Hester gave him, the purpose in life that Notley gave him, and the ever increasing closeness between his brother and him, a mercifully quick end, and a really lovely farewell to the resting place he most desired.

Vivien had introduced me to a man who in an earlier century would have been called an explorer: Quentin Keynes. He had led an expedition to the remotest part of Angola and taken the first photographs ever of the magnificent Giant Sable antelope. One of these creatures had been shot previously by a Spanish hunter, Conde de Yebes, who carefully transported it all the way back to Spain to be preserved by taxidermy for a museum. Quentin went to see him, and after their discussion was invited to find his way to the terraced garden. There was the air of a palazzo, steps between high hedges down to succeeding levels, until eventually he came to a terrace with a fountain, perhaps even with cupids, a chaise-longue beside it, a cigarette at the end of a lengthy holder, and in a negligée was Vivien.

So I became part of the three man expedition Quentin led to retrace Dr Livingstone's Second Journey, which had started a century earlier and plodded beside the Zambezi River and around Central Africa. When we returned three months later Vivien was alone at Notley in tearful despair. Larry was at Stratford and refused to join her. She asked Quentin and me to take her to evensong at Long Crendon church. There she wept and wept.

She implored me to come again the following weekend. I arrived at around tea-time and went into the drawing room. She was with an odd variety of people: Larry's elder sister Sybille, virtually unknown to us, who bored us all about the Olivier family tree; Vivien's oldest friend from convent days, Bumble Dawson; oyster-eyed Bobby Helpmann; and balloons of brandy. They were in a clump on the floor, like Stonehenge, motionless. It had gone on too long.

I sat like a delinquent on the sofa, and asked tragically: 'And have you heard what happened to Helena Rubinstein?'

'No!' they gasped, Vivien with El Greco sorrow. 'Is it too awful?'

'Must've been pretty bad.' I enunciated with precision: 'Max Factor.'

And of course she got the giggles. Sybille gave her an unwelcome hug and said: 'Oh you're so young and beautiful and I'm so old and ugly.' True, but not much help.

Bobby rescued us with tales against himself, his fingers at their most willowy expressive: 'I was in New York, had just had my hair dyed, a leather gunpad stitched into my jacket shoulder, and was walking spritely down Park Avenue. I had a Malacca cane and gold knob. On the cane, dear.

'Feeling watched by one ahead, I saw a redheaded truck driver looking from his cab window down at me. Well. I proceeded in haste. He was *very* rude: "Brush along little fairy with that *wand* of yours." I stopped dead. Feet together, held up the Malacca cane and said: "Vanish!".'

No wonder Vivien adored him.

A few weeks later she was completely alone, busying herself in the rose garden. She smiled brightly: 'Just the two of us.'

'Good,' I said. 'I've brought my dinner jacket.'

'When we're alone?'

'Especially when we're alone' – redolent of Maugham.

Having bathed and changed we met downstairs in the library and she made dry martinis. I added a Coldstream touch: squeezing lemon peel oil through a match flame to settle on the surface with a beautiful aroma. We had two and she preceded me in a long purple dress which she called a 'house-coat', into the dining room. She sat at the far end, a Sickert painting behind her. Behind me was the Harold Knight of Larry as Romeo, and over the empty fireplace was a 'Victory' chimneypiece in blue and white china, with Emma Hamilton gazing out to sea towards Nelson's distant flagship.

'Did you meet anyone on the boat to Cape Town?' she asked.

'A lovely Rhodesian girl with an unlikely name: Iradne.'

'How ravishing. What was her other name?'

'Higgs.'

She burst into laughter. 'What was she like?'

'Long and shapely and fun, with a terrible Rowdeezin iccent. I kissed her and she said: "Torquin, what kin Ah seh?" So I kissed her again to shut her up.'

After dinner I played the piano: some energetic astringent Beethoven to start with. Once I was back in my armchair she asked about Africa and interrupted almost at once: 'What do you mean you *crossed* the Zambezi?'

She was again bringing out what was most interesting from whomsoever she was talking to. The crossing had been fraught: a *jungada* of six dug-out canoes strung together with planks on top, and when loaded with the Land Rover it had only four inches of freeboard. Inside each canoe was an African frantically bailing out with his hands. The river was more than a quarter of a mile wide and a mere gust of wind would have whipped up waves enough to sink everything, and the men would have had to swim for it.

She sought out details. What happened if an African caught one of us in the bush going to the loo? It had happened to me, and the woman turned her back and stood on one foot, the soul of discretion, until I reappeared in the open.

We had some more brandy and I played a Rachmaninoff prelude, No. 10 in B minor, harder than the Beethoven but more forgiving to play. It starts with a fatalistic bell-like langour, develops into double octave fortissimo, dwindles, then scampers regretfully until it settles back to the theme of its birth. She asked me to play it again.

She wanted to know about elephants. She had ridden a tame one in Sri Lanka and was amazed by how hot its flesh was. In Africa, Quentin had been 'elephant-magnetic'. We had spent days filming them. Their size was on a scale far huger than those in Asia, the largest ever shot had feet as big as oil drums, measured 13ft 4in at the shoulder – almost as high as a London bus, and with ears flapping even broader. We had in fact been charged by a phalanx of males and run for our lives. She loved hearing about that.

After a couple of warm and languid Chopin nocturnes I told her about hippos, lions and their idleness, then replenished the brandy. A drink before 4 a.m. can still count as a night cap; any later and it's before breakfast. How early morning hours vaporise!

Time for Debussy, where the blurred sounds accept blurred fingers, vague and impressionistic, full of pictures: 'La Cathédrale Engloutie' where the Cathedral is engulfed by the sea and fisherman can still hear the peal in flat calm, or in tempest. Then 'Voiles' which can mean 'sails' or 'veils' – and of course she guessed I played it as 'veils'. 'La Fille aux Cheveux de Lin.'

'What does she look like?' she asked.

'Flaxen hair? Far eastern do you think? A French overtone, Vietnamese perhaps. Nothing very deep.'

'She'd have to be blonde wouldn't she?'

I finished with 'Clair de Lune' and we went outside.

It was strangely warm, which might have been the brandy. There was a moon. Dawn and rooks and a cow mooing made the whole thing a bit like a Victorian novel. 'Puffikt,' we said, and agreed to meet by the river for brunch.

16

Outward Bound

Larry stayed on in America when 'The Entertainer' closed and began filming with Kirk Douglas and Burt Lancaster in Shaw's 'Devil's Disciple', directed by Guy Hamilton. He was lonely and the only compensation was that Harry Andrews, a friend from the days of the New Theatre, was also in the cast.

He was disenchanted with the film, had convinced himself that Burt Lancaster was mad, and wished someone would tell Kirk Douglas for goodness sake to fill up the crater in his chin. Worse than that, he was furious that such a boring project should attract such expensive talent when his own far more important design for 'Macbeth' had died. His performance as 'Gentleman Johnny' suffered in consequence. He felt he should have been shredded by the critics as the only actor ever to have failed in that fool-proof role.

Not a bit of it. The English newspapers, which had for more than a year thrived on unpleasant stories about him and Vivien, hailed him now, for this of all parts, as the greatest actor in the world. News of a kind, he realised, for them to sell themselves to their public: for once not at the cost of his.

With Vivien still in 'Duel of Angels' he then drove around Europe on his own, a truant and loving it. He sent a card from Portofino on 18 October 1958

> I can't tell you how thrilled I was to get your lovely letter, or how deeply grateful for the sweet thoughtfulness which prompted you to write it. I got here yesterday evening and did the 240 Kms from Florence in 4¾ hours: not too bad over those mountain roads.

I am here with Lili [Palmer, now divorced from Rex Harrison] and Carlos Thomson [a fair haired Argentian Adonis of a film star], and shall move off to Paris on Saturday, where I'll be with the Seidmanns, anyhow till Tuesday. If I get home on Wednesday I'll call you when I get to Notley and maybe come to Oxford if I may . . . I am rather enjoying my little sojourn and love being with my friends. I shall have another week to kill before starting rehearsals for 'Borkman' on the T.V.

Associated Television in England at that time lacked recording equipment so they had to do the play 'live'. The actors were experienced and wonderful: with Irene Worth, Pamela Brown, Maxine Audley, and old George Relph. 'Live' plays on television now are unthinkable for the sheer constraints of studio space, cables to trip over, the different cameras lighting up as they are called into action. There was a moment during one of Larry's long speeches when he skipped a line opposite George, who held him with his eyes and gave him all the steadiness he needed to find his feet again. No critic noticed.

In the New Year he went to New York to *record* a television play of Maugham's 'The Moon and Sixpence', based on the life of Gauguin. He wrote on 17 January 1959 of it being –

. . . the most extraordinarily arduous little affair. After rehearsing 2½ weeks (Very nice people & all friends of yours – including Hume Cronyn and Jessica Tandy) . . . we *taped* it – one act a day – in 3 days.

Sat. Act I from 10 a.m. ready, till 20 to 1 next morning. Sun. Act II from 10 again till 20 to 2. No time to go back to N.Y. as the Cronyns pointed out I would have had one hour in bed only, before getting up to get out again to Brooklyn by 8, at which hour I have to be ready, so I slept on a bed on a set in the studio for 3 hours, and *then* from 8 till five minutes to seven the *following morning*.

I never thought it would be possible to still keep acting & remembering words after 25 hours. From that I had to dash back to the Algonquin, throw things in suitcase, bath & dash straight out to the airport. The papers sometimes complain about actors' salaries, but sometimes we earn it alright.

Vivien had gone to stay with Noël Coward for Christmas at his house in Les Avants sur Montreux, overlooking Lake Geneva and the

Dents du Midi. The shock of Larry's leaving her to take 'The Entertainer' to New York, and then film 'Devil's Disciple', and now again going to California for the part of Crassus in Kirk Douglas's epic film 'Spartacus' left her bereft.

Her coming face to face with reality moved Noël, who was normally implacable with leading ladies who had ever caused him problems, as most of them had; and none more than she, with her mental breakdowns, brainstorms and unexpected pregnancy during the actual run of his previous play. He, like Leigh, her first husband, was a balm to her despite his living at the speed of a cocktail shaker.

The people who surrounded him, even in boring Switzerland, were exciting, mainly because so many of them were theatre people from all over the world, who went specially to see him. He was fun. And so were they. Vivien ceased crying in her room, regained her composure and came downstairs. She joined a teeming drinks crowd in the drawing room.

A huge American woman spotted Coley Lesley, never the most masculine of people, who now had the face of a wrinkled Puck.

'Gee Noël,' she pointed a fat finger, 'who's that nice young man?'

Noël turned, saw Coley and couldn't square the description with *him*.

He turned back: '*Nice? . . . young? . . . MAN???*'

Similar repartee darted out from him when someone wondered about a knighthood for Robert Helpmann: 'Such a come-down for a reigning queen.'

Vivien got better and Noël cast her in his new play, a translation and adaptation of the Feydeau farce 'Occupe-toi d'Amélie', which he called 'Look after Lulu'. He even gave her hope that, now she was as normal and delightful as ever, her marriage might be saved. Neither he, nor more than a couple of people at the time, knew that Larry had fallen in love with Joan Plowright, the Entertainer's daughter.

Larry wrote from 8650 Pine Tree Place, Los Angeles 46, where he had gone for the part of Crassus, in 'Spartacus' together with Roger Furse the designer and his wife Inez.

17 January 1959

Life is extremely pleasant now. The film is supposed to start in about 10 days. I have been *extremely* busy doing nothing much. A press interview almost every day. Wardrobe, make-up, script trouble – all the normal preparagger. To and fro which I swagger in a scarlet Cadillac, and with mild expectancy conduct myself to each social evening.

26 Jan – Mama's birthday – 1959

They started the film proper on location today – out in Death Valley. I shall still not be wanted for work for a few more days. I shall get on with my own work in the meantime. I am starting another film script of my own & have Coriolanus to study – as the director (Peter Hall – husband of Leslie Caron, who will be taking over Stratters next year from Glen entirely) is coming here in a few days and we are going to work a bit on it.

Roger has gone off on location and Inez to relatives in Iowa, so I am alone here a few days. I shall go to the valley on Wednesday for a couple of days – taking Peter Ustinov's wife to him, and discuss the script which at the moment is pretty awful. The more money they pour into a film, the more ordinary and conventional they make it.

We had a long script conference here yesterday with the director Tony Mann, Peter U., Roger and myself. I think Kirk Douglas is a good actor, but he does not feel heroic enough unless he is being fearfully physical all the time, consequently the thing is gummed up with calisthenics & flagellation!

Chateau Marmont, 8221 Sunset Blvd. L.A.46. 19 April 1959

I am here now. When Roger and Inez went back a week ago I decided the house was too lonely, so I'm in an apartment here. It's a bit dowdy but quite alright and I'm beginning to get used to being by myself, (a welcome reminder that one gets used to anything) and am beginning to quite enjoy my little solitary nest with its little singular comforts.

. . . My fucking film goes on and on. I played truant ten days ago & happened across to N.Y. I was so sick of being held on a string. I suddenly found myself free with no warning from my employer and I couldn't bear the thought of the empty house without the Furses & flew East with them. So, for a few shows. Said good-bye to them and came back.

I have now gone on the wagon and feel ten times better & may keep it up indefinitely. I'm due back soon after 1st June & rehearse in Stratford on 8th. Inspite of my longing to see you (& one or two others) I am really rather dreading my return – for reasons that you wot of, & the cowardly part of me wants to run away still further West and bury myself in some South Sea island.

His love of Vivien, and the professional relationship that had locked him to her, died with the stillbirth of 'Macbeth'. With Dickie dead the economics of Notley were falling apart. There remained for him only the need to keep up public appearances and come to some under-standing as to how best to end their marriage.

In her case, she awaited his return as if he were going to bring her another honeymoon. She was radiant, healthy, receiving him in the flat in Eaton Square which she had set up, furnished and decorated. He, after weeks of temperance and regular Californian gym classes looked youthful and well muscled for Coriolanus, which he called his last 'juvenile' part.

'How *are* you?' I asked on the phone.

'Oh,' he said, parodying himself, 'you know.. Um. Well. Very tired.'

He said he had decided to redecorate his bedroom, and make it very masculine: stags' heads, teak chests with brass corners, curtains and carpets of Burgundy, that sort of thing. Within a week he had just what he had always wanted: violet and daffodil chintz, heavily braided swags and little oil landscapes.

The niceties were observed between them, more convincingly by her. They both confided in me and I began to realise that this was only heart-breaking. It was impossible for me to accept that they were through, that it was over, my having so loved the way they had loved one another despite everything. It would have torn me to pieces to be around when it ended.

I seized upon an excuse to go away, not to the Western Pacific as Larry had pondered for himself, but to Southeast Asia, much encouraged by my mother who thought that I ought to become a writer, and start by taking the advice of Somerset Maugham to any twenty-three-year-old: go out and meet the world. This matched a young idealism I had found in Africa that the best thing for a life was to work in developing countries.

My plan was to sail to the Southeast, live with farmers and fisher-men for much of the time, then be one of the first Europeans to live in

China's communes, and after such an immersion in Asia, return slowly across the Soviet Union, gradually coming closer to the familiar. All this called for a great deal of preparation, correspondence and research, especially the Chinese and Siberian ends where introductions were in fact forthcoming. Seldom had my mother been happier.

Weekends at Notley continued but I had so much else on that summer that I rarely went. There were the final exams for my degree, Christ Church First Eight for Eights Week, and then again at Henley for the Ladyes' Plate, and building up a network of contacts for my journeyings in the East.

Vivien opened in 'Look after Lulu' on 29 July at the Royal Court Theatre, directed by Noël and with many old chums in it – Anthony Quayle, Meriel Forbes (Ralph Richardson's wife), George Devine, Max Adrian. With acting and directing talent such as that the hot little stage became a catherine wheel of surprises and gaiety, like an operetta by Mozart.

Vivien had the same dressing room Larry had had there in 'The Entertainer'. She transferred, a few months later, to the New Theatre and further reminders of Larry wherever she looked.

Larry was at Stratford for 'Coriolanus'. He did not really *like* taking direction from Peter Hall, but he admired his intelligence. He had not *at all* liked being directed by Tony Richardson in 'The Entertainer' – the pitying looks bestowed upon him by the younger man who 'knew the today mood'. Perhaps he recalled Ralph not really *liking* being directed by *him*. But, as he wrote from the Chateau Marmont about being all alone, one can get used to anything.

His Coriolanus was acclaimed. The more intellectual critics sounded as if they were unpicking crochet, to identify which thread was Peter Hall's and which Olivier's. The rest of us came away mesmerised yet uplifted by a wonderful show, and astounded by the leap he concocted as a physical climax.

My main memory is of how he looked. Even in his dressing room when stripped, he had the physique of a Roman General. For a long while on stage he stood motionless, leaning back slightly, one naked leg forward, his upstage wrist tucked under his armpit with hand hanging like a gnarled root. It sounds peculiar but it looked wonderful. 'Your leg,' Vivien enthused. 'Just the right position!'

Now about that leap. Below him, a long way downstage, back to the audience, with bandy legs, was his enemy Aufidius played by Richard Johnson. Coriolanus stood back-stage on a platform twelve feet high, bleeding from many stab wounds and determined in one final dying lunge to drive his sword through Aufidius. To reach him he had to leap upwards and far out across to stand a chance. So he literally seemed to fly *up* towards the dress circle: we thought he was going to land in our laps, to be snatched back by strong men grabbing his ankles, gripping and letting him swing down. But that on its own would have ended with his rump towards us. So he had to spin round in mid air, with the restrainers changing hands on his ankles, so that when dangling upside down it would be his dying face we saw, arms swinging in utter defeat. It was difficult, dangerous and a crowning reminder of the physical risks of his career.

To the outside world, yet again, it appeared that Larry and Viv were successful and happy. There was a memorable lunch when Douglas Fairbanks and a few others who loved them both and knew nothing of the 'now', recharged old nerves with love. On the way into lunch she and Larry hung back in the library and kissed passionately.

That evening Douglas wanted to make a note of something. He took out a little pad headed 'Things to do today' with a sketch of a couple copulating. Vivien seized it, 'Let me see!' She turned over to the second page.

'What are you looking for?' Douglas asked.

'To see if it was a different position.'

She was as sexy as ever.

A key contact in my networking behind bamboo and iron curtains was the Head of the Soviet Trade Delegation, and Mrs Kamensky. My mother and I had had them to dinner in Queen's Grove. Dickie Attenborough and his wife Sheila Sim had come too and it had been a congenial evening. The Kamenskys were of peasant stock, barrel-chested, with strong faces, no-nonsense people. I took them up to Stratford to see 'Coriolanus' and they were immensely impressed. We then drove to Notley at midnight, after the show.

I had forgotten the things that could go wrong with a butler such as the character we then had. His name was Salmon. He managed with his clod-hopping feet to make any carpet resound. As we gathered in evening dress for cocktails he would appear in a cloud of black dust, shouldering a sack of coal. In the dining room he would serve from the wrong side, then correct himself in an accusing brogue. If anyone refused what he proffered he would freeze, look as if he had been shot in the stomach and remonstrate: 'No *cheeeese*? We've been to such trouble to get this *cheeeese*.'

When there were ten of us and the first lady took five profiteroles out of a pile of forty he blurted: 'I'm terribly sorry, you'll 'ave to put one back.' She did so immediately.

On the Kamenskys' arrival he was welcoming, helpful with suitcases, every inch the old retainer: a character they had read about in Russian literature. In the dining room all started so well.

'And how is Mrs Salmon?' Vivien asked sweetly. He answered in a manner respectful and engaging, reassuring the Kamenskys of the loyal relationship between master and servant.

'And your son?'

'Oh my son . . .' He became hang-dog. 'My son, your ladyship, the most terrible thing 'appened to my son . . . He was 'ad up by British Rail for ex . . . *exposing* himself.'

Larry quickly cut in: 'What rotten luck,' and changed the subject.

Mr Kamensky did smile to himself. In his letters of introduction to his opposite number in Peking and to the Chinese Foreign Ministry he referred to Larry as 'husband of Vivien Li'.

Larry had begun filming 'The Entertainer' with Joan Plowright as his daughter, directed by Tony Richardson. The location was Morecambe, Lancashire. For every evening performance he commuted to Stratford in an ambulance so that he could sleep. From Archie Rice to Coriolanus and back. The over-exertion thrilled him. When I telephoned and asked how he was he rejoiced: 'I'm alright!!' Still so few knew about Joan.

My mother and I had gone to see her in 'Roots' by Arnold Wesker and we were captivated. Her voice was true and good in the part. She had stayed in Suffolk so as to perfect the accent..When she was on stage the whole production lit up. At one of the turning points in the story she did a dance, by herself, flinging her arms up, a hand-held cloth unfurling, the embodiment of joyousness and youth. We were moved, impressed and excited.

Larry came to dine with us in Queen's Grove before my departure for Manila. We enthused about Joan and then, only then, guessed that she was the one he was after. He was as cool as a cucumber, tight as a clam, his reaction was cliché all over: 'Ye-es, remarkable little performance. I was surprised by the emotional depth she sustained.'

He told us he intended to divorce Vivien. I wept openly, shamelessly, even though it was, and had been for so long, inevitable.

I arrived in the Philippines at the end of September and received a card from him in Morecambe.

I am now here for 4½ weeks & think it's a perfectly lovely place. That thing on the left is my hotel, from the back of which I am looking out across the bay at this moment. The weather is fantastic and the film is going well. 'Shifting Heart' [An LOP production] shifting with undue haste from the Duke of Yorks at end of week and 'One more River' going in. 5 hours drive into Stratford a bit tiring before a show but I sleep on and off in the ambulance coming back. Look forward to your next letters. Same old life here but rather a lot in the papers lately.

In Indonesia I heard from Vivien. I had written to her and Gertrude my condolences on the death of old Ernest.

Notley – Feb 19 '60

. . . Ernest was very fond of you always. It has been a most wretched and miserable time.

. . . Larry's play ['The Tumbler' by Dan Levy, with Charlton Heston and Rosemary Harris] opened in Boston with *fair* notices. He has had a very horrid time poor darling as Tottie Baddeley turned out to be not everyone's idea of the part and has had to be replaced – always a painful and very horrifying procedure. It opens in N.Y. on Wednesday. He will be home by next weekend.

Oh Tarkie darling I just simply cannot live without him and it is an unbearable pain to be parted from him – every minute of every day it seems to become more & more agony. It now seems that I shall *have* to do 'Duel of Angels' in N.Y. rehearsing 12th so that will mean another 4 months separation. I do not know how to begin to think about it or face it. He is most anxious for me to do the play so what can I do?

On top of all this it really seems as if Notley is sold. I can hardly write the words. A Canadian couple saw it some weeks ago, made an immediate and perfectly good offer and want to move in at the end of April. It doesn't seem possible, does it?

Of *course* it is looking particularly beautiful. We have had the most glorious crisp and dazzling winter days. The snowdrops have simply bounced out of the ground in profusion, the violets too, and every tree and shrub has decided to do its stunning best.

I walk from place to precious place and gaze at beloved views with tears pouring down my face. What memories for all one's life – such unbelievable rare happiness, sweetness and quietude there has been here. I don't forget the other times too, but they seem to me outweighed by blissful togetherness. Dear God it is a heartache . . . the fact that we have known for some time now that it would have to go doesn't seem to help in the least.

It is fifteen years – a great part of one's life. Shall you ever forget our walk on that misty moonlit night?

Oh the hundreds of times my beloved Larry and I have wandered here in wonder and grateful amazement at the beauty all around us – the feeling that we were a little responsible for creating it too made it all so doubly dear. It is hard to imagine life without such an oasis. To think that *you* will not see it again seems quite untrue.

If you have felt hurt at my not writing you now know the reason why – for when such upheavals shake one's life in every possible direction it is difficult to assemble one's thoughts and communicate freely . . . Don't blame Larry for not writing, he has had a tremendous amount to do and I think is feeling, in his own way, as uncertain & unhappy.

Her love was palpable, not only for him, but also for Notley. That May, after the new owners had moved in, she could not help herself from going back. In the summer of 1991, when going through some archives which Joan had had put together, I came across a telegram from Vivien when she was on Broadway with 'Duel of Angels'.

NEW YORK, 1960 MAY 2

SIR LAURENCE OLIVIER 54 EATON SQUARE

THANK YOU FOR LOVELY LOVELY NOTLEY MY DARLING BABA

That April in Djakarta I also received a letter from Larry in New York telling me about his love for Joan. It was a secret letter which he asked me to burn lest anyone should somehow find it in my possession and leak it to the papers. His 'great unburdening' of feeling had started a few weeks before in Boston, with an indication of his problems with Charlton Heston's acting ability on stage, then some more from somewhere else, and finally his confession on future plans for marriage and long hoped for happiness. It was very touching. I was sorry to burn it, and wrote back my heartfelt congratulations and wishes, to which he replied:

54 Eaton Square SW1 Sat 14 May 1960

I am so deeply grateful to you for your lovely letter to me, which was so wise it made me feel our positions in life were reversed. It seems that now you love me as I should love you and vice versa, but that feeling perhaps is only temporary.

I can't of course remember how I put things to you in my letter from Boston. I know it was plaguey late at night, & I probably erred on the side of restraint and resisted the risk of embarrassing you by too much youthful idealism. 'Vibrant passions' though does sound not very pleasant – as if I were entirely pre-occupied with that 5% I have always been on at you about.

Seriously and frankly to you my dear this love that I now have is very beautiful to my heart indeed. I need say no more than that to you I know . . . as you would say: 'Nuff said.

Your travels sound so wonderful, at least you make them sound so . . . more and more as time goes by do I feel glad that you set out on them.

The letters from Mama were more frequent but less quotable, except perhaps:

You old devil you, where are you? I know it's only a month since you've written – I can only suppose that she must have been and is very attractive and you are still in Bali – at least I hope that is the reason, and that you are not ill or had some accident – I like to know vaguely within a 1000 miles of where you are – old hen, I know, but I can't help it.

I went to Daddy's first night with Mu Richardson – 'Rhinocerus' by Ionesco. He is quite wonderful in it. He plays an insignificant little man – it's an enormous success – it's a strange play when everybody except Daddy turns into a Rhinocerus.

In late August she wrote to him in New York where he was playing 'Beckett' to wish him all the very best in the world and happiness with Joanie.

His purpose in sitting down to reply must have been to thank her, which he forgets to do. The letter seems more than any other to illustrate the quest of his mind to discover the tone of voice he ought to adopt at the start of a new part, outside himself.

Hers had been a letter from the woman he had . . . etc . . . whose son . . . etc . . . and the woman who caused all that coming in between, destruction, the love of my life . . . is now . . . etc . . .

He was at a loss: very human.

Hotel Algonquin, Sun 4th Oct 1960

Darling

Oh no, oh no no no – you thought this was a *long* letter from me didn't you? But no you see: only some 'olds' from Tark because, I know you have guessed it, I have just got off quite a chunk to him.

It's a good five weeks since you wrote & I'm really sorry about it but I just shall have to (grammar) stop apologising for my sort of corresponding (what have I *said*? Oh no, one R) and my dear ones have to take me the way I am – which is not *good* – don't think I think so, but I honestly do do my *best* – my absolute *best*, I never seem even to get to a movie – and all matinées are the same day here now so it isn't that either.

Is it that I have such a *hell* of a lot to do? Well I do have a bit too much, and that a/c's (smart that a/c's don't you think?) for a lot of it – but the main trouble is & always has been – I AM SLOooooow but about that I do my best too, but it's a bit too late, I should have been whipped into being *quick* when I was a nipper . . .

. . . Well my darling, the divorces came on Friday & you will have read & you will have thought a little thought I dare say, there is nothing I can say that doesn't feel inelegant, but I am glad, glad it's over – but if only I can stop being agonised for V's suffering & the cause for it vanish, then I am in for a hell of a marvellous bloody time.

This girl is so good and so good for me (Even old Noëlie said so last week). She makes me feel I am in a kind of idiot heaven. Life here is perfectly fine, Noël, Binkie, & Ginette are here, and like all waves of such are responsible for an old fashioned nightly round should you wish it. The shows go well, but neither of us enjoy them much – but *no* complaints – they provide a nice expedi-conveni-congenibub.

Almost like a sort of working holiday. Joan [starring in 'A Taste of Honey'] and I are in Margalo's apartment (tho I am *here* at the hotel ostensibub) the audiences have deteriorated here terribly – nothing but expense a/c customers and theatre parties and the acting generally pretty fucking awful in my conceited opinion (Sh! of course) but nobody seems to know much different. 'This town has gone' as Noël says. O do so wonder about Tark – don't you?

. . . Joan just came back from lecturing some college kids and we're *late* for a party at Eileen Herlyburlies so I must stop here & now or she will start that fatal primping & we shan't get anywhere all love darling your L.

Better wish you a happy Christmas *now* darling!

So somewhere between his procrastination and chauvinist objection to Joan's primping is the impression of a man ecstatically in the clouds, and maybe wondering after so many years whether it will be allowed to last.

To me he wrote:

V. must have had a horrid time going through the divorce but she did nobly & bravely & managed alright. Yes sometimes it does seem she can believe in a peaceful & joyful existence for herself, and at others she is obsessed by regret or remorse . . . but now that she has definitely cut the strands and the object of her clinging wish is removed, I pray that the contentment of having settled for something will develop – simply because, as life so often provides – there is nothing else for it but to get on with it.

I am touched and so grateful that you should understand & condone & even bless my wish for a family. Joan is a very natural and splendidly earthy young woman (31), & if I am to make her happy & fulfilled she's simply got to have them that's all, she's that type. She is very very beautiful to me, wonderfully good & good for me.

I don't know if I told you that I bought a house in Brighton for her so that if a dismal occurrence had overtaken me she should have some sort of security. Well that is where we shall live . . . it's all going to be wonderful & lovely to look forward to, and all fresh and new in rhythm. The journey by train is perfect, one can either read or work or sleep or talk, so much better than the nerve-jangling & nowadays literally dangerous car-driving.

My main interest now . . . exists in the National Theatre.

So, his greatest and most lasting achievement for English Theatre was hatched with Joan's energy, youth and forcefulness beside him. His constant efforts to put on play after play had yielded disappointing results for LOP Ltd, and he was realising that for several years now acting itself had had few surprises left for him. Intellectually the repetition was constricting, an exercise in sheer calculated professionalism night after night in 'that most fleeting of all the arts'.

LOP had needed constant nourishing from money he made from acting in films. He could not afford to cast good actors in the smaller roles. The only possible conclusion was that for an audience to be given a perfect experience, which required a limit of not much more than a thousand seats, where the cast was good enough throughout to tempt the public away from television, the cost would have largely to be met out of subsidy. France had a national theatre, so had Germany, why not Great Britain?

> I have worked awfully hard on the National and have been instrumental in its present possibility. I have been one of 3 trustees for about 2 years & have managed to cut out a lot of dead wood, force conciliations & form a small efficient working committee of which Kay [Sir Kenneth Clarke] is now the Chairman & the whole thing is now going up again before the Chancellor of the Exchequer on the 9th of this month.
>
> I wish to God I could be there. After that the Commons may tear it down of course, in which case we've had it – but through this committee we have been able to establish that the Nat. Th., Stratford, Old Vic *and* the commercial theatres are all of one mind about it. And I understand the Prime Minister [Harold Wilson] is all for it.
>
> I get up usually about 11 or 11.30, have breakfast, read papers. I go to a Danish woman for exercises. I go to an osteopath for my back and my knee. I write letters or *do* them with Dorothy. I read scripts or books for film stories. I keep or dodge appointments. I don't have lunch. I talk business. I phone. I sleep before the show. See people after and drink then – late supper, late bed, everything *late* everything, I can't stand it. I shall have to change. What could I do in Singapore?

The last part of my planned peregrination was hostage to China's catastrophic economic collapse in 1960, so the book I wrote was about people I knew in Southeast Asia, called *The Eye of the Day*, partly because 'Tomorrow's another day' and from another world.

When the book was accepted for publication I told the obvious people, including Noël Coward who wrote –

Blue Harbour
Port Maria
Jamaica
W.I.

What wonderful news! I'm absolutely delighted and so very thrilled for you. Watch Heinemann . . . they are liable to translate your favourite lines into Turkish.

I've just been frigging transiently about the Far East. (It is *very* difficult to frig transiently) and I didn't sit by *one* paddy field or hear a single philosophical remark from one slant-eyed oriental. I did however get into a taxi in Singapore and the driver said 'Christ! Another Chinese!'

I'm here finishing a very long short story and putting finishing touches to the 'Sleeping Prince' score. We start rehearsing next week.

Give my love to your poor old Dad and your dear white-headed old mother.

Godfather Noël.

It is good to be reminded of the star quality of the man who gave Larry his first real box office success.

Larry's anguish over Vivien ended when he heard that she was sharing her life with Jack Merivale, Gladys Cooper's step-son. We had all known Jack over many years and always liked him. In August 1960 Larry wrote to him saying he had broken down into tears of heartfelt gratitude on hearing the news.

17

Gemini and Taurus

How, then, could Larry have come to write out of his life so much that he had loved?

Seventeen years were to elapse before he and I were together again for any length of time. We were staying in Anne Bancroft's beach bungalow in Malibu Colony, overlooking the Pacific. It was August 1977, my forty-first birthday. He was filming (hardly 'acting' by his standards) in 'The Betsy', written by Harold Robbins. Appalling illnesses had wrought unimaginable changes in his appearance and character. His eyes had the threatened alertness of the very old.

Some months earlier he had come to stay with me in Hong Kong in Riviera Apartments overlooking Repulse Bay, with its distant islands and occasional Chinese junks sailing between them. I was based there to manage the Asian and Pacific business of Thomas De La Rue, the world's chief security and banknote printers. My marriage had foundered two years before and I was saving up to pay school fees for my son and two daughters: Tristan, Isis and Clavelle, each respectively four years or so younger than his young son and two daughters.

I went to Kai Tak Airport to meet him, early of course, and pondered the effects old age had on the senior citizens labouring down the ramp, hanging on to their luggage trolleys; how the Chinese and European races came to resemble one another at the end of their lives. There was one old Chinese with unlikely high cheek bones who even walked like my father.

He approached me, glasses like fishbowls, a few wisps of black hair.

It was Larry.

'Yes!' he waved. 'I should have warned you about the dyed hair, it is a bit of a baby frightener.'

He loved our early morning swims in the bay, the stately lunch in the Oriental Hotel in Kowloon, and the hey-nonny-no of buying a camera in a Cantonese market. He had been on location in South Korea playing General MacArthur, partly to pay for his own children's education and partly, after his terrible illness, to re-establish himself as a world-class screen actor in a huge part. The film 'O Inshon' was financed by the Moonies and unfortunately never released.

After dinner, cooked by my old Anglo-Chinese housekeeper he put his feet up on my sofa. He wanted to know about my love life and whether being 'Larry's boy' had helped.

'Quite the opposite,' I said. 'They suspect that I use that ruse, you see, so it's a hindrance. In more ways than that, too. You are so often in my thoughts. A lovely American woman was lying over on that sofa, where you are now, and we had been listening to some Scriabin. She asked: "What are you thinking of now?" Can you *imagine*! I said I was thinking of my father and that he was the Beethoven of actors. Now that was a missed opportunity!'

'What happened?'

'Nothing that night.'

He had been riddled by diseases as numerous as asps in a hat, in 1974 the king killer being dermatomiocitis: inflammation of the skin and muscle. In Brighton General Hospital he raged like the dying Falstaff. Anti-inflammatory drugs and cortisones to save his body had brought his mind close to madness. He made little sense. After I had sat with him some time his tall lady doctor beckoned to me.

I followed her down the shiny linoleum corridor, into a glossy white room. 'Perhaps,' I began, 'it would help if I said what I have learned about this disease.'

'It might.'

'It is incurable,' I said with some difficulty. 'He will likely be dead within five or six months.'

'Well at least you know that much. Except that he may not even last six weeks.'

While he was railing in agony, the Board of the National Theatre let it be known that his services as Artistic Director were to be determined, and Peter Hall appointed in his place. He affected to be outraged. Yet for a year he had had other health problems and wondered aloud whether he ought to hand over after his decade at the helm. While he had had mighty disagreements with the first Chairman of the National, Lord Chandos, the successor, Sir Max (now Lord) Rayne gave him no such problems, and when advised of Larry's medical prognosis acted with great understanding.

Larry's reaction to the news was typical. His face was puffed and puce, his eyes like a mad old King Lear, stubbled cheeks, dishevelled, a leather strap suspended above him so that he could grab it if he wanted to move.

I stood for a long time at the foot of the bed. 'Hello, Boysie,' he said frailly. He was even weaker than before. 'Have you heard the news?' he asked.

'What news?'

'That fucking National. They fired me. The relief of it! Shot of that fucking National. How bloody marvellous!'

His defiance made him outface death. Within six weeks he was home, constantly egging everyone on to find him work. Joan's brother David Plowright, head of Granada, arranged for him to put on a series of plays under the title 'Laurence Olivier presents'. He selected them, directed some and even acted in some. Acting to cameras, he could rest between takes. He was unable to stand for long. Yet what for him was a rehabilitation imaginatively conceived by Joan and David, gave British audiences some of the very best in television.

He was told he had to accept that he would never again act on stage: an impossibility for him. How could *he* accept such a death-in-life? He had described the thrill of acting to a live audience as 'like coming for a living', an orgasm. He took the parallel dead seriously. He had earlier had to consider the possible loss of ejaculation when he had had cancer of the prostate.

'How,' he reasoned, 'how can a man lose that ability, a man whose living depends on his audience's belief in his having it in abundance? Acting is largely about sex, you know.'

So rather than lose that sharpest rapture he had risked treatment with radioactive rays, and suffered the pain of being frozen and inserted into a kind of revolving cobalt bomb with the chances of a success about 60 per cent. It worked. There he was, rampant again, perhaps wondering whether Phoenixes feel pity or have contempt for ashes.

By what stages he lost his potency I do not know. When I joined him in Malibu that August of 1977 he was complaining furiously about it. Illnesses had rained down on him like meteors. His nails had fallen out and were only slowly regrowing, great purple blotches spread over his emaciated limbs and body, and he could not walk much. For exercise he took up swimming.

With his extravagance, and the payment of his children's school fees, he needed the kind of money which only Hollywood could pay him, hence 'The Betsy'.

His disciplines and energies were still in place. A typical day would be for me to awaken him at 5.30. While he got ready I cooked a British breakfast. Over the eggs and bacon he would peruse the lines in the script we had been over the previous evening. At 6.15 the stretch limo took him away to location in downtown Los Angeles where there were still Victorian offices with mahogany mouldings.

The climax of the film was a scene with Robert Duval, supremely experienced and with total control of self, and under the veteran eyes of the director Daniel Petrie. Between takes Larry would joke with Bob, or if the lighting had to be changed for another camera angle, he would go away, lie down, or maybe pretend with an attractive minor actress completely to re-write her part, giving her a 'collapse and faint sequence'.

'Why,' she said, 'I haven't had a collapse and faint in years!'

'Stick around darling.'

At the end of the day's shooting Bob went off to play squash. Larry and I returned to the Coast.

In his swimming trunks he managed to walk, with pauses, between the patio furniture to the gate. There he had to support himself on my shoulder as he trod in the sand down to the sea, sometimes singing: 'How I love you, how I love you,' as he blew dried-up kisses to it and pointed out patches of sargasso-like kelp welling up in the rollers.

At about thigh depth his legs were eddied from under him and he splashed around shakily, stroked the sea over his neck and shoulders.

Then: 'Nearly Dada's num-num time.'

We had an American housekeeper who shopped and laid the food out for me to cook. This I had ready by the time we had both showered, dressed and had our whiskies. We dined in the living room, curtainless windows with the sky turned black; and we were cosy in the candle-light, with chops, potatoes, salad and cheese and claret.

I had been reading the John Cottrell biography of him which impressed me as the first serious attempt to tell Larry's story since Felix Barker in the 1950s.

'Of course I won't read it,' he said. 'You have no idea how the subject matter bores me.' What bored him, I think, was not the subject matter of his entire life, but the state to which illness had reduced him.

'So,' he looked challengingly, 'what, if anything, will you write about me. You have that conceit, and I,' a gentle tone, 'have the humble curiosity to wonder.' This was before he had started on his autobiography, and years before my own deepest need to set the record straight.

'So?' he persisted.

'Well, I don't feel comfortable with the idea of a son writing about his father.'

'If, just supposing, anyone ever, by the tiniest possible chance, asked you what were your thoughts about me . . .'

'I should say you were Gemini, cusp of Taurus.'

'What the fuck does that mean?'

'Gemini. The ability to turn disaster into triumph. Twins, the highest and the lowest in every role, surprises in the midst of a predictable sentence, even in conversation you change midstream . . . "*Darling* (to kiss) Jesus Christ you look *awful* (to kill). You poor darling one *never* believes what the critics say (to commune with) the envious little buggers (to quote Noëlie) but it really is a pig of a part (to insult by association)."' Hence the unpredictability he injected into his acting, a reason for the unmatched sense of danger which surrounded him.

'I know that. I learnt very early on it's dramatic. That's why I do it.' A long pause, his all-of-a-piece risen-above-it congenibub.

I cut into that: '*You . . . you could.*'

He sat back, hand to mouth.

'Yes I . . . oh I see . . .' He had a thoughtful sip.

'And Taurus?' he asked gently as a lamb, his eyebrows arched over the glass as if, snake-like, he were wondering where to strike.

'The noble bull. The great ox, fed on choice grasses, a prized beast, to be burned as a sacrifice, take corruption.' And he continued the line: 'For that particular fault.'

We talked of a number of his roles and that evening his favourite seemed to be Othello, the most animal of them all, the most naked and the bravest. Apart from the aspects of it that had been written about – his preparation, characterisation and magnetic, hypnotic energy, which was completely missed when the play was recorded on film – he said there was something he did which no one had ever realised.

'I made them despise Othello, for a long period of time, more and more, because he was a devil-worshipping savage, who became blindly stupid, because he was black and their prejudices were against him. I stretched the elastic of their tolerance to a huge degree, pushed them further and further away from me, and then at the very very end, well into the death scene, I pulled their emotions right back into loving him with an intensity they otherwise would never have felt.'

The ineffectiveness of the filmed version made him wonder whether it would make people laugh at him in years to come. The screen failed to recreate the hypnotism or the danger of his stage performance; it failed to suspend disbelief; you could sit back and watch Olivier at work, in what seemed only a masquerade. We wondered whether such a dangerously 'over-the-top' performance, even if produced on film in a studio with proper lighting, could ever have had its reality decanted through a camera's lens. Its success on stage depended so much on the real presence, which was impossible to recreate on any recording – that special something fed between audience and live actor.

He was also distressed that 'The Entertainer' had not worked on film. It was difficult to know whether it was the writing or the direction or what. He wondered whether the difference in dramatic impact was as simple as that between the immediacy of 'life' and the security of the 'record' – the knowledge that in life things can go wrong any second.

He spoke of his family, the children each in turn, his in their teens. He had little interest in mine, only saw them two or three times, and had made them call him 'Larry' rather than 'grandfather'. His relationship to me had become what he had predicted when Vivien was expecting their baby: more brotherly than fatherly.

I recalled his rushing home to his son Richard, then aged about seven, who leapt up at him, grabbed his neck and hugged him strenuously. 'I can feel him loving me,' Larry cried out in joy, 'I can actually *feel* it.' Whatever had prompted those bitter thoughts on love which he had written to me, about nature's bribe merely to bring children into the world and nature not giving a damn about people, was rapturously replaced when he became a fulfilled father and family man with Joan.

In order to have enough waking hours in the day for his demanding-as-ever schedule, and still get a glimpse of his children at bath-time, he had himself transported hither and yon by ambulance so that he could rest. Even after dermatomiocitis this infrastructure, essential for so committed a man, enabled him to deliver of his love to them, even if only in snatches.

His actual memory of love, on the other hand, had been ravaged. The wasting disease had pillaged his mind as well as his body. The first time I realised this was in May 1975 when I went to tell him my marriage was over and my wife had left with our children. Joan let us have lunch together alone in their Regency dining room in 4 Royal Crescent, Brighton. Dali's portrait of Richard III hung on the wall behind him.

After discussing plans for my children's welfare and education and

establishing that I would be able to be with them or have them in the
Far East for holidays, he helped me to realise that I had not lost them as
well as my wife; not completely. We had some more white Burgundy.

He then said sonorously: 'Don't get married again.'

I had another sip.

'Just a minute,' I said, incredulous. 'You met Mummy at the tender
age of twenty-two, both of you in a virginal state and as soon as you
could you married her. Years before divorcing her, you and Vivien had
been living together virtually as man and wife until twenty-three years
later you and Joanie became enfolded in one another's hearts – the vibrant passions you wrote of. Your union,' I mimicked James Thurber,
'was indeed blessed with issue. Why,' (this was becoming rather fun
as a peroration) 'ever since you burst into puberty, you have been one
of the most constantly married men the world has ever seen, and . . .'

I put it into harmony:

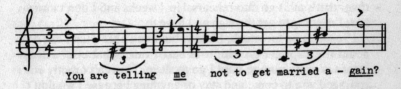

You are telling me not to get married a – gain?

And he said: 'Bloody right.'

Now that was energetic and funny and we laughed: but it was a
denial of love, even when he was at home and in the midst of it.

That disease left him shorn and lost, and on the look-out for
something he could still believe in doing. He cleared his life-raft of
remembered emotion and other baggage, the better to rescue whatever was out there and still have room to take it on board. This
ruthless jettisoning was very much a part of his character, the yes-no
see-saw of mood, the fear of *not* being ready with both hands free, the
recognition that 'You are what you don't throw away, what you don't
excrete.' For there to be room for more births there had to be death.
The consequence was that he had constantly to make room for his
voracious appetite, leaving behind a monumental wake of stardust.

After he married Joan he had somehow to make more time for her
and their children without compromising the new direction of his
career. He had become the first Artistic Director of the Chichester
Festival Theatre, acted, directed, and led the company and indeed
was ultimately responsible for just about everything. This he saw as a
dress rehearsal for the National Theatre at the Old Vic, while the

three auditoria of Denys Lasdun's masterpiece rose so slowly on the South Bank. He cut himself off from all save those who were his immediate concerns.

In Summer 1963 he played Astrov in the Chichester revival of the previous year's production of 'Uncle Vanya', while in London he directed Peter O'Toole in 'Hamlet' at the Old Vic, then brought 'Uncle Vanya' to London, and played Captain Brazen in Farquhar's 'Recruiting Officer'.

His self-renewing rejection of former associates, even those who had been closest to him, is all too apparent in his letter to me –

4 Royal Crescent, Brighton

Oh many days ago now! (Summer 1963)

I don't want to read your book now because I simply haven't time, that's all. I go into rehearsal in 4 weeks and I don't know how I'm going to get through all I have to.

I've taken on too much, I know, but I don't see what I can do about it except get on with it as best I can. What else? All it means is every minute until I go to sleep. I haven't exactly encouraged you to come and stay or anything because I wouldn't be able to give any proper time to you and it's hurting when you take the trouble to come and see people and they don't seem able to take much notice of you.

I had a family of my own, but it was hard to accept the total rejection implicit in his desire to be uninterrupted with his, to the exclusion of what had once been so important.

Again, that night in Malibu, it seemed as if the pruning of earlier friends and relationships, to create space for his brood, had chopped us out of his memory as well. Was this not, I asked, a pity: we would always be there when he had time.

There was a long silence. He looked over at the window, the black night, the waves of the Pacific, then lowered his eyes.

I waited.

'I'm embarrassed by that question,' he said.

It seemed best to remain silent. He cupped his hands and peered into his claret glass.

'The only one I ever loved was Vivien. Oh, and I was rapturously in love with Joan, with the babies.'

The metaphor of his pushing people off his life-raft seems appropriate because he was exceptionally strong and exceptionally storm-tossed. When I heard him his lines for the part Titus Andronicus the words 'I am the sea' excited him. He decided they needed unique emphasis by following them at full volume with an extraordinary rasping intake of breath. He had to practise this again and again to find a way of maximising volume without damaging his voice.

A more youthful image, referring perhaps to 'genteel poverty' comes from the mouth of Brutus:

'. . . lowliness is young ambition's ladder,
Whereto the climber-upward turns his face:
But when he once attains the upmost round,
He then unto the ladder turns his back,
Looks in the clouds, scorning the base degrees
By which he did ascend.'

By the end of the week, we had re-established the closeness which had been suppressed for so long. His rediscovered affection expressed itself unexpectedly. Unbeknownst to me he telephoned my colleagues in Basingstoke and implored everyone in turn, the Managing Director, the Personnel Director, the Sales Director, to allow me an extra week's leave.

'I appeal to you as a father,' he said. He forgot about the eight hours time difference and had a long conversation about me, well after Home Counties' midnight, with a security guard.

Eclipses, however total they seem, always pass. With him it was a question of time and space.

Three years earlier he had written to Jill:

4 Royal Crescent, Brighton, 5th December 1974

Darling Jilly,

Thank you so much for your perfectly adorable letter to me today. I am very glad we are both getting on the mend.

She had cancer of the breast, he thrombosis of the leg; old age made miserable for both of them by constant illness.

Mine is a longish job, I'm afraid – but do you know, the curious thing is I don't seem to mind it one bit. I think that bloody old National nearly killed me, and the idea of being looked after while I write a book would be very welcome.

It is so sweet of you to talk so very kindly about the possibility of a book, and of course I shall long to talk to you about all sorts of things, all sorts of aspects of things. The difficulty I am up against . . . is that I am absolutely determined that every single word in it insofar as I myself am concerned shall be the absolute and utter truth. This is an attitude about which you may possibly have a reservation or two, but I don't know and of course we will have long talkings about it before the final expressions of things are made.

When I say that my own truth will exist in it, this doesn't mean that I intend to deceive anybody, merely that it will be the utter truth as far as I am concerned. I am not going to . . . pull any wool over anybody's eyes or make out things were better than they were, or something was worse luck than it was.

I hope you will like the title: it is to be *Confessions of an Actor*.

All love as always . . .

And two years before, when he was introduced as a Life Peer to the House of Lords, he invited Jill to come with me, along with Joan, their children, and close Olivier relations, for the lunch party beforehand.

He really hated, or affected to hate, writing 'that fucking book'. In the event, despite his promise to share, he never sought to discuss it with Jill. Seven and a half years later, just before its publication, she wrote to him how upset she had been by yet another biography about him.

43 Sutherland Grove, S.W.18

3–4–82

Darling Larry

I have just read that badly written and very inaccurate book by Thomas Kiernan. Very often he makes it read as if I was talking (to him). I just wanted to say I have never met him or heard of him until I was given this stupid book . . .

To which he replied –

> Forgive type, please. I am up to my eyes in a film, so letter-writing times are crowded ones.
>
> How sweet of you to worry. Mr Kiernan's book may be the 11th or 12th – I cannot be sure – and I have never read one of them. My own is a huge tome and, if it comes out in September which it promises to do for the sake of being in time for Christmas, then perhaps it may shut other aspirants up! Thank you so much for bothering, darling. I would not believe a word I read about myself, ever!

The carbon copy of that letter is corrected, and shows that in the last sentence the original word was 'wrote', rather than 'read'. So – 'I would not believe a word that I *wrote* about myself, ever!' Know thyself?

When his own book was published, what he *wrote* about himself and others was in large part untrue, much of it errors of fact which a publisher should have corrected but he was so fed up with the book he was incorrigible. He wanted to be shot of it and get on with something else: 'If the truth be dull, a little imagination won't hurt.'

What he wrote about Jill cannot be so easily dismissed: he chose to ignore all that was good about their relationship and the professional background he derived from her mother and father, who had if anything been rather more than the Lunts of their era, and which he developed day after day with her for seven years. He thrust the memories of romance and love with her so far out of his mind that he did not care to be reminded that they had worked for months on doing 'Romeo and Juliet' together. At no stage did he ever admit to me, or anyone that I know of, that she was the linch-pin of his early dramatic development, and that she had in fact signed his first Holly-wood contract because of his irresolution.

In his autobiography his denial of ever having loved her took the form of saying that it was she who was in love elsewhere and therefore could not love him. According to her, she had never loved before and never fell in love ever again.

After the war, and her failure to make a come-back in theatre or film, and my going to boarding school, her loneliness led her to having an older French woman called Ninette to stay. She still had the occasional fling, sometimes with men friends who were well known and extremely attractive; once with a perfect stranger on a strato-cruiser on her way to Hollywood. In their warm bunk, during the stop-over in Newfoundland, he and she could see the re-fuelling men outside, bowed into a howling blizzard of snow, and felt very happy where they were.

After six years the slightly sinister but well-educated Ninette left. Jill was joined by Joy Pearce, a companion with an infectious laugh who had two sons, liked cooking, watching snooker on television and reading adventure stories by Dick Francis. They lived together until Jill's death. They were a happy couple for thirty years from the age of fifty onwards. Jill's main hobby remained her garden and her reading. On her front door there was a vigorous admonition: 'No car wash, no manure, and no missionaries, thank-you'.

Larry was beastly about this relationship but it was possible to trip him up with anything to make him laugh – that small but most effective shield. His inventiveness for the sake of effect, especially at the cost of truth, more and more frequently made him feel better in his dotage.

Ralph Richardson, his old and close friend, complained to Jill about how much he had come to dislike Larry in absentia, but whenever he was with him, the charm worked yet again and he could not help but love him. The problem was that Larry regarded him as a professional rival and behind his back stamped with disapproval on his work, an ungenerous symptom of the way he aged. Similar dismissiveness was sprayed in many directions. The only words he wrote to describe the relationship between him and me were –

> We were an embarrassment to each other – I to him because I had upped and gallantly left his mother when he was only ten months old, he to me because of the unquenchable guilt that would not leave me, even after twenty years. Only in the last few years have we found untroubled contentment in each other's company and real enthusiasm for it.

His autobiography, written far too late in his life, reflects the terrible personal cost of lost memory.

Larry forever loved hearing about Vivien, being reminded of her even after she had died. He kept saying how pleased he was she had found happiness with Jack Merivale. He still enjoyed sharing old stories about her: how, when Noël was enthusing over his musical of 'The Sleeping Prince', Vivien had said: 'How thrilling! And you must get Dickie Adinsell to write the music.' And for once the Master was speechless.

In his writing of her he was blind with grief, when after her death on 7 July 1967 of tuberculosis, he went to their old flat in Eaton Square, and Jack Merivale left him alone with her in the bedroom.

Jill wrote to me:

31 Queen's Grove, NW8, 15 Aug '67

I went to Viv's memorial service today. You were very fond of her and I thought you would like me to go representing you. Also I wanted to go for myself. I don't quite know why, but I felt an urge. Viv had been part of my life for so long, over 30 years. I wanted to say, I don't quite know what, perhaps good-bye to a great part of my life and with complete sincerity God speed to her soul.

I went with Peggy Webster, going through the side entrance [of St Martin in the Fields] to avoid the vast crowds. We put ourselves on the outside of the very outside pews. The church was packed with those who came because they cared and those who came to rubber-neck.

Emlyn Williams's John Donne was a masterpiece, beautifully spoken and brilliantly picked. John Gielgud's address I thought over emotional and unmoving. The Anthem beautifully sung and of course 'God be in my head' always makes me cry. [Vivien's daughter] Suzanne's little puckered face broke me up.

At the end when I turned to leave I found Larry standing right behind me. In that very large church full of hundreds of people, wasn't it extraordinary that we should find ourselves together. I put my hand on his as I left the pew and he put his other hand on top of mine and gave it three little squeezes. His face looked grey right through.

Problems with her health were almost as terrible as Larry's.

She wrote to Private Patients Plan in September 1986 –

Will you please pay what I am allowed and I will of course settle the rest. I don't see how I can still stay alive and keep on having more and more things wrong with me.

As Larry became older and less able to defend himself, more of an institution to be researched, his sexuality was debated. It was suggested that he had had an affair with Kenneth Tynan his Literary

Manager at the National Theatre, and more recently there has been the titillation of an alleged long relationship with Danny Kaye, delivered perhaps because the authors had nothing new to say and had to invent in order to sell their books.

There is no debate. It is unforgivable garbage.

Larry used to say he didn't mind what homosexuals did so long as they didn't interfere with him. Besides, Vivien was extremely indiscreet about everything, especially his women, or supposed women, and often accused him of being a moral coward for not admitting to them, while the world knew about her and Peter Finch, the only other man she could ever think of marrying. Had there been a whisper of homosexuality about Larry she would have made it as public as her protest in the House of Lords.

For the rest, Larry feared homosexuality as many heterosexual fathers do, until their sons have satisfactorily been laid, as a foundation naturally to adore women. After my walk up the drive with Noël Coward and the question had been popped: 'Not even a little bit?' I laughingly told Larry the story.

'Are you sure you said no?'

'Yes, of course,' I said, 'why?'

'He can be very persuasive.'

'Did he persuade you?'

'Christ no, but he tried, when I was much younger. I've never been queer.'

That would have been during the holiday in Nassau, when Jill was having problems which had to be operated on.

Larry's fear of homosexuality, and what he called its emasculation of many male performances on stage, where an actor's sexual preference is so undisguisedly communicated to the audience, made him uncomfortable with a number of colleagues with whom he should have been closer.

The pious love I had developed for my one-time and lovely French fiancée Jenny, an unfulfilled young love, had rather emasculated me. Before leaving for Southeast Asia I was still a virgin, and he wished to perish the thought: 'If you come back from there, still in that appalling state, I shall cut you off without a penny.'

I wondered how to cable the news to him. The most famous one-word telegram concerned Britain's conquest of Sindh: the one Latin word 'Peccavi' – 'I have sinned'. So I cabled 'Fuckavi'. He at once telephoned Jill and they both congratulated each other that everything was fine, nothing the matter now.

Larry not only lived his life to the fullest, he *re*-lived it through constant repetition. This accounts for the formidable volume of anecdotes so many people remember. Some stories which I felt only *I* knew, because I alone was present, have come bounding back round the houses. About such a man as he there was no possibility of dark secrets.

Visiting him in his *extremis* years was a bit of a gamble. He never accepted his mortality with grace. His defiance was magnificent, his fury noble: he was impossible. From time to time he would settle into recreating some role, anecdote or poem, with a delivery finely timed and tuned as if to crown weeks of rehearsal.

I used to drive old friends of his to see him in his Malthouse near Steyning in West Sussex. He had made the garden like a mini-Notley, a lime 'where'er-you-walk' in the centre, a covered swimming pool between the rose beds and herbaceous borders, a tennis court beyond. Mercia used to go down there with me, Ginette Spanier (Seidmann), Rosemary Harris and her husband, the writer John Ehle and many others. It gave his family and New Zealand nurse a bit of a break.

While at lunch there I once complained about the mess some builders were making in my Kensington flat, and wondered why on earth Rupert Brooke had included dust as an object for affection in his poem 'The Lover'. Larry drew a deep breath and recited the piece in its entirety. We all, Joan, his nurse, Ginette Spanier, with his children Richard, Tamsin and Julie-Kate now in their twenties, watched agog. His gestures were there, the exuberance, the cadenced voice hitting the climax precisely. We were astounded.

'Where *did* you do that?' I gasped.

He snapped: 'In the Albert Hall in 1942, of *course*.'

Sometimes he used his old age as a disguise. At the Garrick Club the members might pass him in the corridor, or even stand next to him in the loo and not recognise him. Occasionally he enjoyed his worn-out appearance as a kind of make-up. Once, when at the club's main table after a very late lunch, there were a number of other members stretching down each side of him. Just then the porter showed in some Americans by appointment to see the portraits, and said: 'Here we have the Zoffany collection'.

Larry wiped his mouth with a napkin, became the old Italian from the Eduardo de Felipe play he was in ('Saturday, Sunday, Monday') and all hunched up, struggled to his feet.

'I am Papa Zoffany,' he bowed. He indicated the others at table. 'And these are my sons, Rocco, Luigi, Paulo . . .'

His raunchiness never left him. He concocted two epithets in 'franglais': 'Whatever will they think of next' became 'Que jamais penseront-ils de prochain'. He was even prouder of 'Baisez cela pour une alouette' – 'Fuck that for a lark'. As Dickens wrote: 'Tastes differ, for if not, what would happen to the makers of fancy waistcoats?'.

He tried everyone's patience. The family had continually to leave it to the long-suffering nurse to answer his demands. There was a long time of pain and anguish, years in fact, yet even then he reassembled his energies to do 'Lear' on television.

My mother wrote to me of him again:

43 Sutherland Grove, Southfields SW18, March 22 78.

I hear Daddy is not well but about, and talked to Donald Sinden at the Garrick till 2.30 a.m., which fascinated Donald and Diana – he had his taxi waiting. I hear about him from Mu Richardson. He has spent hours with Ralphie, frail but full of humour, stayed so late he had to be turned out.

I don't think he will be with us much longer. I haven't seen him much in the last 40 years. It's funny after all that time how I can still love him so much.

The chairman of my company, Sir Arthur Norman, sent me a wonderful photograph of Larry he had used to promote the World Wildlife Fund. I showed it to her and she burst into tears: 'How beautiful, how old. He has become a beautiful old old man.'

I last saw Larry two days before he died, on Sunday, in a room as tiny as the one he was born in. He was lying shrunken, unshaven, face to the wall hardly breathing, his nose 'as sharp as a pen'. I was told he could be peppery so I refrained from touching him, only called him softly: 'Daddy?' He turned and opened his eyes, glanced at me sideways, eyebrows arched to carry his eyelids outwards, a gleam of defiance, rejection and welcome at once, laughter longed for, rage at the fading of the light.

He died on 11 July 1989 aged 82. Before his funeral, as friends of the family were gathering in the garden, I sought out the young male nurse who had been with him in the last stages. I explained how Larry had loved recounting the alleged dying words of King George the Fifth – 'What's on at the Empire' and 'Bugger Bognor'. The nurse then recalled that a day before his death Larry had been lying speechless on his back. His parched mouth was open and the male nurse, to introduce some fluid, cut an orange in half, held it over the parted lips and squeezed. A few drops fell wide and trickled under the cheek and round to the temple. The eyes opened and the voice crackled: 'This isn't fucking Hamlet, you know. It's not supposed to go in the ear . . .'

At his memorial service in Westminster Abbey, Jill was there in a wheel chair, frail but still strong enough to mourn him. She died scarcely a year later. I took her casket to Apple Porch, now an old people's home. A beech hedge hid the view. The matron had the key for the gate to Temple Golf Course but the lock had rusted solid. I went into the orchard and found a way through the spinney, to scatter her ashes over the fairway.

The best lines after his death were by Bernard Levin in *The Times*, and these Joan and I chose for Alan Bates to read two years later, when his ashes had been laid to rest in the Abbey, and there was a service to dedicate the Memorial Stone in Poets' Corner.

Let us be clear about what exactly we have lost with the death of Laurence Olivier. Theatre goers have lost the greatest of modern actors, and one of such gifts that perhaps only three or four in all history could have counted themselves his peers . . . What we have lost with Laurence Olivier is *glory*.

He reflected it in his greatest roles, he walked clad in it – you could practically see it glowing around him like a nimbus . . .

Part of it is optimism – not the facile optimism that ignores reality, but the profound kind that accepts it but believes that the world may yet be saved. 'Clenching his fist at the death-pale stars'; such an optimist faces always outwards, and in his heart it is always noon.

Such a picture points inevitably to further qualities. Chief among these is courage and Olivier radiated it. One of the roles with which he will always be associated is Henry V . . . He did in truth embody and personify the virtues of Shakespeare's Hal, and courage was foremost of these.

Optimism; courage; the third quality of glory is romanticism. Again not the sentimental or bombastic kind, but the romanticism of those who live always above the clouds.

Laurence Olivier's work was glorious in the same way as the Fifth Symphony of Beethoven is glorious . . . No one will ever fill the place he leaves in the hearts of those who knew him; no one will ever play the roles he played as he played them; no one will replace the splendour that he gave his native land with his genius.

As my father quoted me to him:

> As you would say: ''Nuff said'.

INDEX

More bestselling non fiction from Headline

THE MURDER YEARBOOK	Brian Lane	£5.99 □
THE ENCYCLOPAEDIA OF SERIAL KILLERS	Brian Lane & Wilfred Gregg	£6.99 □
ONE LIFETIME IS NOT ENOUGH	Zsa Zsa Gabor	£5.99 □
GINGER: My Story	Ginger Rogers	£6.99 □
MICROWAVE GOURMET	Barbara Kafka	£5.99 □
PLAYFAIR CRICKET ANNUAL 1992	Bill Frindall	£2.99 □
PLAYFAIR FOOTBALL ANNUAL 1992-93	Jack Rollin	£3.99 □
DEBRETT'S CORRECT FORM	Patrick Montague-Smith	£7.99 □
DEBRETT'S ETIQUETTE & MODERN MANNERS	Elsie Burch Donald	£7.99 □
SUNDAY EXPRESS GENERAL KNOWLEDGE CROSSWORD BOOK Volume 1	*Sunday Express*	£2.99 □

All Headline books are available at your local bookshop or newsagent, or can be ordered direct from the publisher. Just tick the titles you want and fill in the form below. Prices and availability subject to change without notice.

Headline Book Publishing PLC, Cash Sales Department, Bookpoint, 39 Milton Park, Abingdon, OXON, OX14 4TD, UK. If you have a credit card you may order by telephone — 0235 831700.

Please enclose a cheque or postal order made payable to Bookpoint Ltd to the value of the cover price and allow the following for postage and packing:
UK & BFPO: £1.00 for the first book, 50p for the second book and 30p for each additional book ordered up to a maximum charge of £3.00.
OVERSEAS & EIRE: £2.00 for the first book, £1.00 for the second book and 50p for each additional book.

Name ....

Address ....

....

....

If you would prefer to pay by credit card, please complete:
Please debit my Visa/Access/Diner's Card/American Express (delete as applicable) card no:

Signature ....Expiry Date ....